THE
MAGIC
of
FIRE

THE MAGIC of FIRE

Hearth Cooking

One Hundred Recipes for the
Fireplace or Campfire

WILLIAM RUBEL

Illustrations by IAN EVERARD

A PORCH CAFÉ BOOK

Ten Speed Press
P. O. Box 7123
Berkeley, California 94707
www.tenspeed.com

Distributed in Australia by Simon and Schuster Australia, in
Canada by Ten Speed Press Canada, in New Zealand by Southern
Publishers Group, in South Africa by Real Books, in Southeast
Asia by Berkeley Books, and in the United Kingdom and Europe
by Airlift Book Company.

A Porch Café Book

Designed by Jim MacKenzie

Library of Congress Cataloging-in-Publication Data
Rubel, William.
The magic of fire : hearth cooking : one hundred recipes
for the fireplace or campfire / William Rubel ;
illustrations by Ian Everard.
p. cm.
ISBN 1-58008-453-2
1. Fireplace cookery. 2. Outdoor cookery. I. Title.
TX840.F5 R83   2002
641.5'8—DC21   2002005953

First printing, 2002
Printed in Hong Kong

1 2 3 4 5 6 7 8 9 10 — 06 05 04 03 02

In winter, Snow-white lit the fire and put

on the kettle, which was made of brass, but

so beautifully polished that it shone like gold.

ANDREW LANG, *Snow-white and the Seven Dwarves*

I gave them fire.

AESCHYLUS, *Prometheus*

And I said, Tell on, my Lord. Then said he unto me, Go thy
way, weigh me the weight of the fire, or measure me the blast of
the wind, or call me again the day that is past.

The Apocrypha, 2 Esdras 4:5

She burn'd with love, as straw with fire flameth;

WILLIAM SHAKESPEARE, *Sonnet VII*

As I sat there in that now lonely room; the fire burning low in
that mild stage when, after its first intensity it has warmed the
air, it then only glows to be looked at; the evening shades and
phantoms gathering round the casements, and peering in upon us
silent, solitary twain; the storm booming without in solemn
swells; I began to be sensible of strange feelings. I felt a-melting
in me. No more my splintered heart and maddened hand were
turned against the wolfish world.

HERMAN MELVILLE, *Moby-Dick*

Some brought bowls with the blood of slaughter, others took up
baskets of meat and offal, while others kindled the fire and set
cauldrons upon the hearth, and the whole roof rang.

EURIPIDES, *Electra*

CONTENTS

INTRODUCTION

Hearth cooking
is an ancient and
wonderful craft.
It is the craft that
stands at the center
of European cuisine.
With few exceptions,
all recipes that
originated in Europe
were first created
on an open hearth . . .

On the hob, a kettle steamed; on the hearth, a cat reposed.

CHARLES DICKENS, *Our Mutual Friend*

IT IS DIFFICULT TO COMPARE HEARTH COOKING with cooking on a modern kitchen stove because the open hearth is so much more than a place to cook. The firelight that casts its spell over the room—that entwines lovers—infuses everything cooked on the hearth with a touch of magic.

Hearth cooking is an ancient and wonderful craft. It is the craft that stands at the center of European cuisine. With few exceptions, all recipes that originated in Europe were first created on an open hearth and only adapted comparatively recently to the modern kitchen. All adaptations involve a shift—however subtle. When translating languages, even when the meaning of the words remains precisely the same, there is an inevitable shift in feeling, a shift in the poetry of sound: ocean, *le mer, el mar, il mare.* In making the move from the open hearth to the modern kitchen, recipes undergo two shifts: always a shift of poetry and often a shift in flavor.

This book is about the poetry of fire and the extraordinary flavors and textures that develop through cooking on the open hearth. Compared with the fireplace, the modern kitchen stove and oven, even taken together, are one-dimensional. As you begin to cook on your fireplace, and as you begin to adapt your repertoire from the kitchen stove to the open hearth, you will discover that the hearth is a cooking tool of undreamed potential. On the open hearth everything can be made to taste better: stronger, deeper, richer, more striking.

The open hearth offers a range of cooking temperatures from barely hot to intensely hot. You can cook at 160°F (70°C) or at 700°F (370°C), or any temperature in between, and you can make the shift quickly from one temperature to another. Compared with the stovetop, the open hearth is a cooking tool with spatial dimension. You can cook beside the fire, under the fire, over the fire, on the hearth in front of the fire, and on the hearth over embers. In many cases, you can apply heat to what you are cooking from more than one direction at the same time, and you can control the heat from each of the directions independently of one another. All of this means that the hearth cook has unparalleled nuanced control over the application of heat to dishes, which translates to unparalleled control over taste, texture, and presentation.

I selected recipes for this book that, each in their own way, call out one or another of the strengths of the open hearth. They provide you with the skills you need to apply hearth cooking to your own recipe repertoire. This book is written for a general audience—everyone who likes to eat—and also for anyone with a special interest in hearth cooking, such as those interested in the cuisine of the hunt, early American cooking, the rustic table of southern Europe, or the cooking of the Middle Ages.

I have drawn the recipes from a wide range of sources: ancient literature; medieval manuscripts; novels; scholarly works on the history of cooking; modern cookbook literature; field research in Europe, Asia, and Africa; and my own experience cooking on my hearth. I hope this book will lead each of you to your own hearth, and that many readers, beginning where I have left off, will use it to create new worlds of flavor for friends and family. I also hope that through this book you will find in the flames of the hearth fire dreams and visions that will bring a sparkle to your eyes and a smile to your lips.

I selected recipes that, each in their own way, call out one or another of the strengths of the open hearth.

But what if you don't have a fireplace? In historic terms, the fireplace is the campfire brought indoors and built under a chimney. Every recipe in this book can be cooked equally well on a campfire or in a fire pit, and many of the recipes can be cooked on a barbecue. Hearth cooking is for anyone with access to an open fire.

Ember-roasted artichoke (see page 136)

HOW TO USE THIS BOOK

My own suggestion for how to use this book strikes a balance between that of no advance preparation, and waiting to begin cooking until you have read every word of the reference material that precedes and follows the recipes.

ONE APPROACH TO USING THIS BOOK is to "jump right in." Find a recipe that interests you, light the fireplace fire, and start cooking. My own suggestion for how to use this book strikes a balance between that of no advance preparation, and waiting to begin cooking until you have read every word of the reference material that precedes and follows the recipes. I advise you to proceed as follows:

1   **Before browsing through the recipes, review the table of contents** to get a sense of what is included and where you can find it.

2   **Become familiar with basic hearth cooking methods** by reviewing *Illustrated Methods* on page 14. The methods are cross-referenced with detailed descriptions beginning on page 254. If your hearth is a campfire or fire pit, imagine the illustrations without the fireplace. The cooking methods remain the same.

3   **Review *Illustrated Equipment* on page 12** to set your mind at ease regarding what equipment is required, and to provide a mental image of the equipment as you read the recipes. The equipment is cross-referenced with more detailed descriptions beginning on page 247.

Next, browse through the book to find recipes that interest you. As you do, familiarize yourself with the reference material that supports each recipe. Key words in the margins are linked to information sections appearing after the recipe chapters, including Equipment (page 247), Methods (page 254), Key to Cooking Venues (page 270), and Unusual Foods and Special Techniques (page 274).

While I have done my best to structure this book for the many readers who are impatient with technical manuals, some material should be read before beginning to cook. This information falls into the category of text that, when discovered after you have run into trouble, causes you to exclaim, "Oh! It said that on page 264? Wow! If only I'd read that before!" Please review the section called All About the Fireplace (page 240) for information that will be useful to you. Be sure to read the entries on Ash, Embers, Fireplace Preparation, Fireplace Safety, Firewood, and Lighting the Fire. In addition, read the entry Radiant Heat on page 264.

The fireplace fire is the great variable in hearth cooking. Learning to manage the fire for cooking is the primary skill of the hearth cook. Many of my recipes include cooking times. If you follow my cooking instructions, and match my cooking times, then you will know that your fireplace fire and mine are calibrated. This will help you to determine what is feasible to cook for a given meal. Each recipe begins with a description of the fire, which should always be read before you begin making the recipe. The first few times, please also read The Fire (page 16), which discusses fire management for hearth cooking in general, and also includes the definitions of the terms I use in the description of the fire. Understanding these terms is critical to using this book successfully.

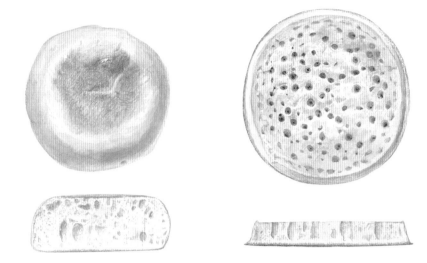

Hearth-baked English muffin (left) and crumpet (see recipe, page 165)

Learning to manage the fire for cooking is the primary skill of the hearth cook. Each recipe begins with a description of the fire, which should always be read before you begin making the recipe.

While experience will be your most effective teacher, please read the section called Cooking Multicourse Meals (page 19) for tips on preparing multiple dishes for the same meal.

When you are ready to begin cooking, make any changes necessary to ready your fireplace as described in Fireplace Preparation (page 244). If your hearth is a campfire or fire pit, make the changes suggested on page 272. Next, assemble the equipment specified in the recipe you have selected, light the fire as described in Lighting the Fire (page 245), and proceed to cook according to the recipe's instructions.

As you become more experienced with hearth cooking, you will find that the process is a collaboration among the fire, the cookware, and the cook. Use this book, the recipes and the reference material, as a guide to get you started. But in the end, let your intuition guide you as you take part in the adventure of reviving the ancient tradition of cooking with live fire.

ILLUSTRATED EQUIPMENT

Hearth cooking is a hobby with almost no entry barrier. With basic pots and pans, the shovel and tongs from a standard fireplace set, a Dutch oven with legs, a small barbecue grill, two bricks, and a hook with a length of looped string, you can cook every recipe in this book. While the number of tools required is few—and many are easily improvised—one of the pleasures of the open hearth is the opportunity to use handsome handmade tools. This book includes all the information you need to commission basic tools from a local blacksmith. A list of suppliers of hearth tools and equipment are included at the back of this book. A more extensive list is available on my Web site, *williamrubel.com.* Antique tools can be found through Internet auction houses, and through antique stores, particularly in the northeastern United States and in Europe.

The Basic Tools

1 Small shovel

2 Long-handled tongs

3 Long-handled fork

4 5- and 7-quart (5- and 7-l) Dutch oven

5 Iron tripod with 2½-inch (6-cm) legs, or 2 common red bricks

6 Iron grill with 2½-inch (6-cm) legs, or 2 common red bricks and a small barbecue grill

7 Pair of Kevlar gloves

8 Ceiling hook, 2 short skewers, and a length of string for string roasting

9 Pot hook to lift the lid of the Dutch oven

10 Griddle and other pots and pans from your kitchen

11 Blow pipe or bellows

ILLUSTRATED METHODS

Chicken, duck, and meat roast on the edge of the hearth, near the fire. Of the three roasting methods introduced in this book, two of them— String Roasting, page 62, and Roasting on a Stand, page 124— require no special equipment. Only Spit Roasting, page 127, requires an investment in equipment.

CAUTION: Read Fireplace Safety, page 244, before under- taking any of the recipes in this book. You cannot assume that the cooking methods described in this book accord with current international or national safety standards. Do not follow any instruction that may be unsafe.

THE ILLUSTRATIONS ON THESE TWO PAGES show most of the hearth techniques called for in this book. The techniques are linked to extensive reference material in the back of the book. In the painting, above, a frittata (page 82) cooks on the hearth over embers in a frying pan set on a tripod 8 inches (20 cm) from the fire. When the frit- tata is done, the embers are shoveled back into the fireplace (see Hearthside Tripod, page 262). Beans (page 34) are cooking in the bean pot set on the hearth 4 inches (10 cm) from the fire. The beans simmer from the heat of the flames falling on the side of the pot. On the right, a saucepan sits inside the firebox 2 inches (5 cm) from the fire. The stewed fruit (page 198) is cooking both from the fire's side heat and from embers that are pushed up against the saucepan where it is closest to the flames (see Pot Beside the Fire, page 263).

Beans bake in a pot buried in hot ash (Pot Buried in Hot Ash, page 263).

A crêpe bakes on a griddle with embers spread evenly underneath (Hearthside Griddle, page 260).

Fish, poultry, and meat are among the easiest foods to cook on the hearth (Hearthside Grilling, page 261).

I MPROVISATION SITS AT THE HEART OF HEARTH COOKING. Two common red bricks can be used as an improvised stand for kebabs, a grill, a frying pan, a griddle, or a pot. In this illustration, chopsticks function as skewers for kebabs (page 112). A barbecue grill set over the bricks lets you grill (see Hearthside Grilling, page 261). A hot fire in the fireplace pulls smoke generated by grilling up the chimney. Many foods, including Flat Bread (page 162) and Roasted Onions (page 22), can be cooked directly on the embers (see Ember Baking, page 260). Many foods can also be baked buried in hot ash, either directly, such as potatoes (page 154) or Ash Cakes (page 158), or wrapped in oiled paper, large leaves, or clay (see Ash Baking, page 255). Since any pot can be pushed near the fire as illustrated in the painting opposite, it is possible to cook complex meals with no specialized equipment.

THE FIRE

AN ORNAMENTAL FIRE IS ABOUT FLAMES. A cooking fire is about heat. The heat for cooking comes from embers, from flame, and from a combination of embers and flame. Managing a cooking fire means having the heat you require for a recipe in the form and intensity you require it when you are ready to cook.

The hearth techniques in this book rely heavily on embers both as a portable heat source and as a source of radiant heat. To a great extent, managing the fire for cooking means managing the fire to produce embers.

For most of the recipes, plan to start the fire one to one and one-half hours before you begin to cook the first dish. Assuming you are burning well-seasoned, dry hardwood logs, this is usually the amount of time it takes for the first set of logs to have been largely reduced to embers. Add new logs as needed, one, two, or three at a time, to maintain a hot bed of embers, and to develop the "gentle," "moderate," or "high" flames required by the food you will cook.

You may start the fire long before you are ready to begin cooking and maintain the fire "at rest" for as long as you like, but the fire should always be hot enough to ignite fresh logs quickly. If it is indeed kept this hot, there will always be two or three small shovelfuls of embers to place under a pot, grill, or griddle on the hearth as soon as you are ready to begin cooking.

At the start of each recipe is a painting of fire, and then a description of the optimum fire for that recipe. When making several recipes for a single meal, the challenge is to coordinate the management of the fire with the order in which the recipes are to be cooked. If they cannot all be cooked at the same time, either because their fire requirements are different or because there isn't enough room, then a sequence for cooking the recipes must be decided. When working in sequence, the fire needs to be managed in a way that provides both the embers and the radiant heat for the recipes at hand, and that also anticipates, as much as possible, the needs of the recipes that will follow. This sounds more complex in words than it is in practice.

It usually means nothing more than keeping the wood burning fast enough, usually at the "moderate flames" rate as defined on page 18, to replenish embers as they are being used.

Can you make a "mistake" with the fire? No, the state of a fire can always be changed. A slow fire can rapidly be made a hot one through burning kindling and logs split into small pieces. Wood that is sound, dry, well seasoned, and of a small diameter quickly generates embers. A fire can be slowed by banking it with ashes.

Here is a typical description of the fire, taken from the recipe for Frittata (page 82):

 The Fire: A moderately mature fire with gentle to moderate flames.

The terms used in these fire descriptions are defined as follows:

New fire: *15 to 30 minutes after lighting the fire.* A recently lit fire in which there are no embers and the heat comes entirely from flames. A new fire does not radiate as much heat toward the hearth as a mature fire and has limited use in hearth cooking.

Moderately mature fire: *30 to 60 minutes after lighting the fire.* The fire has been burning for a while and it has generated some embers, enough to provide one or two shovelfuls to be placed under a grill, tripod, or griddle. It is still "new," however. This fire is appropriate for dishes that only require a modest quantity of embers.

Mature fire: *60 to 90 minutes after lighting the fire.* The first five logs used to light the fire (see Lighting the Fire, page 245) have been largely reduced to embers, leaving a gentle fire; embers represent a substantial component of the heat radiating out of the fireplace; the combination of embers and gentle fire is hot enough that a log added to the fireplace will quickly light; and you cannot long hold your hand at the edge of the hearth near the fire. This fire is appropriate for any recipe that requires a generous quantity of embers and/or a significant amount of radiant heat projecting out of the fireplace toward the hearth. Most hearth recipes start with a mature fire.

To a great extent, managing the fire for cooking means managing the fire to produce embers.

The intensity of the flames is also critical because the flames are a component, along with embers, in the amount of heat radiated out of the firebox toward the hearth.

Long-burning fire: *More than four hours.* The fire has burned through many logs and has therefore heated a substantial portion of the ash base on which it sits. Depending on the fire's cycle, the flames from the logs will be gentle, moderate, or high, as defined below. There will always be a significant amount of heat projected toward the hearth, and you will be unable to hold your hand at the edge of the hearth near the fire for more than a few seconds. The primary difference between a long-burning fire and a mature fire is the former's greater quantity of hot ash, making it the preferred fire for recipes that call for ash baking.

Once the fire is established, you need to determine how robust the flames should be. For many of the recipes, the rate at which the fire is burning is important because it determines how quickly fresh embers are created. The intensity of the flames is also critical because the flames are a component, along with embers, in the amount of heat radiated out of the firebox toward the hearth.

Three terms describe the flames: gentle, moderate, and high. When logs are set on top of either a mature fire or a long-burning fire, they are assumed to be resting on a substantial bed of embers. Even when the flames can be described as gentle, the combination of the fire and the embers will radiate a substantial amount of heat toward the hearth. For the ultimate guidance on my fire definitions, look to the recipes themselves. I provide cues, particularly cooking times, that will help you calibrate actual fires to my descriptions of them. Here are the basic characteristics of each type of flame.

Gentle flames are one or two logs burning lazily on a bed of hot embers. Fresh embers are produced slowly.

Moderate flames are two or three logs with flames that have some energy to them, but the flames are only a few inches (about 7.5 cm) long. The logs are burning on a hot bed of embers. This fire burns rapidly enough to permit harvesting of fresh embers for use on the hearth every ten to fifteen minutes.

High flames are three or four logs burning fiercely on a substantial bed of embers. This is a roaring fire, a fire with a great deal of energy—the flames are long, and the heat projected into the room on the border between the hearth and the firebox is intense. Embers are produced rapidly.

COOKING MULTICOURSE MEALS

I HAVE A VERY SMALL FIREPLACE, one that I am sure is smaller than the fireplace of most of my readers. My fireplace is only twenty-six inches (65 cm) wide. I routinely cook multicourse meals for eight to twelve guests entirely on my hearth. When I try to think about what I do that makes this possible, I think the most valuable answer is that I create ferociously hot fires that produce a prodigious quantity of embers. An anecdote might make this statement about "ferociously hot fires" seem more real: at one meal, a guest took off his shirt because, even in winter with a window open, the dining room was too hot.

Embers and flame are the raw materials of open-hearth cuisine. A large supply of embers, and a fire burning fast enough to replenish them as they are used, is analogous to having both money in the bank and a good-paying job. With enough embers and enough radiant heat pouring out of the fireplace toward the hearth, one can produce more food in a shorter amount of time than is possible in a standard kitchen, even if your fireplace is small.

A few recipes are so demanding of one or another hearth resource — of embers, of the space within the firebox, or of the space on the hearth — that, at least when working on a small fireplace, a single demanding recipe, such as Chicken in Clay (page 75), can prevent others from being cooked at the same time. As you plan multicourse meals, try to visualize each recipe's space requirements, and its need for resources, particularly embers. Manage the space and the fire to meet these needs.

When serving guests, remember that they will be interested in how you cook the meal, and so, unlike a dinner prepared in the kitchen, it does not all have to be ready when they arrive. In fact, it is better if it is not. Setting aside the matter of hearth cooking's incomparable taste, pulling food from the ashes, taking vegetables off the embers, shoveling embers off the lid of a Dutch oven and lifting it to release a cloud of steam — these are among the elements in the theater of hearth cooking that make it so memorable for guests. When it comes to dessert, I often choose one that can be cooked while my guests and I are eating dinner, such as Clafouti (page 194) or *Tarte Tatin* (page 186).

With enough embers and enough radiant heat pouring out of the fireplace ... one can produce more food in a shorter amount of time than is possible in a standard kitchen.

It was a pretty scene in the red fire-light; for there were no candles—why should there be, when the fire was so bright and was reflected from all the pewter and the polished oak?

George Eliot, *Adam Bede*

APPETIZERS

Roasted Onions

BASIC METHOD
Ember Roasting

EQUIPMENT
Shovel
Long-handled tongs

PRIMARY VENUE
Firebox

ALTERNATE VENUES
Barbecue
Campfire
Bread Oven

MEDIEVAL COOKS WERE HEARTH COOKS. To create their sophisticated cuisine, they took advantage of all the hearth cooking techniques, including the rustic method of roasting onions on the embers. The shock of high heat changes onions. Caramelized sugars combine with a hint of smoke to give them unexpected complexity. The roasting process is a sensual delight. When the charred onions are ready, spear one with a fork and hold it close to your ear. You will hear the juices churning and smell an intoxicating fragrance.

Of all the hearth-cooked dishes I most often serve my friends, this one remains a favorite. I developed the recipe before I found what is a closely related treatment in a book on medieval cooking. In that version from the latter part of the fifteenth century, the salad includes a little vinegar, oil, salt, and some spices. A complementary medieval spice mix for this recipe would include pepper, cinnamon, ginger, saffron, and clove, a blend not unlike the modern French *épices fines*. Use spices with a light touch to fuse with the warm tones of the hearth-roasted onions.

The Fire: A mature fire with moderate to high flames and a substantial bed of embers.

INGREDIENTS

(Serves 8 to 12 as an appetizer, 4 to 6 as a side dish)

6 medium to large yellow onions

Olive oil

1 to 2 tablespoons finely chopped fresh thyme or sage

Salt, preferably a gray sea salt

Use the shovel to spread embers beside the fire and immediately use the long-handled tongs to place each onion on the embers 4 to 8 inches (10 to 20 cm) from the flames. The embers contribute to the cooking, but the primary cooking comes from the onions' proximity to the fire. The ideal distance will char the outer skin, but also gives the heat time to penetrate to the center.

As the outer shell of each onion begins to blister, turn the onions with the tongs, rotating them several times during the roasting process. The onions are done when the outer skin is charred and the onions can easily be pierced to their center with a sharp fork. Aim for a cooking time of 20 to 40 minutes.

Remove the cooked onions from the fire, place on a plate, and take to the kitchen. When cool enough to handle, use a sharp knife to cut off the bottom of each onion. The burnt outer layers will often slip off like a glove. Quarter, separating all the leaves. While still warm, transfer to a bowl, drizzle lightly with an aromatic olive oil, toss with the herbs, and season with salt. Serve at once.

Roasted Red Peppers

BASIC METHOD
Ember Roasting

EQUIPMENT
Shovel
Long-handled tongs

PRIMARY VENUE
Firebox

ALTERNATE VENUES
Barbecue
Campfire
Bread Oven

THE CHARRED SWEET RED PEPPER is one of the miracles of the open hearth, a dynamic flavor in its own right, and a combination of color and taste that distinguishes any dish to which it is added. In my own fireplace cuisine, roasted red pepper joins with roasted onion and roasted eggplant to form a foundation of flavors that is all but impossible to create in the typical kitchen.

Many Italian cookbooks include instructions for roasting red peppers on the stovetop. Fireplace roasting is faster, easier, and produces a more flavorful result. The ember-charred skin is brittle and easily peels off.

Serve strips of roasted red pepper as an appetizer. They are excellent eaten as is, or on crackers, flat breads, or toast. The better the underlying pepper, the better the roasted pepper will be. Create a beautiful and vibrant antipasto salad with strips of roasted pepper, anchovy fillets, thinly sliced roasted onion, flat-leaf parsley, a fruity olive oil, and salt to taste. Or make a soup by puréeing 6 roasted red peppers with a roasted onion and a boiled potato. Simmer for half an hour, adding water as needed. Top each serving with a tablespoon of heavy cream or crème fraîche.

Raw

55 seconds

3 minutes

The Fire: A mature fire with moderate to high flames and a substantial bed of embers.

INGREDIENTS
(Serves 6 to 8)

4 sweet red peppers
(The smoother and more uniform the shape, the more evenly the peppers will roast. The deeper the red, the better the flavor.)
Salt (optional)
Olive oil (optional)

Use a shovel to spread embers beside the fire and use the long-handled tongs to immediately place each pepper on the embers 2 to 4 inches (5 to 10 cm) from the flames. The embers contribute to the cooking, but the primary charring comes from the peppers' proximity to the fire. At the ideal degree of hotness, when you first begin charring the peppers, you will hear popping sounds as the skin blisters. As each side is charred, use the tongs to turn the pepper, exposing a fresh side to the flames. Each side should char in a maximum of 3 minutes.

When the entire pepper is black, use tongs to remove it from beside the fire to a plate. When cool enough to handle, peel off the burnt skin. Your hands will get covered with black, so do this near the kitchen sink.

After the skin is peeled, rinse your hands and cut off the top of the pepper. Next, slice the pepper down one side, open it flat, and remove the seeds. The peppers can be rinsed to remove every last speck of char, but rinsing dilutes the flavor, so I don't recommend it. Cut the peppers in long strips, place on a small plate, and serve. Red peppers purchased out of season are better when lightly dressed with salt and an aromatic olive oil.

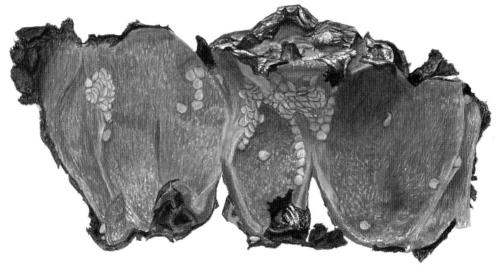

9 minutes

Bruschetta

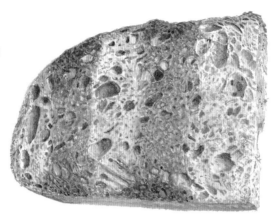

BASIC METHOD
Hearthside Grilling

EQUIPMENT
Grill
Shovel

PRIMARY VENUE
Hearth

ALTERNATE VENUES
Barbecue
Campfire

INGREDIENTS
(Serves 6)

6 bread slices, hand-
cut from a *pain de
campagne*–style loaf

Olive oil

2 or 3 cloves garlic,
peeled but left whole

I CAN'T THINK OF ANYTHING more perfect than bruschetta for those times when you are hungry and need something that is quick and delicious. Grill both sides of a piece of bread over moderate embers, brush one side with an aromatic olive oil, and rub the same side with a clove of garlic. That's all there is to it. Crisp hot grilled bread is a masterpiece of the Italian grill—a blend of fire, toasted wheat, olive oil, and the aroma of garlic made volatile by heat.

With a good bread, a flavorful olive oil, and sweet garlic, it is difficult to improve upon the classic preparation. Cooks being cooks, however, there is always the temptation to experiment. My rule is to keep the toppings simple. In a restaurant near Spoleto, I was served bruschetta with grilled mushrooms, specifically with grilled saffron milk caps *(Lactarius deliciosus)*, a recipe included in this book. I often serve bruschetta topped with Grilled Chicken Livers (page 27) or with Ember-Roasted Vegetables (page 136).

 The Fire: A mature fire with gentle flames.

Place the clean grill on the hearth. Shovel an even layer of embers underneath to create gentle heat. Lay the bread on the grill and grill until both sides are light brown, turning once. Add additional embers as needed. Different breads toast differently, some burning very easily, so be cautious with the embers. When the bread is toasted and still hot, brush one side with olive oil and rub with the garlic cloves. Return the embers to the fireplace and serve the bread.

Grilled Chicken Livers

CHICKEN LIVERS MARINATED IN OIL AND HERBS and then grilled on the hearth over smoldering rosemary sprigs are fabulous whether eaten as a topping on bruschetta or from the end of a fork. The best livers to grill are firm and pink. Even so, livers are delicate and can be difficult to handle on the grill. That is why, before grilling, I advise sautéing them just enough to firm them up.

The Fire: *A mature fire that has produced several shovelfuls of embers, enough both for the initial sautéing and for grilling, and a moderate to hot fire to pull smoke up the chimney.*

To make the marinade: In a mortar, pound the garlic, salt, and thyme into a coarse paste. Add the olive oil and mix. Place the livers in a bowl, add the marinade, mix well, cover, and let rest for 2 to 4 hours in the refrigerator.

When ready to grill, place the tripod ond the clean grill on the hearth close to the fire. Put the livers with their marinade in the frying pan on the tripod, and shovel embers underneath to create high heat. Cook the livers, stirring as needed, until they just begin to firm on the outside, but are still raw in the middle, 2 to 4 minutes. Just before they are done, preheat the grill by shoveling an even layer of embers underneath the grill to create moderate to high heat. As soon as the livers are ready, remove the frying pan from the heat, brush the grill with olive oil, and, using a fork, place the livers on the grill.

When you can hear the livers cooking again, begin placing rosemary sprigs on the embers, 1 to 2 half-branches at a time to produce a thin stream of smoke. Turn the

livers as needed. If additional embers are required, add them with the shovel a sprinkling at a time. Livers are done when they are firm and hot all the way through but still show some pink in the middle. Transfer from the grill to a plate, return the embers to the fireplace, and serve.

BASIC METHOD
Hearthside Tripod and
    Hearthside Grilling

EQUIPMENT
10-inch (25-cm)
    frying pan
Grill
Tripod
Shovel

PRIMARY VENUE
Hearth

ALTERNATE VENUES
Barbecue
Campfire

INGREDIENTS
(Serves 6)

2 cloves garlic

1 teaspoon salt

4 thyme sprigs,
    coarsely chopped,
    or 1 teaspoon dried
    thyme

¼ cup (60 ml) olive oil

1 pound (450 g) firm
    chicken livers,
    halved, and fat and
    sinew removed

1 bunch rosemary
    sprigs cut in half, or
    small handful of dried
    rosemary, soaked
    in warm water

BASIC METHOD
Dutch Oven

EQUIPMENT
5-quart (5-l) Dutch oven
    with legs
Shovel

PRIMARY VENUE
Hearth

ALTERNATE VENUES
Campfire
Bread Oven

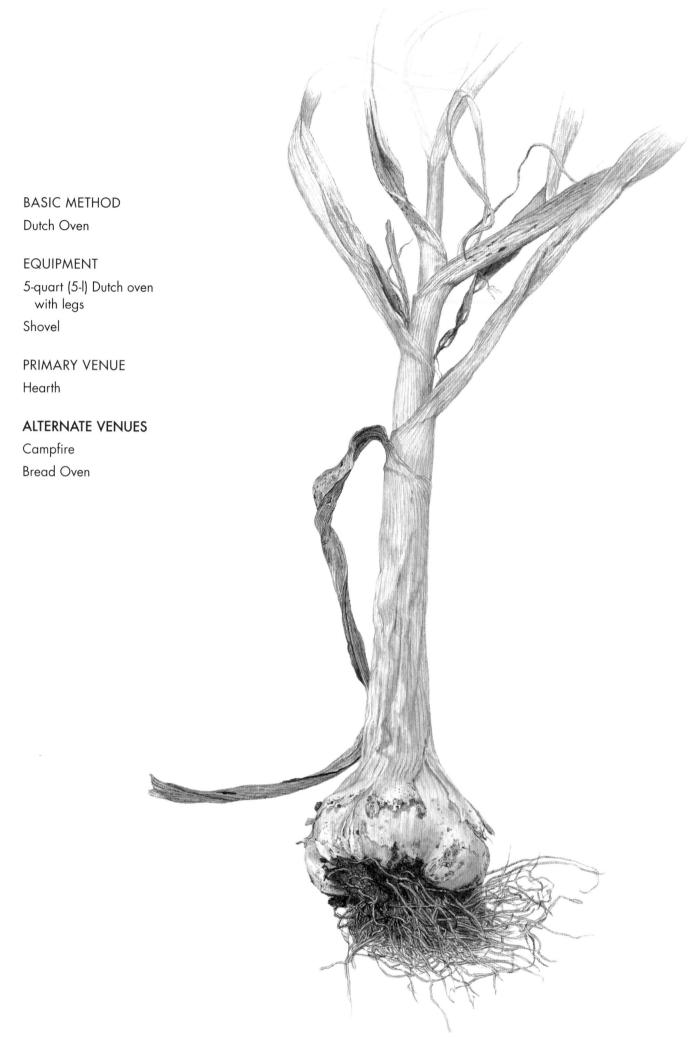

Baked Garlic

INGREDIENTS
(Serves 6)

Thyme sprigs, to cover
    the bottom of the
    Dutch oven
6 large heads garlic
1 teaspoon salt
¼ cup (60 ml) olive oil
2 cups (75 ml) water

FRESHLY HARVESTED GARLIC IS THE SWEETEST, most delicious garlic to roast. In the United States, most of the garlic comes from California, where it is harvested in the spring. By the following midwinter, it is past its prime. Even so, slow roasting transforms the hard, hot, stinking weed into a soft, sweet purée that blends nicely with the other roasted and grilled appetizers recommended in this book. Slow-roasted garlic of any age and variety is excellent spread on grilled toast.

The two simplest methods for roasting garlic require no equipment. One calls for roasting the heads on the edge of the hearth in front of a gentle fire. If the fire is too hot, the heads will show you by splitting open and oozing caramelized pulp. If the roasting is going too slowly, correct by pushing the garlic closer to the fire. As a rule, start the garlic 10 to 12 inches (25 to 30 cm) from the flames. Garlic can also be baked, like potatoes, buried in hot ash. Garlic does best when baked slowly, so try to intuit where the ash is 300° to 325°F (150° to 160°C), or use an infrared thermometer to check. The recipe I provide here is one for garlic baked in a Dutch oven over a bed of herbs. It makes a delicious treat on a wintry day, a reminder that the summer sun once warmly shined.

 The Fire: A mature fire with gentle flames that has generated at least a few shovelfuls of embers.

Line the bottom of the Dutch oven with the herbs. Cut the top one-fourth off of each garlic head and place the heads, cut-side down, on the herbs. Add the salt, olive oil, and water. Cover and bring to the hearth.

Place the Dutch oven on the hearth where it will receive moderate side heat from the fire, usually 4 to 6 inches (10 to 15 cm) back from the edge of the firebox. Begin by shoveling a thick layer of embers underneath the Dutch oven to create high heat. Bring the water to a boil and then let the heat fall so the water simmers. Add additional embers as necessary to maintain the water at a simmer. When the garlic is soft, 35 to 40 minutes, remove the cover and increase the heat under the Dutch oven. Boil away the water and continue cooking the garlic, adding embers as required, until the exposed face is browned. When done, remove the garlic heads to a serving platter and shovel the embers back into the fireplace. Serve the garlic warm.

Roasted-Eggplant Spread

BASIC METHOD
Ember Baking

EQUIPMENT
Shovel
Long-handled tongs

PRIMARY VENUE
Firebox

ALTERNATE VENUES
Barbecue
Campfire
Bread Oven

ONE APRIL I WAS IN ISTANBUL with a friend researching the Turkish morel harvest. On this particular day, we were following separate leads, and by early afternoon I was in the Kadiköy district, on the Asian side of the Bosporus, and very hungry. I selected a restaurant situated on a narrow street overhung with grapevines and outfitted with a grill topped by an impressive copper hood. I ordered what I saw everyone else ordering: flat bread, grilled ground lamb, grilled tomato, and grilled eggplant served with a sauce of yogurt and garlic. The lunch came, I ate, and it was one of those rare memorable meals. Each taste of the eggplant was a revelation, the tomato was fabulous, the flat bread excellent. I sat eating in that almost drugged state that one sometimes reaches on a long trip. I was happy. I was floating. I was smiling. I made eye contact with the waiter, who had been watching me. He came over. I had been eating the lunch incorrectly. Very friendly, he took it upon himself to be my instructor. I wasn't supposed to eat each ingredient separately; instead, they were to be mashed together. He took the fork from my hand and mixed everything up. I appeared thankful, but that amazing eggplant was now masked by many other flavors. Lunch was not the same.

Cooking eggplants until their skins char—on a grill or, more traditionally, on embers—creates one of the warmest and most distinctive tastes of the open hearth. Ember-charred eggplants, like Roasted Red Peppers (page 24), cannot be cooked too hot, and can even withstand flame. Fire, like a lens, focuses and intensifies the flavor. This recipe for eggplant pounded with garlic and olive oil is memorable because the sharp, deep, complex flavor of the fire-touched eggplant is so striking. The spread is simple to make, can be made several hours in advance, and merits making often. Serve with flat bread or crackers. In northern India, an almost identical dish is a standard restaurant dish.

 The Fire: A mature fire, moderate to high flames, and a substantial bed of embers.

Use the shovel to spread embers beside the fire and immediately use the long-handled tongs to place the eggplant on the embers 2 to 4 inches (5 to 10 cm) from the flames. The embers contribute to the cooking, but the primary charring comes from the eggplant's proximity to the fire. After 4 to 7 minutes, even the largest eggplant should be thoroughly charred on one side. Using the tongs, turn the eggplant to expose the uncooked side to the flames. After another 4 to 7 minutes, the eggplant should be charred on all sides and very soft. The eggplant must be thoroughly cooked for the best flavor. If you have any doubts, cook it until the eggplant has lost a little weight. When done, transfer the eggplant to a plate. If it has collapsed, you may need to use the shovel to remove it from the fireplace. (Japanese eggplants are cooked the same way, but because they are smaller, they need to be watched carefully. They should be turned frequently and are usually done in 4 to 5 minutes.)

When the eggplant is cool, lift it up so you are holding it in the palm of your hand. Using a dull knife or a spoon, split it open lengthwise. At this point, especially when working with large eggplants, you may feel that you have a disaster on your hands. You don't. Still holding the eggplant in your hand, spoon the pulp into a measuring cup and discard the charred skin. You should have at least 1 cup (240 ml) pulp. Some of the charred skin may end up in the cup, but you can pick it out later.

In a mortar, pound the garlic into a smooth paste. Add the eggplant pulp and the olive oil, and season with salt. If the eggplant yielded more than 1 cup (240 ml) pulp, adjust the other ingredients proportionately. Mix thoroughly, then serve.

Long-handled Tongs

INGREDIENTS
(Serves 4 to 6)

2 large eggplants, or 6 Japanese eggplants, about 1½ pounds (650 g) total weight
1 clove garlic
1 to 3 teaspoons olive oil
Salt

A great fire was burning on the hearth, and from afar over the isle there was a fragrance of cleft cedar and juniper, as they burned; but she within was singing with a sweet voice as she went to and fro before the loom, weaving with a golden shuttle.

HOMER, *The Odyssey*

BEANS
and
SOUPS

Beans

BASIC METHOD
Pot Beside the Fire

EQUIPMENT
Terra-cotta bean pot,
 Dutch oven, or
 other pot with lid
Shovel

PRIMARY VENUE
Firebox or Hearth

ALTERNATE VENUES
Campfire
Bread Oven

B OILED BEANS—AS A MAIN COURSE, as a substantial side
dish, as the heart of a soup—are the invaluable friend of the country farmer and fireside cook. Given time, and a steady, gentle heat,
beans cook with minimal supervision. A pot of beans placed on the hearth
in front of the fire will cook in the fire's radiant heat while you do something else.

At its simplest, the recipe for beans can be easily told: simmer with
water and salt until done. This is how millions of people prepare the beans
they eat as the central portion of every meal. As a staple food—as someone
else's staple food—this is the kind of recipe that is poorly served by cook-

books. In a book, the telling is over too soon, and the true weight of the recipe is not conveyed. Staple foods acquire deep personal associations that go far beyond cooking technique and flavor. For bean eaters, no book has enough pages to hold all those associations.

Beans and fire work well together, and fire-cooked beans are well worth a frequent visit. I provide a slightly more elaborate recipe than beans with salt. In keeping with the tonalities of this book, I follow a French practice of boiling beans with aromatics. Even so, the recipe remains lean and unadorned, at one with the spirit of one of the world's great staple foods.

 The Fire: A mature fire with gentle to moderate flames.

Place the beans in the pot along with the water, onion, garlic, bouquet garni, and salt. The pot should be at least three-quarters full. Cover the pot.

Place the bean pot 4 to 6 inches (10 to 15 cm) from the fire, either on the hearth or set beside the fire within the firebox. If the pot is sitting on the hearth, at your discretion, use the shovel to push embers against the base of the pot where it is nearest the flames. If it is sitting within the firebox, you may ring the pot with embers. When the beans first begin cooking and there is plenty of water, they may boil on the side of the pot nearest the flames, but as the water is absorbed, let the heat fall to a simmer. When the beans have plumped, begin tasting to judge the cooking time. At any point, you can quickly adjust the cooking speed by adding or subtracting embers from the base of the pot. As the beans absorb the water, they become increasingly at risk from burning, so stir from time to time and add water to prevent sticking.

The beans are done when they are soft and no longer starchy. The timing, which depends on variety and on how recently the beans were dried, can range from one hour to many hours. Remove the pot from the fireplace and remove and discard the onion, garlic, and bouquet garni. Season with salt and serve. If there is excess liquid, reserve it for use in soups.

INGREDIENTS
(Serves 4 to 6)

2⅓ cups (450 g) dried beans

6 cups (1.5 l) water

1 yellow onion, studded with 3 whole cloves

1 head garlic, halved

Bouquet garni of 1 celery stalk, a few parsley stems, 1 thyme sprig, and 1 bay leaf, tied together with kitchen string

1½ teaspoons salt

Bay leaves

Fagioli al Fiasco

BASIC METHOD
Radiant Heat

EQUIPMENT
Glass flask, such as
    a 750-ml Chianti
    bottle
Cotton ball or
    rag and string
Shovel

PRIMARY VENUE
Hearth

ALTERNATE VENUES
Campfire
Bread Oven

THE TUSCAN *fagioli al fiasco* is one of the most strikingly flavored and elegantly simple fireplace dishes. It requires, almost literally, no work at all. Put the ingredients—beans, water, olive oil, garlic, salt, sage—into a Chianti bottle, the kind that has a bulbous base, then, when banking the fire down for the night, surround the bottle with hot ash. When you wake in the morning, remove the bottle from the ashes. The beans will have cooked to perfection in the gentle heat of the embers. The flask's closed atmosphere produces beans that are soft, intensely flavored by the garlic and sage, and often lightly caramelized—beans that have much in common with the similarly long-cooked American baked beans.

You do not need a Chianti bottle. Any bottle with a comparatively wide base will work. I have had good luck with brandy bottles, but you could also use a Mason jar. Flasks impose a single limitation: the beans must be small enough so that, when cooked, they can still be shaken out of the narrow neck. A variant to surrounding the bottle with hot ash is to place it on the hearth and bake the beans in the radiant heat of the daytime fire. The results are the same, but the daytime method is easier to master—you can see what is happening within the bottle—and is the method called for here.

The Fire: A mature fire with gentle flames.

Place the flask inside a bowl to catch any beans that miss the opening. Using your hand to guide them, pour the beans into the flask. Add the garlic, sage, and salt. Using a funnel, add the water and olive oil. Cap the bottle with a stopper made out of the cotton ball, using string to tie the stopper lightly in place. A little steam must be able to escape during the cooking process. If the bottle is stoppered too tightly, pressure can build and the bottle can explode.

Place the flask on the hearth on a shallow mound of ash with the leading edge 8 to 10 inches (20 to 25 cm) from the fire. While the flames may be described as "gentle," you should not be able to hold your hand near the bottle for more than a few seconds. Reduce the risk of cracking the glass by turning the bottle a half-turn a few times during the first 15 minutes. After about 40 minutes, you should begin to see an occasional small bubble rising to the surface; after about an hour, there should be a gentle simmer on the side of the bottle closest to the fire. Once the beans begin to simmer, a few will float to the surface and the visible cooking process begins.

Since cooking in a glass bottle is a visible process, you can see precisely what is happening and thus maintain fine control over the speed of the cooking. During the 9- to 10-hour cooking process, the fireplace fire will go through many cycles of getting hotter when a log is added and cooler as the wood burns down. The fire should never get so hot that the beans boil rapidly on the side nearest the flames. If the fire cools to the point that the beans stop simmering, you can increase the heat by shoveling embers around the base of the bottle. Once most of the water has been absorbed, the beans become very sensitive to small changes in temperature. By maintaining a sprinkling of hot embers around the base of the bottle, you can keep the beans simmering throughout the bottle, not just on the side nearest the flames.

The beans are done when all the water has evaporated—the only liquid will be the olive oil—and the beans are a beautiful caramel color. Remove the flask from the hearth and shovel the embers back into the fireplace. When the bottle is cool enough to handle, but the beans are still warm, shake the beans out of the bottle. Serve warm or reheat on the hearth for a later meal.

Note: Sometimes the beans become mushy and will not come out of the bottle intact. When this happens, add a little water, cover the top, shake, and pour the beans out into a saucepan. Reheat on the hearth to enjoy a tasty bean soup.

INGREDIENTS
(Serves 2 to 4)

¾ cup (185 g) cannellini, navy, or other small white dried beans, picked over and rinsed

2 to 6 cloves garlic

6 fresh sage leaves

½ teaspoon salt

2 cups (475 ml) water

¼ cup (60 ml) olive oil

Sage

Garlic

Winter Bean Soup

BASIC METHOD
Pot Beside the Fire

EQUIPMENT
5-quart (5-l) terra-cotta
    bean pot or other
    appropriately sized
    pot
Shovel

PRIMARY VENUE
Firebox or Hearth

ALTERNATE VENUES
Campfire
Bread Oven

INGREDIENTS
(Serves 4 to 6)

2⅓ cups (450 g)
    dried beans, picked
    over and rinsed

2 quarts (2 l) water

2 yellow onions,
    1 studded with
    2 whole cloves and
    1 finely minced

2 heads garlic, halved

Rind of a hard cheese
    such as Parmesan,
    or 6-ounce (175-g)
    piece salt pork

(continued)

BEAN SOUPS LEND THEMSELVES to an improvisational style of preparation—a bit of this and a bit of that yield a rich soup laden with flavor. Alternatively, if you have a lot of something on hand, the soup can be given a more singular identity: tomato-bean soup, nettle-bean soup, kale-bean soup. Country women traditionally add additional fat and flavor to soups with a piece of salt pork or the rinds of hard cheeses.

My recipe for a winter bean soup calls for nettles, a winter green where I live, and a handful of dried mushrooms. Neither ingredient is crucial in terms of flavor, but both are important in terms of an idea. Wild foods were part of the lives of most people who lived and cooked with an open hearth. Foraging, even in

Nettle

your own garden, or on the edge of a parking lot, draws you closer into the world of the country farmer who, until quite recently, always married what was grown in the field with what grew beside the field. Even a small amount of foraging adds a component to the meal that cannot be bought. I refer not to flavor, but to a layer of memory, the where and when of what you find.

With a steady, gentle fire, this richly flavored soup cooks on the hearth with minimal supervision. Start it in the morning for the evening meal; it will never let you down.

Any dried beans can be used. If you have a vegetable garden, plant more beans than you can eat fresh, let them dry on the vine, and then use them dried in this soup.

Serve with a salad, bread, and red table wine.

The Fire: A mature fire with gentle to moderate flames.

Place the beans in the pot along with the water, the clove-studded onion, the garlic, cheese rind, and bouquet garni. The pot should be at least three-fourths full. Cover.

Place the pot 4 to 6 inches (10 to 15 cm) from the fire, either on the hearth or set beside the fire within the firebox. If the pot is sitting on the hearth, at your discretion, use the shovel to push embers against the base of the pot where it is nearest the flames. If it is sitting within the firebox, you may ring the base of the pot with embers. When the beans first begin cooking and there is plenty of water, they may boil on the side of the pot nearest the flames, but as the water is absorbed, let the heat fall to a simmer. When the beans have plumped, begin tasting to judge the cooking time. At any point, you can adjust cooking speed by adding or subtracting embers from the base of the pot. As the beans absorb the water, they become increasingly at risk from burning, so stir from time to time and add water to prevent sticking.

The beans are done when they are soft and no longer starchy. The timing, which depends on variety and on how recently the beans were dried, can range from 1 hour to several hours. Remove the pot from the fire; remove the onion, garlic, and bouquet garni and discard. Add the minced onion, potatoes, tomatoes, and mushrooms. Re-cover and put the pot back near the fire. Shovel embers against the pot where it is nearest the flames so the contents begin to simmer. Cook the soup, stirring as needed to distribute the heat, for an additional 20 minutes, or until the potatoes are tender.

While the vegetables are cooking, make the toast according to the directions for Bruschetta (page 26).

When the potatoes are tender and the toast is finished, add the greens to the soup. Heat uncovered for a few minutes, stirring as needed, until the greens are limp and tender. Season with salt. Place the toast, one piece per bowl, in soup bowls and ladle in the soup. Reserve the other pieces of toast for second servings. Serve with grated Parmesan, if desired.

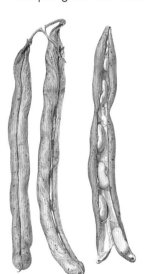
Dried beans

Bouquet garni of
  1 celery stalk,
  few parsley stems,
  1 thyme sprig, and
  1 bay leaf, tied
  together with
  kitchen string

1 large or 2 medium-
  sized potatoes,
  unpeeled, diced

2 cups (350 g) fresh
  or canned tomatoes,
  chopped

Handful of dried
  porcino mushrooms

2 cups (175 g)
  chopped mixed
  greens such as kale,
  mustard, cabbage,
  and, season permit-
  ting, a wild green
  such as nettles

Salt

Grated Parmesan
  (optional)

Toast

2 slices bread
  per person

Olive oil

2 to 4 cloves garlic,
  peeled but left whole

Baked Beans

BASIC METHOD
Pot Buried in Hot Ash

EQUIPMENT
3½-quart (3.5-l)
    terra-cotta bean pot,
    Dutch oven, or
    other pot with lid
    (or improvised lid
    of aluminum foil)
Shovel

PRIMARY VENUE
Firebox

ALTERNATE VENUES
Campfire
Bread Oven

The meal is for men who toil. At one end of the table stands a pot of ample dimensions, smoking from the great oven flanking the fireplace, of that most excellent of New England cookeries, "A dish of baked beans," crowned with a great square piece of salt, fat pork, crisped and rich.

THE NATIONAL ERA, *October 30, 1851*

IF YOU HAVE ENOUGH hot ashes to bury a bean pot up to its neck, you can bake beans in your fireplace. In Puritan New England, beans were often served for the Sabbath, which began on Saturday at sundown. The classic preparation is a long, slow baking of navy beans mixed with molasses and pork, either in a pot buried in the ashes of the fireplace, or in the dying heat of the bread oven after the bread is baked. The gentle all-day baking in ash is alchemical. With virtually no human intervention other than keeping a side fire burning, and, from time to time, adding small amounts of water to the pot, the beans become, in the eighth, tenth, or twelfth hour, more than just beans—they become something dark, buttery, and dense with flavor. That is when baked beans are done. Eat them the day they are baked, or keep them for the next day and reheat on the hearth.

The bread most associated with baked beans is Brown Bread (page 180), a steamed loaf made with molasses and a mixture of corn, wheat, and sometimes rye or barley flours. A side dish of sautéed vegetables, such as cabbage, kale, or collards, provides contrasting flavor and texture.

 The Fire: Ideally, bake beans in the morning in hot ashes from a fire banked the night before at bedtime. Alternatively, after the pot is surrounded with ashes, light a fire next to the pot. Once a solid quantity of embers is produced, maintain gentle flames beside the pot throughout the cooking.

Place the beans and water in a large bowl and let soak overnight.

In the morning, drain the beans into a colander, reserving the liquid for use throughout the cooking. In a large bowl, mix together the molasses, mustard, salt, and pepper, using some of the reserved bean water as needed to thin the mixture. Stir in the beans, mixing well.

Place the beans and one-third of the salt pork in the bottom of the bean pot. Add the onion. Fill the pot with the remaining beans and salt pork. Ideally, the beans should come within 1 or 2 inches (2.5 or 5 cm) of the pot's rim. Add the reserved bean water just to cover the beans. Cover with the lid.

Using the shovel, dig a depression in the ashes 12 to 18 inches (30 to 45 cm) from where you will build the fire. Place the covered bean pot in the depression and mound the pot on all sides up to its neck with ashes (ideally, hot ashes from the previous night's banked fire).

Build a robust fire near the ash-mounded bean pot to develop a solid mass of embers. Let this fire die down and maintain it as a gentle fire throughout the day to provide steady, even heat to the mound of ashes surrounding the pot. Maintain the beans at a very slow simmer—just a few bubbles around the mouth of the bean pot on the side nearest the fire. To get the pot up to temperature, mix fresh embers into the ash and pile embers on top of the ash, making certain that the back of the bean pot—the side away from the fire—is piled with a substantial quantity of embers. Once the beans begin simmering, the side fire will maintain the temperature.

Cook for 8 to 12 hours, adding the reserved bean liquid as needed to keep the beans barely covered with liquid. Stir lightly every couple of hours to make sure no beans are sticking. If, after a couple of hours, you feel the beans are not cooking quickly enough, add additional embers to the ash mound on the sides that are not exposed to the fire. For the purposes of this dish, the beans are not done until they have darkened, become very soft, and absorbed the flavor of the surrounding sauce, which itself has become dark and thick. When done, remove the bean pot from the ashes, wipe the pot clean with a cloth, and bring to the table. These beans are also excellent reheated the next day.

Brown Bread

(Serves 6 to 8)

2 pounds (1 kg) dried navy beans or other small white dried beans, picked over and rinsed

2½ quarts (2.5 l) water

1 cup (300 g) dark molasses

1 tablespoon dry mustard

2 teaspoons salt

1 teaspoon pepper

¾ pound (350 g) salt pork, cut into several pieces

1 yellow onion, peeled but left whole

Bread Soup

BASIC METHOD
Boiling and
    Hearthside Grilling

EQUIPMENT
Saucepan with lid
Tripod
Grill
Shovel

PRIMARY VENUES
Firebox and Hearth

ALTERNATE VENUES
Barbecue
Campfire
Bread Oven

FOR THOSE OF US WHOSE choice of cuisine is based on arbitrary personal decisions, it is difficult to imagine the larder of a subsistence farmer for whom the choice of what to eat is closely prescribed by circumstances. Although most of us like bread and eat it daily, it is at the edge of our cuisine. "Give us this day our daily bread" is a prayer we now understand metaphorically. Money, not bread, is our staff of life.

To find the inspiration that is at the heart of bread soup, you have to imagine yourself living in a different time and place, and in very different circumstances. One of fire's magical properties is its ability to transport us out of our time into another. And so, one evening, with darkness at your back, look into the flames and imagine that it is some years ago and you are living on a small farm with poor land. It is a cold evening in early spring; a cuckoo is issuing its call into the gathering night as the pine forest closes in. There is bread on the shelf from last week's baking, a little salt pork, enough potatoes to last until early potatoes can be harvested, and, if you imagine yourself in southern Europe, olive oil. Wild chicory shoots are growing by the path to the barn. There is a store in the village, but money is scarce and the road is muddy. What's for dinner can only be what you have on hand—tempered by an eye on tomorrow. That is the soul of bread soup.

Russian kale

Bread soup was found throughout Europe. The version I present here is from northern Italy. It is a flavorful soup with a rich texture that can be made at the last minute. It always makes converts among my guests.

 The Fire: A mature fire, gentle to moderate flames, with a good supply of embers both to boil the greens and to toast the bread.

Place the clean grill on the hearth. Shovel an even layer of embers underneath to create gentle to moderate heat. Lay down the bread and grill, turning once, until both sides are light brown, adding additional embers as needed. Different breads toast differently, some burning very easily, so be cautious with the embers. When the bread is toasted and still hot, rub one side with the garlic cloves and set aside. Return the embers to the fireplace.

Pour the lightly salted water into the saucepan, cover, and place the tripod on the hearth so the saucepan sits within 4 to 6 inches (10 to 15 cm) of the fire. Push embers against the base of the saucepan where it is nearest the flames. In 10 to 15 minutes, the water nearest the heat will simmer. Lift the saucepan and shovel a thick layer of embers under and around the tripod. Replace the saucepan. In 2 to 3 minutes, the water will boil. Uncover, add the greens, re-cover, and cook until the greens are limp but still firm, 3 to 5 minutes. Remove the pan from the heat, shovel the embers back into the fireplace, and drain the greens in a colander, reserving the water.

To assemble the soup in a serving bowl: Dip a slice of the garlic toast in the vegetable water until it is soggy and place it in the bottom of the bowl. Lightly dress with olive oil, a layer of greens, and a sprinkling of Parmesan. Repeat the layering until the ingredients are used up, ending with a layer of cheese. Spoon the remaining vegetable water over the bread until a small amount of water pools in the bottom of the bowl. Using a large serving spoon, break up the bread, mixing the ingredients together, and serve in individual bowls.

INGREDIENTS
(Serves 4 to 6)

8 to 12 slices bread

4 to 6 cloves garlic, peeled but left whole

3 cups (725 ml) water, lightly salted

2 pounds (1 kg) mixed greens such as chard, kale, broccoli rabe, or chicory, trimmed and coarsely chopped

Olive oil

1/3 pound (150 g) Parmesan, grated

Aïgo Bouido

EVERY CULTURE HAS its tonics and revivers. In American cuisine, chicken soup is the tonic and a glass of water with sodium bicarbonate is the reviver—what we take when we have eaten or drunk too much the night before, and our stomachs don't feel quite right.

There is a great tradition of soups in Mediterranean Europe that combine tonic and reviver into one. These soups are based on tonics made from one or more of a group of ingredients, often the common culinary herbs—thyme, sage, rosemary, bay leaves—alone or with garlic, egg, salt, olive oil, and bread. While we tend to adopt the fancier fare of a region—the festival foods, the more elaborate restaurant creations—it is in the dishes that exist on the cusp between food and medicine that I find the essence of my Mediterranean dream: wild herbs, strong flavors, simple combinations. In southern France, *Aïgo Bouido*, literally "boiled water" in Provençal, is made with garlic and herbs picked in the hills or by the roadside.

The essence of a tonic, of course, is that it suits your mood, so adjust the flavors accordingly. If you need reviving on a day when the very thought of egg yolk would make you sick, leave it out. *Aïgo Bouido* was the daily drink of many a Provençal family. It was credited with a wide range of curative powers including, but not limited to, curing a hangover, the common cold, melancholy, and the effects of aging. This recipe calls for a single variety of herb in the soup, but combining herbs is well within the *Aïgo Bouido* tradition.

Simmer the soup on the embers of the fire, toast the bread on the end of a fork, and drink the soup sitting in front of the hearth. Quietude before the hearth is part of the cure.

The Fire: A mature fire with moderate to high flames.

Put the water, garlic, and herbs in the covered saucepan. Place the pan in the fireplace with one side pushed within 2 to 4 inches (5 to 10 cm) of the fire. At your discretion, use the shovel to push embers against the base of the pot where it is nearest the flames. Bring the water to a simmer on the side that is closest to the heat and maintain the soup at a simmer for 15 to 20 minutes, or until the broth is aromatic and the garlic is soft.

Make toast while the broth is cooking. Either toast the bread before the flames on the end of the long-handled fork or toast them on the hearthside grill. If using the grill, shovel embers underneath to create gentle to moderate heat. Lay down the bread and grill, turning once, until both sides are light brown, adding additional embers as needed. When the bread is done, set it aside. Shovel the embers back into the fireplace.

When the soup is done, season with salt. Place a piece of toast in the bottom of each bowl and place an egg yolk on top. Pour the soup through a sieve over the egg. If you are extremely fond of garlic, press the garlic through the sieve into the soup. Use a fork to mix in the yolk. Break up the now-sodden bread, and serve.

INGREDIENTS
(Serves 2)

3 cups (25 ml) water

8 cloves garlic, peeled but left whole

3 fresh or dried sage sprigs, or 6 fresh or dried thyme sprigs, or 4 to 8 bay leaves

2 slices bread

Salt

2 egg yolks

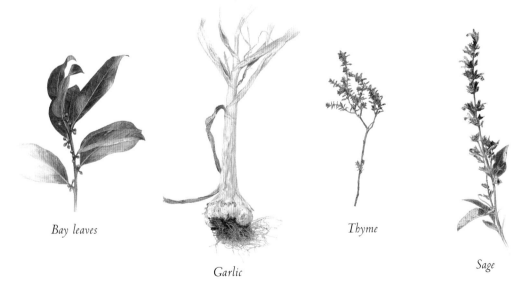

Bay leaves

Garlic

Thyme

Sage

Heaped up on the floor, to form a kind of throne, were turkeys, geese, game, poultry, brown, great joints of meat, suckling-pigs, long wreaths of sausages, mince pies, plum-puddings, barrels of oysters, red-hot chestnuts, cherry-cheeked apples, juicy oranges, luscious pears, immense twelfth-cakes, and seething bowls of punch, that made the chamber dim with their delicious steam.

CHARLES DICKENS, *A Christmas Carol*

FISH,
POULTRY,
and
EGGS

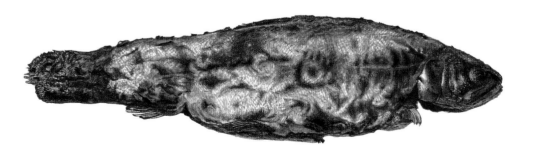

Ember-Baked Fish

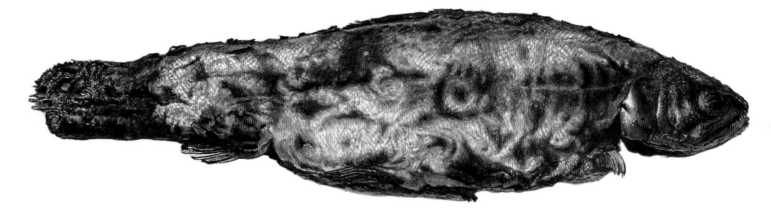

As soon then as they were come to land, they saw a fire of coals there, and fish laid thereon, and bread.

John 21:9

BASIC METHOD
Ember Baking

EQUIPMENT
Shovel
Spatula

PRIMARY VENUE
Firebox

ALTERNATE VENUES
Barbecue
Campfire
Bread Oven

FISH AND FLAT BREAD BAKED ON EMBERS are ancient foods of the Middle East. It is the meal Jesus is said to have fed his disciples on the shore of the Sea of Tiberius. It is a meal of today's Bedouin fishermen, and it is a meal you can make at home on a thick layer of embers spread across the fireplace floor.

The fish is browned, even charred by the embers, but because it cooks so quickly, the flesh remains soft and moist. Served with flat bread and chile paste, this is a specialty of restaurants in the cities of the Red Sea, Sana'a, Aden, and Massawa. In Sana'a, where natural gas is cheap, restaurant cooks thread the fish onto sticks and lower them into tandoor ovens heated by a roaring jet of gas. In Massawa, the fish is cooked in the same way, but the ovens are built of adobe and fired with wood. In both cities, after the fish is removed from the oven, dough is slapped onto the white-hot walls of the oven and baked in one to two minutes.

If you are preparing fish and Flat Bread (page 162) on the embers, I suggest prebaking the breads on a hearthside griddle before baking the fish, and then finishing the breads on the embers after the fish is done. In this way, both the fish and the breads will be hot when served. In keeping with an ancient practice, if you live near the sea, add seawater in lieu of salt.

Fish cooked on embers is a meal that can be eaten with a knife and fork, but I recommend that you sit on the floor in front of the fire with newspapers as the tabletop and your fingers as the fork. Let your house become a fisherman's hut, the floor the desert sand, the time two thousand years ago.

In traditional societies, a pitcher of water, soap, a bowl, and a towel are passed around to the seated diners both before and after the meal so hands can be washed.

The Fire: A mature fire, gentle to moderate flames, and a substantial bed of embers. If, after baking the fish, you plan on finishing flat breads on the embers, maintain a moderate side fire while the fish bake to supply fresh embers for the bread.

About 4 hours before baking: Rub the cavities of the fish with the olive oil and salt. Divide the parsley-tomato mixture evenly among the fish cavities or rub the cavities with the chile paste. Pat the exteriors of the fish dry and place in the refrigerator.

About 45 minutes before baking: Remove the fish from the refrigerator so that they come to room temperature before baking.

To bake the fish: Use the shovel to create a flat bed of embers beside the fire that is big enough to allow room for turning the fish. Using your hands, immediately place the fish on the embers. When you judge the fish are half-cooked, 3 to 4 minutes, use the spatula to turn them. Bake on the second side for 3 to 4 minutes. Depending on the heat of the embers, the outer skins may be completely charred. Use the spatula to transfer the fish from the embers to a plate. Remove any embers that may be sticking to the fish, bring to the table, and serve with salt. If preparing flat breads, leave the fish on the hearth to stay warm while you refresh the embers and finish off the breads. This should take 5 to 8 minutes. Serve the bread and fish together.

INGREDIENTS
(Serves 6)

3 trout or other
   whole fish,
   1 pound (450 g)
   each, cleaned

Olive oil

Salt

9 flat-leaf parsley
   sprigs, coarsely
   chopped, mixed
   with 1 ripe tomato,
   diced, or harissa
   (North African chile
   condiment)

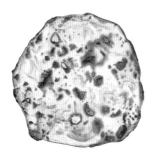

Flat bread

Grilled Fish

BASIC METHOD
Hearthside Grilling

EQUIPMENT
Grill
Shovel

PRIMARY VENUE
Hearth

ALTERNATE VENUES
Barbecue
Campfire

GRILLED FISH IS ALWAYS delicious, and if you already have a fire going in the fireplace, it is quickly made. A single overriding rule prescribes what fish to cook: the more recently caught, the better. Ideally, buy whole fish with eyes that still retain the look of life. Different fish have very different qualities, some being thick, some thin, some fatty, some lean. In this recipe, I provide a basic grilling method and three variations to suggest how to match more precisely the heat under the grill to the qualities of the fish that is placed on it.

The Fire: A mature fire with moderate to high flames to pull smoke up the chimney while grilling.

This first step is optional, but if you have the time, it can make a difference in the ultimate flavor of the fish. Rub the whole fish, fish steaks, or fish fillets with salt, and let them rest in the refrigerator for 4 hours before grilling. Fish can absorb a lot of salt. The oilier the fish, the more salt it can absorb. I suggest a generous 1/4 teaspoon per 1 pound (450 g).

Remove the fish from the refrigerator. If you rubbed the fish with salt, omit the salt from this instruction. Lightly rub the fish with salt, olive oil, and herbs. If the fish is whole, stuff with herbs that are tossed with salt until the fish is lightly plumped out— 2 tablespoons for a 1-pound (450-g) trout. Let the fish come to room temperature before grilling.

The basic method: Place the clean grill on the hearth close to the fire. Shovel an even layer of embers underneath to create gentle to moderate heat. When the grill is hot, brush it with olive oil and lay down the fish. Throughout the cooking, add embers, a sprinkling at a time, to maintain the desired temperature. When you judge the fish is half-cooked, use a spatula to turn it. To test if the fish is done, try to flake it with a fork. It should break apart easily. Plan on about 15 minutes per inch of thickness. When done, return the embers to the fireplace. Serve the fish hot as a main course or at room temperature as an appetizer.

Here are three variations on the basic method. In each case, start by placing the clean grill on the hearth close to the fire and shovel embers back into the fireplace when you are done.

1   **Fish steaks, fish fillets with no skin, and lean whole fish:** Start by shoveling a thin, even layer of embers under the grill. When the grill is hot, brush with olive oil and lay down the fish. Add additional embers over a period of a few minutes, building the heat up to the point that you can see or hear the fish cooking. From that point on, only add embers to maintain the temperature. Grilling lean fish on the cool side tends to create a moister, more flavorful fish. Baste with olive oil at your discretion and turn the fish when you judge it is half-cooked. You can also create a bed of fresh herbs such as dill, thyme, bay leaves, or rosemary on the grill and place the fish on top of it. It can make turning the fish easier and will also impart flavor. Be careful not to make the embers so hot that the herbs catch fire.

2   **Fish fillets with skin:** Grill the fillets on the skin side. For lean fish, build up to the heat you want, as described in the procedure above. For oily ocean fish, such as mackerel and salmon, cook over hot embers as described below. As a rule, I prefer cooking fillets on one side only. Baste with olive oil at your discretion. As soon as you see the top flesh has set, the fillet is done. If you feel that the fillet must be turned, turn just before the top sets and cook for only a few minutes on the second side.

3   **Oily ocean fish with skin:** Sardines, mackerel, and salmon are examples of oily ocean fish. They benefit from being cooked over very hot embers. Charring the skin of the larger fish such as mackerel and salmon is acceptable. Smaller fish, such as sardines, are usually grilled whole and are browned but not charred. To grill oily fish shovel a thick bed of embers underneath the grill to create high heat. When the grill is hot, brush it with olive oil and lay down the fish. Cooking times can be surprisingly short.

INGREDIENTS
(Serves 4 to 6)

2 to 3 pounds
   (1 to 1.5 kg) whole
   fish, fish steaks,
   or fish fillets

Salt

Olive oil

Coarsely chopped
   fresh aromatic herbs
   such as thyme, dill,
   or flat-leaf parsley

Thyme

Steamed Mussels

BASIC METHOD
Steaming

EQUIPMENT
Small saucepan
Large saucepan
   or stockpot with lid
2 common red bricks
Shovel

PRIMARY VENUE
Hearth

ALTERNATE VENUES
Barbecue
Campfire

AT MY FAVORITE MUSSEL BEACH, the biggest mussels are at the far end of a rock shelf that gently slopes from the base of a cliff, topped with fields of artichokes and Brussels sprouts, down to the ocean and a ferocious surf. At the base of the ledge, you have the illusion that the waves are above, and that you risk being raked across the mussel bed and swept into the ocean. In fact, during low tides, the waves and the windsurfers are at a safe distance, and although it is prudent to reserve some attention for the sea, you can safely pry mussels off the rocks until your bucket is full.

Small quantities of mussels can be served in the pot in which they are steamed. Larger quantities are best served in several bowls. Since many people consider the steaming broth to be the best part, provide easy access to the broth and plenty of bread for soaking it up. The easiest way of getting mussels out of their shells is by using another mussel as a pincer, so this part of the meal requires no silverware.

In the Northern Hemisphere, wild mussels are usually safe to collect during the months that, in English, contain the letter "r," but always check with the local health department, and also the fish and game authorities, before gathering shellfish. Wild California mussels (*Mytilus californianus*) have orange flesh. The mussels grown commercially in the Northern Hemisphere are *M. edulis* and *M. galloprovincialis.* These have pale flesh and, like the California mussel, dark shells. There is a green-shelled mussel (*Perna canaliculus*) native to New Zealand that is widely sold in North America. These mussels gape, that is, when you buy them, they will often be open. None of the wild or farm-raised Northern Hemisphere mussels are safe to eat if they gape. Whichever variety of mussel one cooks, mussels that don't open when steamed should not be eaten.

If you have gathered a large quantity of mussels for a party, there are two approaches to scrubbing them clean. Everyone can pitch in, or, if you know someone with a cement mixer, pour the mussels into it, add water, turn it on, and come back in twenty minutes to clean mussels.

For a one-pot meal, serve with plentiful bread, wine, and salad.

The Fire: A mature fire, moderate to high flames, and a substantial bed of embers.

If you collect wild mussels or buy mussels that have not been cleaned, scrub them as clean as you can. Remove the "beard" by either pulling it out or cutting it off with scissors. Pour the wine into a small bowl and add the saffron. Push the small saucepan with the 1 cup water next to the fire. When the water is hot, but not necessarily simmering, pour it into a bowl over the dried tomatoes. Set aside.

To cook the onion: Place the 2 bricks parallel to each other and pointing toward the fire, each of them resting on its broadest face, and positioned with the leading edge of both bricks touching the ash of the fireplace. Add the olive oil, onions, garlic, and salt to the large saucepan, and place the saucepan over the bricks. Shovel embers under the pan to create gentle to moderate heat and slowly sauté the onions until they are translucent, about 15 minutes. Remove the pan from the heat and set it aside. Shovel the embers between the bricks back into the fireplace.

To steam the mussels: When you are ready to cook the mussels, add the sun-dried tomatoes and water, wine and saffron mixture, parsley, and mussels to the saucepan holding the cooked onion and cover. Shovel a thick bed of embers between the bricks to create the highest heat you can. Place the covered pan over the bricks, with one edge pushed a few inches into the fireplace itself. Push embers against the base of the pan on the side nearest the flames. The mussels should cook as hot as possible—a rolling boil is ideal. Check often and maintain the hottest pile of embers you can under the pot. Once the mussels begin to open, stir every couple of minutes to distribute the heat. At a rolling boil, the mussels will steam open in 5 to 10 minutes. Remove when all of the mussels are opened wide. Discard any that have failed to open. Alternatively, steam in a pot hanging from a crane over the hottest part of the fire. Serve the mussels from the cooking pan or transfer them and their cooking liquid to a ceramic serving bowl.

Variation: If you make more mussels than you can eat at one sitting, let them cool, remove from the shells, mix with a light vinaigrette, and refrigerate. Serve as an appetizer.

INGREDIENTS
(Serves 4 as a main course, or 12 as an appetizer)

4 pounds (1.75 kg) mussels

1½ cups (250 ml) dry white wine

Pinch of saffron threads

1 cup (250 ml) water

Handful of dry- or oil-packed, drained, sun-dried tomatoes

⅓ cup (80 ml) olive oil

2 medium yellow onions, minced

4 cloves garlic, minced

½ teaspoon salt

1 bunch flat-leaf parsley, coarsely chopped

BASIC METHOD
Dutch Oven

EQUIPMENT
1½-quart (1.5-l)
   saucepan (for cod)
2-quart (2-l)
   saucepan (for
   potatoes)
9-inch (23-cm)
   frying pan
5-quart (5-l)
   Dutch oven with legs
2 tripods
Shovel
Pot hook

PRIMARY VENUE
Hearth

ALTERNATE VENUES
Campfire
Bread Oven

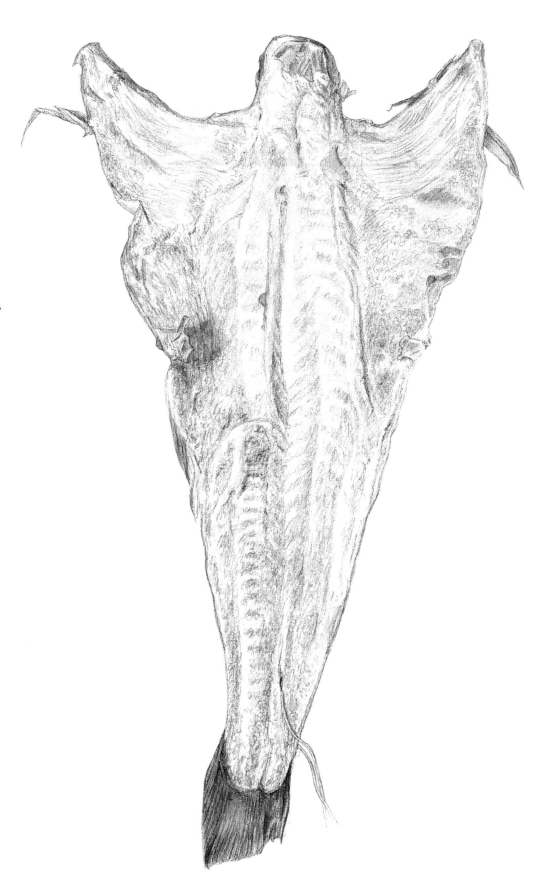

Salt Cod Stew

I FIRST BECAME AWARE OF PRESERVED COD in a local fish market, where dozens of stockfish hang from the ceiling—a flock of white birds frozen in midflight. For hundreds of years, preserved cod was the ocean meat of Europe's landlocked hearths and the winter fish of its storm-bound ports. Along with dried mushrooms, it remains common in the cooking of a significant portion of the European countryside, from Scandinavia to the southern countries of Greece, Italy, France, Spain, and Portugal, but it holds only a minor place in the North American imagination.

The two forms of preserved cod, air-dried cod—stockfish—and the more commonly available salt-dried cod, can be used interchangeably in most recipes. The flesh of air-dried cod is typically yellow. It is often beaten with a hammer and then soaked for days in water before being cooked. The flesh of salt-cured cod is typically white, and twenty-four hours of soaking with a few changes of water is sufficient to render its flesh edible. In whichever form, this much-loved preserved fish brings a universe of flavor and texture to many European cuisines.

This recipe is based on that of a Portuguese friend. It makes a wonderful hearth-cooked stew and is a good place to begin making your acquaintance with preserved cod. If you have a choice, buy salt cod that is the whitest and thickest.

 The Fire: A mature fire with gentle to moderate flames.

The day before: Soak the salt cod pieces in water to cover in the refrigerator for 24 hours, changing the water 3 or 4 times. Drain.

About 1½ hours before baking: Most of the ingredients are cooked separately, then put together in the final stew. Boil the potatoes and the cod at the same time.

To prepare the potatoes: If your fireplace is equipped with a crane, boil the potatoes in a pot of lightly salted water hanging over the flames. Otherwise, place the covered 2-quart saucepan with lightly salted water on a tripod so the saucepan sits within 2 to 4 inches (5 to 10 cm) of the fire. Push embers against the base of the

INGREDIENTS
(Serves 4 to 8)

1 pound (450 g) salt cod fillets

2 pounds (1 g) potatoes

2 tablespoons olive oil

1 large yellow onion, thinly sliced

6 cloves garlic, finely chopped

Salt

1 cup (175 g) canned tomatoes, drained and quartered

½ cup (100 ml) liquid from drained tomatoes

1 small bunch flat-leaf parsley, minced

2 tablespoons chopped fresh rosemary leaves

Rosemary

saucepan where it is nearest the flames. In 10 to 15 minutes, the water nearest the heat will begin to simmer. Lift the saucepan and shovel a thick layer of embers under and around the tripod. Replace the saucepan on the tripod. In 2 to 3 minutes, the water will boil. Add the potatoes and refresh embers as needed to maintain the covered pan at a simmer or low boil. Remove the potatoes from the heat when they can be pierced with a fork but are still a little firm. Drain, cool, and thinly slice.

To prepare the cod: Put enough water in the 1½-quart saucepan to cover the cod. Follow the same procedure for bringing water to a boil as described for the potatoes, above. Once the water is boiling, add the cod and simmer, covered, until the cod flakes at the touch of a fork, 15 to 20 minutes. Drain, remove any pieces of skin or bone, and use a fork to break into small pieces.

To cook the onions: After one of the tripods is freed up, place the frying pan on a tripod and shovel an even layer of embers underneath to create moderate to high heat. Add the olive oil, onion, garlic, and a sprinkling of salt. Let the heat under the pan fall to gentle as you sauté the onions until they are translucent, about 15 minutes. Transfer to a plate and set aside.

To assemble the stew: In a well-oiled Dutch oven, begin with a layer of potatoes and follow with a layer of the onion, the cod, and the tomatoes. Sprinkle with the parsley, rosemary, and a little salt. Continue until all of the ingredients are used up, finishing with a layer of potatoes. Add the reserved liquid from the tomatoes. Cover the pot.

Baking the stew: Place the Dutch oven on the hearth where it will receive gentle side heat from the fire, usually 6 to 8 inches (15 to 20 cm) back from the edge of the firebox. Begin by shoveling a thick layer of embers underneath the Dutch oven and onto the lid to create high heat. Allow the embers underneath to cool a little, refreshing them as needed, a sprinkling at a time, to maintain gentle heat. At the same time, maintain moderate to high heat on the lid. After 20 minutes, use a pot hook to lift the lid and check the progress. Adjust the temperature according to what you see. The total cooking time should be between 30 and 40 minutes. About 10 minutes before you think the stew will be done, replace all the embers on the lid with a substantial pile of fresh embers in order to brown the top. When the stew is done, shovel all the embers back into the fireplace and serve the stew.

Fish Baked in Salt

EW DISHES ARE MORE VISUALLY DRAMATIC than the elegantly simple fish baked in rock salt. Salt can store a huge amount of heat. Pack a fish in rock salt and then nestle it into the embers. Long after the embers themselves have cooled, the salt remains hot. Salt-baked fish can be cooked in a conventional oven, but the genius of the method becomes evident when you prepare it in the fireplace. Here is a way to create an oven where there is none.

Steam from the fish combines with the salt to create a hard pack, making testing for doneness difficult. Thus, the success of the recipe depends on consistency of approach—a measured thickness of salt, a measured thickness of fish, and a known cooking temperature, which in this case, as in the case of crusts made of clay or dough, is "hottest."

The ultimate quality of the recipe, however, rests with the fish. Freshness is the ineluctable key to good eating.

 The Fire: A mature fire with gentle flames and a substantial bed of embers.

Rinse the fish and pat dry. Rub the stomach cavities with olive oil and salt and then stuff with the chopped herbs so the bellies are slightly plumped out.

Line the bottom of the pan with a layer of rock salt 1 inch (2.5 cm) deep. Lay half the sprigs from the herb bunches on the salt, place the fish side by side on top of the herbs, cover with the rest of the sprigs, and then cover with a 1-inch (2.5-cm) layer of salt.

Use the shovel to spread a deep bed of embers beside the fire in the shape of the pan. Place the pan on top of the embers and mound embers around the sides of the pan. Fish the thickness of a 1-pound (450-g) trout cooks in 20 minutes. If using a thicker fish, bake longer. A warning: rock salt explodes when exposed to high heat, so do not lay embers directly on the rock salt.

When the fish are done, transfer the pan from the firebox onto the hearth. At the hearth or in the kitchen, use a stout knife or metal serving spoon to pull away the salt covering the fish and using a spatula, transfer the fish to a serving platter. If the fish is undercooked, finish cooking it on a hearthside grill.

BASIC METHOD
Ember Baking

EQUIPMENT
Disposable aluminum
    pan modified if
    necessary to fit fish
Shovel

PRIMARY VENUE
Firebox

ALTERNATE VENUES
Barbecue
Campfire
Bread Oven

INGREDIENTS
(Serves 2 to 4)

2 trout or other small
    whole fish,
    1 pound (450 g)
    each, cleaned
Olive oil
Salt for seasoning
Coarsely chopped
    mixed fresh aromatic
    herbs such as thyme,
    sage, rosemary,
    and dill, plus
    2 to 4 bunches of
    any of the herbs
Several pounds (kilos)
    rock salt for pan

Chicken or Fish Baked in Wrappings

BASIC METHOD

Ash Baking
    or Radiant Heat

EQUIPMENT

Heavy brown paper
    saturated with
    vegetable oil,
    parchment paper,
    banana leaves, or
    large brassica leaf
    such as cabbage,
    collard, or broccoli

Shovel

Long-handled tongs,
    if cooking beside
    the fire

PRIMARY VENUE

Firebox

ALTERNATE VENUES

Barbecue

Campfire

Bread Oven

THE FIRST TIME I saw foods wrapped in leaves and baked in the embers of a kitchen fire was while studying mushroom cookery in China, near Myanmar. The cooking in this region is different from what most people associate with Chinese food. For example, pastes pounded in a mortar are common. A typical paste is made by first roasting mushrooms on the embers, and then pounding them with salt, garlic, and chile. Many pastes are wrapped in a banana leaf and then roasted on the embers beside the fire until the leaf is browned, and even a little charred.

Foods wrapped in leaves, and later paper, have a long lineage in European cuisine. Pike wrapped in oiled paper and baked in hot ash was a popular dish in colonial America, and the recipe is still found in European cookbooks. Most foods of moderate size can be wrapped in large leaves or oiled paper and then baked surrounded by hot ashes or on embers beside the fire, as in China. These methods produce the clean flavors that come from foods steaming in their own juices. Fish, chicken pieces, and whole small birds, such as Cornish game hen and wild duck, do well in wrappings, readily absorbing flavor from spices and aromatics included in the packet. It is a practical method to use if you want to cook in a fireplace, but don't have any equipment.

When large leaves are not available, wrap foods in heavy brown paper cut from grocery store bags and rubbed with oil. Oiling the paper is a crucial step because it raises the temperature at which paper burns.

The Fire: At least 4 inches (10 cm) of ash in which to bury the packets, a mature fire with gentle to moderate flames, and a substantial bed of embers.

INGREDIENTS
(Serves 6)

6 pieces chicken
  or fish, each
  6 to 8 ounces
  (175 to 225 g)

Olive oil

Salt

6 cloves garlic

12 herb sprigs
  such as dill, thyme,
  rosemary, marjoram,
  or basil

In a bowl, coat the chicken or fish pieces with olive oil and salt. If you are using stiff leaves, such as cabbage or collards, for the wrappers, you may have to first wilt them in hot water. The best way to do this on the hearth is to steam them in a small amount of water in a covered pot hanging from a crane over the fire or on a hearth-side tripod over hot embers.

To assemble the packets: Have ready the 12 wrappers, each large enough to wrap a piece of chicken or fish. Lay 6 wrappers side by side on a work surface. Place on each wrapper a piece of the chicken or fish rubbed with olive oil and salt, 1 garlic clove thinly sliced, and 2 herb sprigs. Fold the wrapper around the food and enclose each in a second wrapper. Tie each packet closed with kitchen string.

There are two approaches to baking wrapped foods—buried in hot ash and beside the fire. To bake in hot ash, use the shovel to dig a trench in the ashes to the side of the fire. Line the trench with a thin layer of embers. Cover the embers with a 1/2-inch (1-cm) layer of ash and lay down the packets. Cover the packets with a 1/2-inch layer of ash and pile with a thick layer of embers. A chicken leg or piece of fish wrapped in paper baked under high heat will be ready in about 20 minutes.

To cook beside the fire, use the long-handled tongs to place the packets on the ashes 6 to 12 inches (15 to 25 cm) from the fire. Adjust the distance as necessary so the packets cook without the outer wrapper charring. Turn the packets often. A chicken leg or a piece of fish wrapped in paper cooks in about 20 minutes.

Whichever of these two methods you choose, when done, use tongs or the shovel to remove the packets from the fireplace. Dust off the ash, place the packets on a plate, and take the plate into the kitchen. Discard the outer wrapping and bring the inner packets to the table on a serving platter. If you have misjudged the cooking time and the food needs to be cooked longer, set up a grill on the hearth near the fire. Place the food on the grill, shovel embers underneath, and cook the food until done.

Variations: *Use this method to cook small birds such as quail; small, lean wild ducks; and Cornish game hens, as well as whole fish such as trout or pike. Cooking times will vary.*

Garlic

Rosemary

Chicken in a Pot

BASIC METHOD
Pot Beside the Fire

EQUIPMENT
8-quart (8-l)
terra-cotta pot or
other good-sized
cooking pot
Shovel

PRIMARY VENUE
Firebox or Hearth

ALTERNATE VENUES
Campfire
Bread Oven

CHICKEN CAN BE BOILED OR STEWED IN ANY POT, open or covered, that will comfortably hold the chicken and any vegetables to be cooked with it. The spirit of this, and all rustic one-pot meals, is improvisation. Use what you have, in terms of both ingredients and cooking equipment. Ironically, I think that improvisation is more of a burden to us who have, for all practical purposes, unlimited choices, than it was to subsistence farmers who faced external restrictions on what they could bring to the table. We have the saying, "Necessity is the mother of invention." Our challenge is how to guide culinary invention when necessity provides no guide.

One of my more memorable experiences of cooking on the hearth was when, a couple years ago, I was staying in Lithuania with a friend in his forest cabin. It was winter. I needed two weeks without interruption to write. Being a native Californian, with a native Californian's lack of understanding about seasons, I brushed off my friend's concern about the winter weather. I shouldn't have. It was cold. Really cold. It snowed every day, which meant clearing paths every day, including the one kilometer track to the road. It was also dark. The sky was overcast, the sun came up around nine, and it was already dusk at three-thirty in the afternoon. It was hard to work. When I was indoors, I sat close to the fire, often just looking into the flames trying to feel warm. One afternoon I put a chicken in an old ceramic milk jug, along with potatoes and carrots from the root cellar, and Jerusalem artichokes

INGREDIENTS
(Serves 6 to 8)

1 chicken,
    4 to 5 pounds
    (1.75 to 2.25 kg),
    or 3 Cornish game
    hens

1½ pounds (750 g)
    potatoes, peeled and
    quartered lengthwise

2 yellow onions,
    quartered through
    stem end

3 to 5 heads garlic,
    halved

Handful of dried
    porcino mushrooms

1 pound (450 g) fresh
    tomatoes, or handful
    of dry-packed
    sun-dried tomatoes

6 thyme sprigs

2 bay leaves

1 globe artichoke,
    quartered lengthwise
    and choke removed

½ pound (225 g)
    Jerusalem artichokes,
    peeled and
    quartered

1 celery stalk

1½ teaspoons salt

1½ pounds (750 g)
    deep-colored greens
    such as kale or
    collards, coarsely
    chopped

I dug from under the snow. I added water and salt, and placed the jug on the hearth a few inches from the flames.

Few places are quieter than a snowbound clearing with an early dusk descending—no sounds, and no movement except that of the fire. I was being warmed by the same light that was cooking my dinner, a feeling that is deeply moving and, at least for me, an integral part of what makes hearth cooking so extraordinarily satisfying.

 The Fire: A steady mature fire with gentle to moderate flames.

Rinse the chicken. Layer the bottom of the pot with half the potatoes, half the onion quarters, half the garlic, the mushrooms, half the fresh tomatoes or all the dried tomatoes, and the herbs. Place the chicken, breast-side up, on top and place the remaining ingredients except the salt and greens around and on top of the chicken. Sprinkle with salt, add water to cover, and cover the pot.

Place the pot 6 to 8 inches (15 to 20 cm) from the fire, either on the hearth or set beside the fire within the firebox. At your discretion, shovel embers against the base of the pot where it is nearest the flames to bring the chicken more quickly to a simmer on the fire side of the pot. If it is sitting within the firebox, you may ring the pot with embers. Maintain the chicken at a low simmer until done, 1½ hours. Add the greens 10 to 20 minutes before the chicken is done, depending on the greens and the speed of the cooking. Serve the chicken in a large, shallow bowl surrounded by the vegetables. The stock, with the surface fat spooned off, may be served as a first course soup.

String Roasting

EQUIPMENT

Ceiling or mantle hook

Two 8-inch (20-cm)
  skewers

String

Dutch oven

Shovel

PRIMARY VENUE

Hearth

ALTERNATE VENUE

Campfire

I N COOKING, as in other aspects of life, the most elegant solution is often the simplest. When it comes to hearthside roasting, the elegant solution is to roast from a loop of cotton string hanging from a hook, a practice that lasted well into the nineteenth century. Today, it is only in France that the system the French call *à la ficelle*—on a string—remains more than a historical curiosity. Leg of lamb turned on a string, *gigot à la ficelle*, is a Provençal specialty, a preparation about which restaurants boast. It is also the system used by many French hunters at their country houses to roast haunch of boar and the small birds they so enjoy eating.

What is amazing about this roasting method is that, in many cases, once the loop of string is weighted down by the meat, it begins turning of its own accord. Watching the meat turn is mesmerizing. The string unwinds and then winds again, seemingly on its own power. After many minutes, it slows down, stops, hangs motionless, and then, somehow, begins turning again in the opposite direction. When, finally, the meat does stop turning, the slightest touch sets it back in motion. While I could say, "On each wind from a five-foot loop a chicken will turn for ten minutes," the fact is that from the perception of the cook, the chicken seems to never stop turning. The barest touch keeps the system in play, and since you have to attend to roasting meat anyway—to baste it, to check the fire—you never have the sense of doing anything to keep it going. The meat seems to turn magically, silently, without help. Of all the methods of roasting before the open hearth—on a clockwork spit, on an electric spit, on a spit turned by hand, meat resting on a stand—this way is the most lyrical. When backlit by the fire in a darkened room, the bronze glow bathing the rotating meat, whatever you are roasting appears to float in front of the fire as a golden apparition.

The Fire: A mature fire with moderate to high flames combined with a substantial bed of embers to radiate a significant amount of heat onto the hearth.

See page 267 for instructions on setting up the string-roasting system, including placement of the hook, making the string handle, and making the string loop.

After preparing the roasts, poultry, or lamb according to one of the suggested recipes, truss them with string so they are as compact and as symmetrical as possible. String roasting requires even more attention to symmetry than other roasting methods, so truss as tightly and compactly as you can. If the looped string is not already on its hook, place it on its hook at this time.

To position the skewers: Set the bird or roast on a counter so it stands upright. Push a short skewer through the top and bottom thirds of the meat. On a bird, this generally means one skewer passes through the thighs and the other through the wings. The skewers should be parallel to each other, pass through the meat's center of gravity, and extend 1 to 2 inches (2.5 to 5 cm) on either side.

To test for balance: Take 1 string handle of the right length (see page 267) and attach it the top skewer so you can lift the meat like a purse. When you lift the meat by this handle, it should hang vertically. If it tilts toward you or away from you, reposition the skewer and test again. If it hangs correctly, test the second skewer.

Pour 1 cup (250 ml) water into a drip pan and place the pan on the hearth under where the meat will spin. If you instead plan to make Vegetables in Drippings (page 140), set up a tripod and pan as described in that recipe.

With the string still attached, carry the meat in a bowl to the hearth. With an assistant holding the bowl, slip the string handle off one end of the skewer and pass it through the bottom of the loop that is hanging from the hook. Slip the string back over the skewer and slowly lower the bowl until the meat is hanging from the looped string. The meat should hang 6 to 8 inches (15 to 20 cm) above the hearth. If necessary, adjust the height by using a looped string of a different length. Once positioned, press the loops that hold the skewers flush against the meat and give the meat a spin to start it turning.

How hot should the fire be? The air at the edge of the hearth, where the meat is turning, is equivaleant to the air of the oven. The hotter this air, the faster the roasting. I prefer roasting very hot. When I roast, I cannot hold my hand near the meat for more than a few seconds. Experience must be your guide. The consequences for cooking cooler, rather than hotter, is longer cooking times. At some point the cooking times can become so long as to be impractical. My advice is to roast as hot as you feel comfortable roasting. For me that means roasting in the equivalent of a moderately hot oven, with the air in which the meat turns being approximately 375°F (190°C).

Refer back to individual recipes for details about basting. As a rule, if the fire is intensely hot, the meat will roast faster than what you are used to in a conventional oven. Add wood, including kindling, as needed to maintain high heat, and add water to the drip pan as needed to prevent the drippings from burning.

Flipping the meat: With string roasting, the lower portions of the meat are exposed to significantly higher temperatures than the upper portions, thus the bird or roast requires turning at least once. Flip the meat by switching the string handle from the top to the bottom skewer. It is always helpful to have an assistant who will hold the meat so you can make this change. Once the string handle is attached to the bottom skewer, slowly let go of the meat and it will reverse its orientation. What was the bottom will now flip to the top. Once the string handle is in place, push the loops flush with the side of the meat and give the meat a push and continue roasting.

It is possible to stop the meat from spinning. For example, if you feel the breast of a chicken needs more time to cook, but the rest of the bird is done, stop the string so the breast meat is closest to the fire for a few minutes. However, to avoid burning the skin, do this only when the fire is below its peak temperature.

When the meat is done, remove it from the hearth, remove the skewers, and let the meat rest for 10 minutes before serving. If you will be serving the drippings, skim the fat while the meat is resting and pour the drippings into a small pitcher to serve at the table.

String-Roasted Turkey

BASIC METHOD

String Roasting
(or, if you have a
spit that can turn the
turkey, Spit Roasting)

EQUIPMENT

Large frying pan

Small saucepan

Ceiling or mantle hook

Two 8-inch (20-cm)
skewers

String

Drip pan

Tripod

Dutch oven

Shovel

PRIMARY VENUE

Hearth

ALTERNATE VENUES

Campfire

Bread Oven

THE THANKSGIVING MEAL IS THE AMERICAN MEAL most tied to tradition. Turkey, stuffing, sugared sweet potatoes, cranberry sauce—these are the fixtures of the holiday table—and it is possible to bring them all back to the hearth where they began. If you are new to roasting on a string, I suggest first practicing with a chicken (Roasted Chicken, page 70). When you are confident working with a chicken, then, before roasting a twenty-four-pound (11-kg) behemoth, roast a small turkey, one about twelve pounds (5.5 kg). Then, based on your experience, decide how heavy a bird you can handle. I find that twelve pounds is a comfortable-sized bird to work with, and I encourage you to stay with a turkey in that range. Hearthside roasting is often faster than in an oven. On my fireplace, a stuffed twelve-pound (5.5-kg) turkey roasts in a little over two hours.

INGREDIENTS

(Serves 8 to 12)

1 turkey, 12 pounds
   (5.5 kg)

Stuffing

2 pounds (1 kg)
   chestnuts

½ cup (100 g)
   unsalted butter

¼ cup (60 ml)
   olive oil

3 yellow onions, diced

2 celery stalks,
   thinly sliced

1 head garlic,
   cloves separated,
   and crushed

2 teaspoons salt

7 cups (350 g) cubed
   stale bread (1-inch/
   2.5-cm cubes)

Light chicken stock,
   as needed to wet the
   bread thoroughly

1 bunch sage,
   coarsely chopped

1 bunch flat-leaf
   parsley, coarsely
   chopped

Basting Sauce

½ cup (100 g)
   unsalted butter

4 cloves garlic, minced

4 sage sprigs,
   coarsely chopped

 The Fire: A mature fire with moderate to high flames combined with a substantial bed of embers to radiate a significant amount of heat onto the hearth.

Remove the turkey from the refrigerator. Remove the neck and any organs that have been stored in the stomach cavity and reserve for the drip pan, then rinse the turkey and pat dry.

To make the stuffing: Prepare and roast the chestnuts as described in the recipe for Roasted Chestnuts (page 206). Of the three methods described, the most practical for this quantity of nuts is to roast them in the Dutch oven. If you have not previously roasted chestnuts in a Dutch oven, I suggest experimenting with ½ pound (225 g) to be sure there are no problems. The most difficult part of this recipe is peeling the chestnuts. The more crisply they are roasted, the easier it will be to peel them. It is also helpful to have an assistant. Once the nuts are peeled, coarsely chop them.

Put the butter and olive oil in the large frying pan placed on the hearthside tripod. Shovel an even layer of embers underneath to create moderate heat. When the butter has melted, add the onion, celery, garlic, and salt. Cook slowly, stirring as needed, until the onions are limp but not browned, about 15 minutes. Add the bread cubes. When the oil has been absorbed, add the chestnuts, and add the chicken stock, a little at a time, until the bread is no longer dry. Add the sage and parsley and cook for 3 minutes. Remove the pan from the fire and set aside to cool. Return the embers to the fireplace.

To make the basting sauce: Put the butter, garlic, and sage in the small saucepan and push it close to the fire. Stir to prevent burning. When the butter has melted, set the pan on the hearth to keep warm.

To stuff, sew, and truss the turkey: When the stuffing is cool, spoon it into the stomach cavity and the neck cavity. Do not pack the stuffing tightly, or it will not cook properly. Sew the cavities closed, leaving a small space in the tail where you can add drippings during the roasting. Truss the turkey, tying the legs and wings close to the body. The more compact you can make the turkey—the closer its shape is to that of an egg—the more evenly it will roast. Bake any extra stuffing in a small Dutch oven placed on the hearth where the heat of the fire is gentle. Begin by shoveling embers underneath the Dutch oven to create moderate heat, but let those embers die down. Rely on side heat from the fire to do the cooking. From time to time, lift the lid and spoon drippings onto the stuffing.

Roasting: See page 267 for instructions on setting up the string-roasting system. This is the best time to place the looped string on the previously positioned hook. Insert the skewers in the top and bottom third of the turkey as described in String Roasting (page 62). Pour 2 cups (500 ml) water into a drip pan along with the reserved neck and organs and place the pan on the hearth under where the meat will spin. If you instead plan to cook Vegetables in Drippings (page 140), set up a tripod and pan as described in that recipe.

When the turkey has reached room temperature, and the fire is ready, bring the turkey to the hearth and set it up on the string as described on page 63 of String Roasting. You need an assistant for this step. Baste the turkey often throughout the roasting and maintain water in the drip pan to keep the drippings from burning. To ensure even roasting, flip the bird at least once (see page 64 for details). When the turkey is hanging legs up, spoon drippings into the hole you have left near the tail.

Cooking time: A stuffed 12-pound (5.5-kg) turkey roasting in front of the hottest fire will cook in a little over 2 hours. Roasting in front of a more moderate, but still hot fire, you can expect the turkey to roast in 3 to 3½ hours. Always remember that the fire can be quickly built up, so if you find the turkey is roasting too slowly, add kindling to immediately make the fire hotter. The turkey is done when the breast temperature is 160°F (70°C) and the thigh is 180°F (82°C). When done, remove the turkey from the hearth, transfer to a serving platter, and let rest for 10 minutes before carving and serving. If you will be serving the drippings, skim the fat while the turkey is resting, and pour the drippings into a small pitcher to serve at the table.

Sage

Chicken in an Inedible Flour Crust

BASIC METHOD
Ash Baking

EQUIPMENT
Shovel

PRIMARY VENUE
Firebox

ALTERNATE VENUES
Campfire
Bread Oven

DOUGH AND SALT are two long-standing substitutes for the traditional clay used to enclose chickens baked in embers. At the extreme edge of refinement are the edible crusts of French haute cuisine. At the other extreme are meats baked in coarse salt. In between are infinitely varied combinations of flour, salt, egg white, spices, and oil, each of them forming the basis for a quick and wonderful way to envelope chicken, fish, and large cuts of meat for baking in the fireplace.

This recipe results in an intensely flavored chicken. It is stuffed under the skin, in the stomach cavity, and wrapped with herbs before being baked in an inedible flour crust. The dough is easy to make, easy to handle, and consistently gives good results. Bake the encrusted chicken by surrounding it with ash and embers, and maintain the heat with a steady side fire. When done, the flour crust will be rock hard. Since you cannot penetrate the crust to test for doneness, this is a recipe in which you must rely on time and temperature. The easiest temperature to re-create—which is essential for predictability—is "hottest." Follow my instructions, keeping this cue in mind, and the chicken will be done in two hours. It may, in fact, be done in less time. Based on your first experience, adjust the timing for subsequent bakings to suit your own hearth cooking style.

The Fire: At least 4 inches (10 cm) of ash on the fireplace floor, a mature fire that has produced a substantial bed of embers to begin the baking, and moderate flames beside the chicken while it bakes.

Remove the chicken from the refrigerator. Remove any organs in the stomach cavity, rinse the chicken, and pat dry. Remove any clumps of fat from around the tail. Proceeding carefully so as not to tear the skin, work your fingers under the skin to separate it from the flesh over the breast and, as much as possible, over the legs and thighs. Distribute half the garlic, several lemon slices, all of the thyme sprigs, and 2 tablespoons of the butter under the loosened skin. Place the remaining garlic and lemon in the stomach cavity along with the 1 teaspoon salt and the remaining 2 tablespoons butter. Rub the chicken with olive oil and salt. Sew up the stomach cavity and any tears in the skin. Truss the chicken with string.

To make the crust: Mix the flour and salt in a bowl. Make a well in the center. Add the water and mix with a spoon or with your hands until the stiff dough forms a homogenous mass. Add additional water if necessary. Turn the dough onto a floured work surface. If your hands are sticky, rinse them in water, then knead the dough until it is smooth and elastic. Let rest for 10 minutes. On a floured work surface, roll out the dough until it is big enough to wrap the chicken. It should be ½ inch (1 cm) thick. Surround the chicken with aromatic leaves and cover with the dough, being careful to seal the seams.

To the side of the fire, use the shovel to dig a trench in the bed of ash large enough to place the chicken. Line the trench with a thick layer of embers. Place the dough-wrapped chicken on top of the embers, and cover with 1 inch (1 cm) of ash followed by as thick a layer of embers as possible. Maintain moderate flames to the side of the mound. In a small fireplace, you might have to rearrange the fire to fit beside the chicken. As fresh embers are created by the fire, shovel them over the mounded chicken, paying particular care to add hot embers to the side of the chicken that is not facing the fire. Check in 45 minutes. The crust should be firm on all sides. The first time you bake the chicken, bake it for 2 hours. Based on that experience, you may wish to adjust the timing the next time you make it.

When the chicken is done, place it on the hearth and brush off the ash and embers. On the hearth or in the kitchen, use a hammer or a cleaver to strike the first blow. Be cautious. The crust is very hard. Young children should not be standing nearby. Once you open up the crust, transfer the chicken to a serving platter, bring to the table, and serve. If, by chance, it is not fully cooked, let the chicken cool, and cut it into pieces. Place a grill on the hearth near the fire, put the chicken pieces on the grill, and shovel embers underneath to finish the cooking.

INGREDIENTS
(Serves 4 to 6)

1 chicken,
  4 to 5 pounds
  (1.75 to 2.25 kg)

4 to 8 cloves garlic,
  thinly sliced

1 lemon,
  thinly sliced

6 thyme sprigs,
  finely chopped

4 tablespoons (60 g)
  unsalted butter, at
  room temperature,
  or olive oil

Salt

Olive oil

Aromatic leaves or
  herbs to place
  between the chicken
  and the inedible
  crust, such as dill,
  sage, thyme, rose-
  mary, grape, or fig

Flour Crust

7 cups (1 kg) flour

2½ cups (600 g) salt

3 cups (725 ml) water

Roasted Chicken

BASIC METHOD

Spit Roasting
or String Roasting

EQUIPMENT

See equipment list
for selected method

Drip pan

PRIMARY VENUE

Hearth

ALTERNATE VENUES

Campfire

Bread Oven

N O BOOK ON HEARTH cooking is complete without a roasted chicken. Whether using a mechanical spit or a loop of string, roasting is the method that transforms the barnyard fowl into the golden roast—the jewel of the country table. Accompany roasted chicken with Grilled Vegetables (page 134) or Ember-Roasted Vegetables (page 136), Baked Apples (page 204) for dessert, and Mulled Wine (page 224) for later, to create a meal woven out of the deepest flavors of fire, ember, and ash.

My approach to hearth-roasted chicken builds on the strengths of live fire to create a bird that is unusually deep flavored. I use an intensely hot fire to crisp the skin and push flavors stuffed under the skin deep into the meat of the breast and thigh. But no matter how rich the flavors are that the live fire releases, they are always enhanced by the setting in which they are presented. In the chiaroscuro of the premodern house, in a room illuminated only by firelight and candlelight, the cook enlists the magic of fire—its yellow light and dancing shadows—to cast a spell that stops time and bends space. Roast chicken, typically a meal for family and best friends, can also be a meal of poetry to serve when you want to share something private with a stranger.

The Fire: A mature fire with moderate to high flames, combined with a substantial bed of embers to radiate a significant amount of heat onto the hearth. At its hottest, you may not be able to hold your hand near the chicken for more than a few seconds.

Remove the chicken from the refrigerator. Remove the neck and any organs that have been stored in the stomach cavity and reserve for the drip pan; then rinse the chicken and pat dry. Remove any clumps of fat from around the tail. Proceeding carefully so as not to tear the skin, work your fingers under the skin to separate it from the flesh over the breast and, as much as possible, over the legs and thighs.

To make the paste: In a mortar, pound the garlic and salt into a rough paste. Add the thyme and parsley and pound until well bruised. Add the olive oil and pound into a thick paste. Use your hands to distribute the paste evenly under the skin over the breast, thigh, and leg. Place a bay leaf over each breast. Sew up any tears in the skin.

To make the stuffing: Squeeze the juice of the lemon into a bowl, and add the spent lemon quarters, garlic, thyme, salt, and olive oil. Mix well and spoon into the stomach cavity.

Sew the stomach cavity closed, rub the skin with olive oil, salt, and pepper, and truss the chicken, tying the legs and wings close to the body. The more compact you can make the chicken—the closer its shape is to that of an egg—the more evenly it will roast.

To roast the chicken: Insert the skewers if string roasting (page 62) or the spit if spit roasting (page 127). Pour 1 cup (250 ml) water into a drip pan along with the reserved neck and organs, and place the pan on the hearth where it will catch the drippings. If you plan to cook Vegetables in Drippings (page 140), set up a tripod and pan as described in that recipe instead. Set up the equipment around the hearth as required for your selected roasting method.

When the chicken has reached room temperature and the fire is ready, bring the chicken to the hearth and set it up on the string or on the spit. This chicken does not need basting. Add water to the drip pan as needed to keep the drippings from burning. If roasting from a string, to ensure an even roasting, flip the chicken at least once (see page 64 for details). Chicken is served well done—180°F (80°C) in the inner thigh, about 1 hour before a very hot fire, and 1½ hours before a more moderate fire. At at any time you may quickly speed up the roasting by boosting the fire with kindling. When done, remove from the hearth, transfer to a serving platter, and let rest for 10 minutes before carving and serving. If you will be serving the drippings, skim the fat while the chicken is resting, and pour the drippings into a small pitcher to serve at the table.

INGREDIENTS
(Serves 4 to 6)

1 chicken,
    4½ pounds (2-kg)

Paste Under Skin

4 to 6 cloves garlic

1 teaspoon salt

Leaves from 8 thyme
    sprigs

1 small bunch flat-leaf
    parsley, coarsely
    chopped

4 tablespoons olive oil
    or unsalted butter

2 bay leaves

Stuffing

1 lemon, quartered

1 head garlic, cloves
    separated but left
    unpeeled, then
    crushed

1 bunch thyme,
    coarsely chopped

1 teaspoon salt

2 tablespoons olive oil

Rub for Skin

Olive oil

Salt

Pepper

The human heart will desire
a bite of meat, a meal of flesh. . . .
Then they roasted the birds and
cooked them until they were brown,
dripping with fat that oozed from
the back of the birds, with an
overwhelming fragrant aroma.

Popul Vuh

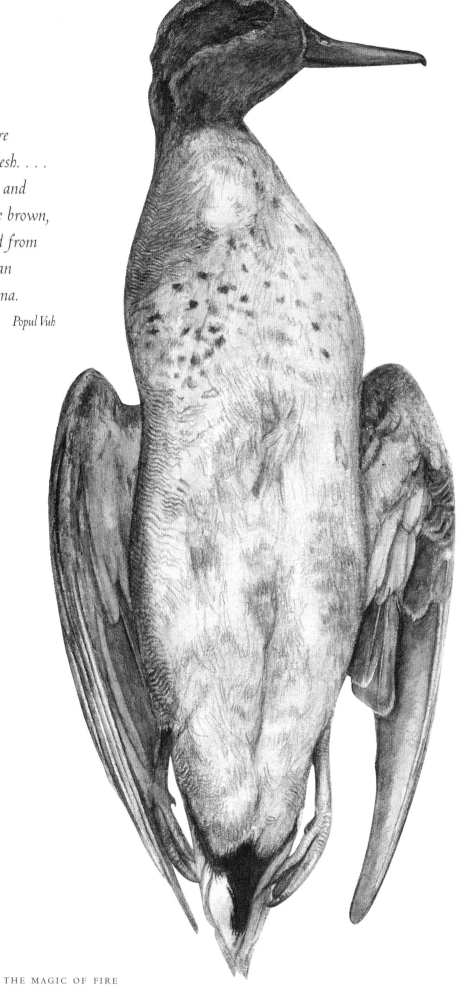

Roasted Duck

ROASTED DUCK IS ONE OF THE GREAT FOODS. I don't know of any country that has ducks that doesn't celebrate the roasted bird. The French adore their ducks, the Chinese go to great lengths to roast them crisp, and in the United States, roasted duck with wild rice is one of the iconic foods served at state dinners.

The world of duck divides cleanly between farm raised and wild. Farm-raised duck is always fat and very simple to prepare: rub with salt and roast on a mechanical spit or string before a robust fire until most of the fat is rendered out. Wild ducks are more variable. They get fatter as the season progresses, but, as a rule, wild ducks are both leaner and smaller than domestic ducks, are cooked for much less time, and may require basting. Wild ducks are easily and successfully baked on the embers beside a gentle fire wrapped in a double layer of oiled paper (see Chicken or Fish Baked in Wrappings, page 58).

To stay within American culinary tradition, serve duck with wild rice, Sautéed Greens (page 141), and Spider Corn Bread (page 160). Duck holds its own with a full-flavored red wine.

The Fire: A mature fire with moderate to high flames, combined with a substantial bed of embers to radiate a significant amount of heat onto the hearth. At its hottest, you may not be able to hold your hand near the chicken for more than a few seconds.

The basic duck: Remove the duck from the refrigerator. Rinse and pat dry. Rub with salt, both inside and out, and sew up the stomach cavity. Sew up any holes in the skin of the wild duck. Using kitchen string, tie the legs and wings close to the duck's body to create as compact a form as possible.

Garlic-sage duck: This recipe is for domestic duck or a very fat wild duck. In a mortar, pound together 4 cloves of the garlic and the 1 teaspoon salt to form a rough paste. Strip the leaves from the sprigs of 1 bunch of the sage and add them to the mortar. Pound until they are well bruised and somewhat shredded. Add the olive oil and pound into a smooth paste.

Using a thin, sharp knife, make a small incision right above each wing. The incision should be parallel with the wing and just below the edge of the fat that covers

BASIC METHOD
Spit Roasting
    or String Roasting

EQUIPMENT
See equipment list for
    selected method
Drip pan

PRIMARY VENUE
Hearth

ALTERNATE VENUES
Campfire
Bread Oven

INGREDIENTS
(Serves 4)

1 domestic duck,
    or 1 or 2 wild ducks

For the Basic Duck
Salt

For Garlic-Sage Duck
6 cloves garlic

1 teaspoon salt,
    plus salt for rubbing
    on duck

2 bunches sage

1 tablespoon olive oil

Basting Sauce for
Wild Duck

¼ cup (120 ml)
    olive oil

1 teaspoon salt

Roasted Duck
(continued)

the breast. Make the incision exactly large enough for you to insert a couple of fingers under the fat to loosen it over the breast. When the fat is loose on both sides of the breast, spread the paste under the fat.

Cut the remaining 2 garlic cloves into slivers. Using a skewer or a thin, sharp knife, make incisions in the breast meat and in the leg, and insert garlic slivers into the holes. If the duck is fat enough, also try to insert garlic slivers into the fat itself. Rub the interior of the duck with salt and stuff with the sprigs of the remaining bunch of sage. Sew up the stomach cavity and, using string, tie the legs and wings close to the duck's body to create as compact a form as possible. Rub with salt.

Roasting: Insert the skewers if string roasting (page 62) or the spit if spit roasting (page 127). Pour about 1 cup (250 ml) water into a drip pan, and place the pan on the hearth where it will catch the drippings. If you instead plan to cook Vegetables in Drippings (page 140), set up a tripod and pan as described in that recipe. Set up the equipment around the hearth as required for your selected roasting method.

When the duck is at room temperature, and the fire is ready, bring the duck to the hearth and set it up on the string or spit. Add water to the drip pan as needed throughout the roasting to keep the drippings from burning. Domestic duck does not need basting, but wild duck may, depending on how fat it is. Use the basting sauce of oil and salt. Domestic duck is done when the fat has melted away, 35 to 45 minutes before a fiercely hot fire. Wild duck may be done in as little as 20 minutes. When roasted hot, domestic duck quickly takes on a golden hue. When roasted before a more moderate fire, domestic duck will take 1 to 1½ hours and will not be as deeply browned. At at any time during the roasting you may quickly speed up the cooking by boosting the fire with kindling. If roasting from a string, to ensure an even roasting, flip the duck at least once (see page 64 for details). Duck may be served rare. When the duck is done, remove from the hearth, transfer to a serving platter, and let rest for 10 minutes before carving and serving. If you will be serving the drippings, skim the fat while the duck is resting, and pour the drippings into a small pitcher to serve at the table.

Chicken in Clay

THE MOST BASIC OVENLESS OVEN is one made of clay. A small bird or animal is packed in clay and buried in hot embers. Fur or feathers are left on to separate the flesh from the clay itself, and to provide structure so the clay won't crack while baking. Chicken packed in clay is traditionally prepared by people who are traveling light. It's the "Gypsy chicken" of Europe and the "hobo chicken" of the United States.

For those of us not on the move, who buy plucked chickens from the market and clay from the art store, Chicken in Clay is a way to create a bird of exemplary flavor. A plucked chicken wrapped in clay reinforced with cheesecloth (in lieu of feathers) can be triple stuffed: in the stomach cavity, under the skin, and between the skin and the clay. When the clay shell is broken open with a hammer, the bird emerges accompanied by a cloud of richly scented steam—a dish, if not of elegance, then of intense flavor and high drama, which is always better. Crusts made of salt or dough are alternatives to the clay. You can also bake this chicken on the hearth close to the fire, turning the clay package to promote even baking.

The Fire: At least 4 inches (10 cm) of ash on the fireplace floor, a mature fire that has produced a substantial bed of embers to begin the baking, and moderate flames beside the chicken while it bakes.

Remove the chicken from the refrigerator. Remove the neck and any organs in the stomach cavity and reserve for a soup stock. Rinse the chicken and pat dry. Remove any clumps of fat from around the tail. Proceeding carefully so as not to tear the skin, work your fingers under the skin to separate it from the flesh over the breast and, as much as possible, over the legs and thighs.

To stuff the stomach cavity: Rub the stomach cavity with the salt, squeeze the lemon quarters into it, and add the spent lemon quarters, garlic, and butter.

To stuff under the skin: In a mortar, pound together the garlic and salt until the garlic is well crushed. Add the herbs and pound until they are well bruised. Pound in the lemon slices, followed by the butter to form a rough paste. Evenly distribute the

BASIC METHOD
Ash Baking

EQUIPMENT
Heavy brown paper
   saturated with
   vegetable oil or
   parchment paper
25 pounds (11 kg) clay
About 3 feet (1 m)
   cheesecloth
Shovel

PRIMARY VENUE
Firebox

ALTERNATE VENUES
Barbecue
Campfire
Bread Oven

INGREDIENTS
(Serves 6 to 8)

1 chicken, 4 to 6 pounds
   (1.75 to 2.75 kg)

Stuffing for Cavity

1 teaspoon salt

1 lemon, quartered

2 heads garlic, cloves
   separated but left
   unpeeled, then crushed

2 tablespoons (30 g)
   unsalted butter, at
   room temperature

(continued)

Chicken in Clay
(continued)

Stuffing for
Under the Skin

4 cloves garlic, peeled

1 1/2 teaspoons salt

1/4 cup coarsely
   chopped fresh herbs
   such as thyme, dill,
   sage, or savory,
   or 2 tablespoons
   dried herbs

1/2 lemon,
   thinly sliced

4 tablespoons unsalted
   butter

Stuffing for Between
Chicken and Paper

Olive oil

Salt

Pepper

2 to 3 bunches
   fresh or dried herbs
   such as dill, rose-
   mary, or thyme,
   and/or aromatic
   leaves such as
   chestnut or fig
   (rehydrate dried
   leaves in warm
   water)

paste under the previously loosened skin over the breast, legs, and thighs. Sew up the stomach cavity and any tears in the skin. Truss the chicken with string.

To stuff between chicken and oiled paper: Place the chicken on the oiled brown paper. Rub the chicken with olive oil, salt, and pepper and surround with the herbs and/or aromatic leaves. Enclose the chicken in the paper, and tie with string.

To cover with clay: So the clay will not stick to the work surface, cover the work surface with oiled paper and place the clay on it. Roll out the clay so it is 1/2 inch (1 cm) thick and large enough to surround the chicken fully. Press a piece of loosely woven cheesecloth into the rolled-out clay. This step must not be skipped, as the cheesecloth provides the structure that keeps the clay from cracking. Place a bowl of water next to the work area. With wet hands, surround the chicken with the clay. The edges should overlap a little. Dampen the edges before overlapping, and use water to smooth over the seams. Leave a single small hole through which steam can escape.

To the side of the fire, use the shovel to dig a trench in the bed of ash large enough to place the chicken. Line the trench with a thick layer of embers. Place the clay-wrapped chicken on top of the embers and cover with as thick a layer of embers as possible. Maintain a moderate fire to the side of the mound. In a small fireplace, you might have to rearrange the fire to fit beside the chicken. As fresh embers are created by the fire, shovel them over the mounded chicken, paying particular care to add hot embers to the side of the chicken that is not facing the fire. Check in 30 minutes. The clay should be firm on all sides. The chicken is done when the clay sounds hollow. I bake a 4-pound (1.75-kg) chicken in 1 hour. I suggest, the first time you bake the chicken, that you bake it for 1 1/2 hours. Based on that experience, adjust the timing for subsequent bakings.

When the chicken is done, place it on the hearth and brush off the ash and embers. On the hearth or in the kitchen, use a hammer, or a hammer and screwdriver, to strike the first blow. Be cautious; the clay is very hard and very hot. While the cheesecloth prevents the clay from shattering, young children should not be standing nearby when you strike the first blow. Once you open up a crack in the casing, you may need to cut the cheesecloth with a knife before you can fully open the clay. Transfer the chicken in its paper wrapping to a serving platter, bring to the table, open the wrapping, carve, and serve. If it is not fully cooked, let the chicken cool and cut it into pieces. Place a grill on the hearth near the fire, put the chicken pieces on the grill, and shovel embers underneath to finish the cooking.

Grilled Quail

QUAIL ARE SMALL, QUICKLY ROASTED, and good tasting. They have a reputation for being an expensive gourmet food. Perhaps they were, and perhaps in some parts of the country they still are. However, if you live near a good-sized Chinese or Mexican community, you will be able to buy packages of four to six farm-raised quail for less than the price of a premium chicken.

It is easy to grill quail on the hearth. While many recipes call for wrapping them in fat, an initial rubbing with olive oil is all that is necessary for farm-raised birds. When cooked over gentle to moderate heat, they stay moist even without basting. One of the most beautiful presentations at my table is a platter of polenta topped with sautéed greens and circled with grilled quail. When it is time to eat, you will find that it is more practical to eat quail with your fingers than with a knife and fork.

 The Fire: A mature fire with moderate to high flames to pull smoke up the chimney while grilling.

About 4 hours before grilling: Using a sharp knife or poultry shears, butterfly the quail by cutting them open along the spine. To make the marinade, in a mortar, pound together the garlic, salt, and thyme into a rough paste. Add the olive oil and pound until all the ingredients are well mixed. Rinse the birds and pat dry. Put the quail in a bowl and cover with the marinade. Set aside in a cool place for 2 hours.

To grill the quail: Place the clean grill on the hearth close to the fire. Shovel an even layer of embers underneath to create gentle heat. Lay the birds on the grill so they are open, with the rib cage up. Wait a few minutes, and then, over the next 5 minutes, add embers under the grill, a sprinkling at a time, until you hear the birds cooking. Once they begin to cook, roast for 5 to 10 minutes on each side, replenishing embers as needed to maintain the temperature. Quail are done when the meat is no longer bloody at the bone. If the quail are done before they are browned, brown them by returning the embers under the grill to the fireplace and replacing them with a thick bed of fresh embers. The quail will now brown in only a few minutes. When done, shovel the embers back into the fireplace, and transfer the quail to a serving platter.

BASIC METHOD
Hearthside Grilling

EQUIPMENT
Grill
Shovel

PRIMARY VENUE
Hearth

ALTERNATE VENUES
Barbecue
Campfire

INGREDIENTS
(Serves 4 to 6)

6 quail

Marinade
6 to 12 cloves garlic
2 teaspoons salt
6 thyme sprigs,
   coarsely chopped
¼ cup (60 ml)
   olive oil

Fried Eggs

BASIC METHOD
Cooking over Flame

EQUIPMENT

Egg spoon, modified
ladle, or small
frying pan

PRIMARY VENUE
Hearth

ALTERNATE VENUES
Barbecue
Campfire

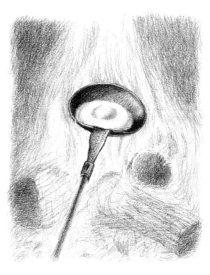

A FRENCH EGG SPOON is essentially a small frying pan on the end of a long handle. The highly ornamented spoon illustrated here was forged in the early eighteenth century and is a much more complex work of the blacksmith's art than was strictly necessary for the task of frying an egg. It was likely commissioned as a gift for someone who enjoyed sitting alone by the fire and adored fried eggs.

In the United States, fried eggs are exiled to the breakfast menu. This is not the case in France. Fried eggs, bread, and wine make a respectable French lunch. If you are alone by the fire, there are few meals that I can recommend more highly. While an egg fried on the kitchen range often seems indifferent or uninspired, an egg brought to the hearth, sprinkled with herbs and coarse salt, and fried in a spoon on the light of the fire is always special.

Improvise an egg spoon by bending the handle of a metal ladle so the bowl of the spoon can be held over the fire like a frying pan. An egg spoon makes a practical first commission from a blacksmith.

 The Fire: A new fire with high flames.

The basic recipe: Put a little butter or olive oil, or a mixture of the two, into the egg spoon and heat over the flames. When the butter is melted, or the oil is hot but not smoking, pull the spoon out of the fire, lay it on the hearth, and break an egg into it. Sprinkle with a little salt and chopped herbs. Put the spoon back over the flames and cook until done, usually 2 to 4 minutes.

Truffled eggs: Store up to 12 eggs in an airtight box in the refrigerator with several truffles for 2 days. The eggs will absorb the flavor of the truffles. When ready to cook, proceed with the basic recipe with one change: after sprinkling with salt, shave some truffle as thinly as possible over the yolk, covering it completely, and over some of the white. Assuming the truffles are ripe and in good condition, the egg will have a sweet and memorable flavor. See page 276 for information on buying, storing, and handling fresh truffles.

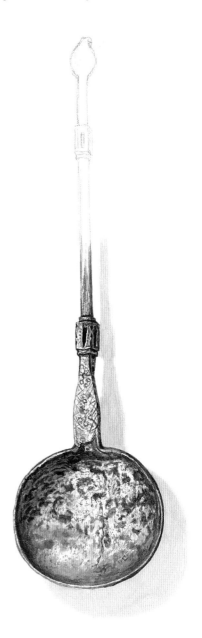

*This elaborately crafted egg spoon
is from France, circa 1720.*

INGREDIENTS

(1 or 2 eggs
per person)

Butter or olive oil

Chicken or duck eggs

Salt

Finely chopped
    aromatic fresh herbs
    such as parsley,
    dill, chervil, thyme,
    or tarragon

Black truffle (optional)

Roasted Eggs

BASIC METHOD

Radiant Heat
or Ash Baking

EQUIPMENT

Shovel, If ash baking

Infrared thermometer, if
ash baking (optional)

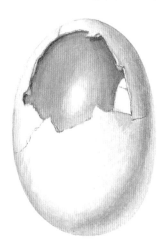

PRIMARY VENUES

Firebox and Hearth

ALTERNATE VENUES

Barbecue

Campfire

Bread Oven

I set up my sail, the wind being fair, with a design to reach the nearest of those islands, which I made a shift to do, in about three hours. It was all rocky: however I got many birds' eggs; and, striking fire, I kindled some heath and dry sea weed, by which I roasted my eggs. I ate no other supper, being resolved to spare my provisions as much as I could. I passed the night under the shelter of a rock, strewing some heath under me, and slept pretty well.

JONATHAN SWIFT, *Gulliver's Travels*

YOU CAN MAKE A SIMPLE HARD-ROASTED EGG, like Gulliver did, by placing eggs on the hearth to absorb heat from the fire. As long as the eggs are well back from the flames—too close and they may explode—they cook to perfection with a few turnings in an untimed hour. In a beautiful scene in *Metamorphosis* that takes place around a hearth, Ovid describes this same method for cooking eggs:

> *And new-laid eggs, which Baucis' busie care*
> *Turn'd by a gentle fire, and roasted rare.*

Another way to cook eggs is to roast them long and slow, buried in the ashes of the nighttime fire. This creates the most distinctive egg of the open hearth, *huevos haminados*, the *beitzah* of the Passover plate and the egg of everyday Sephardic cooking. Overnight roasting turns the whites a caramel color, the cooked yolk retains its familiar texture, and the egg picks up an ineffable flavor. Each egg roasts to a slightly different color, so a bowl of *huevos haminados* presents a magnificent array of golden hues.

Serve long-roasted eggs as an appetizer accompanied with salt, an anchovy or herb vinaigrette, or other dipping sauce. *Huevos haminados* contribute flavor and contrasting texture to stews and particularly complement chicken. Boiling eggs for several hours in water with onion skins mimics the look of long-roasted eggs, and is the way they are commonly prepared in Israel.

The Fire: For roasting eggs on the hearth, a mature fire with gentle flames. For roasting eggs in ashes during the night, a deep bed of warm ashes, the product of an all-day fire.

INGREDIENTS
(Serves 3 to 6)

6 large chicken or
 duck eggs if using
 radiant heat, or
 8 to 10 eggs (to
 get 6 perfect ones)
 if ash baking

Hearth-roasted eggs: Start eggs resting on the hearth 12 inches (30 cm) from a gentle fire. Turn every 10 to 15 minutes to promote even heating. After the eggs have become hot to the touch, and too hot to hold in your hand, begin to move them closer to the fire. Be cautious, however, as eggs heated too quickly may explode into the room, an experience to be avoided at all cost. Having said this, I have roasted many eggs on my hearth without a single explosion. Eggs roasted on the hearth will be done in about 1 hour. After 40 minutes, break an egg open to see whether it is hard-cooked and adjust the position of the eggs accordingly. When done, run eggs under cold water while they are still hot; this will make peeling easier. The risk of explosion can be reduced by using a pin or the end of a skewer to prick a hole in each end of the egg.

Eggs roasted overnight: Bank the fire for the night by covering embers and unburned wood with a layer of at least 2 inches (5 cm) of ash. Use the shovel to dig a trench in moderately hot ash a few inches from the banked embers. Place the eggs in the trench and cover with at least 2 inches (5 cm) of moderately hot ash. Dig the eggs out of the ash in the morning, run under cold water, and either peel and serve, or reserve for later use.

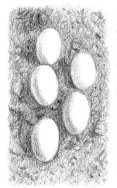  

LEFT: *Eggs are placed in a trench of hot ash.*
CENTER: *The eggs are partly covered with hot ash.*
RIGHT: *The fully buried eggs bake in hot ash overnight.*

While these instructions are easily stated, this is, in fact, one of the most difficult recipes in this book to master. If the buried eggs get too hot too quickly, they soon explode with a muffled "pop." If they are less hot, but still too hot, and especially if too hot for too long, they dry out in the all-night baking. But if the ashes are too cool, the eggs don't cook fully. Perfect warmth maintained for 8 hours results in eggs of lovely golden hues and a delicate flavor. A bed of ash that registers 300° to 350°F (150° to 180°C) on an infrared thermometer and is within about 4 inches (10 cm) of a mound of buried embers reliably produces beautiful eggs. Until you have repeated success, it is prudent to bake several more eggs than you need. When you remove the eggs from the embers in the morning, run them under cold water to make peeling easier.

Frittata

BASIC METHOD
Hearthside Tripod

EQUIPMENT
11-inch (28-cm)
    frying pan
Tripod
Shovel

PRIMARY VENUE
Hearth

ALTERNATE VENUES
Barbecue
Campfire
Bread Oven

A FRITTATA, THE THICK ITALIAN OMELET, is an excellent introduction to cooking everyday foods on the hearth. Like so many Italian preparations, frittatas are beautiful and straightforward. Flavorings, which can be as simple as salt and herbs, are combined with eggs. Even a young child can do the mixing. Cooking a frittata is also simple—the omelet or egg cake, depending on how one thinks of it, is cooked on one side, flipped, and briefly cooked on the other. The slower the eggs set, the more tender the frittata will be.

What makes the hearth an attractive place to prepare frittatas is not the flavor the hearth imparts to the dish—the flavor is the same as a frittata prepared in the kitchen—but the flexibility the hearth provides in terms of heat. The small ring of a stovetop burner is not ideal for cooking frittatas. On the stove, frittatas cook more quickly in the center than on the edge. On the hearth, embers are spread evenly underneath the pan, so a frying pan of any size can be used to make frittatas that are always evenly cooked. Adjusting heat is instantaneous—simply add or subtract embers.

Frittatas are a favorite Italian antipasto when cut into small wedges and served at room temperature. By thinking about flavorings in terms of appearance, you can influence how beautiful the omelet will look on the plate—add black olives for black, tomato or roasted peppers for red, kale for green. A frittata also makes a light lunch or dinner served with salad and bread.

 The Fire: A moderately mature fire with gentle to moderate flames.

Prepare a filling—herbs, greens, or leftovers—and let cool if necessary. Set aside. Break the eggs into a bowl. Mix lightly with a fork or a whisk until the eggs are a uniform yellow. Add the filling and mix well. Season with salt.

Put the frying pan on the tripod placed on the hearth where the side heat will not significantly affect the cooking. Shovel an even layer of embers underneath to create gentle heat. Brush or wipe the pan with oil. When the pan is hot, pour in the eggs. The frittata should be ½ to 1 inch (1 to 2.5 cm) thick. Cook slowly, adding additional embers sparingly. A thick frittata may take 15 minutes. When well set, and only a little raw egg is left on top, shake the pan, or use a spatula to loosen the frittata before flipping.

To flip the frittata, insert a flat plate over the pan. Holding the plate and pan, invert them together so the frittata falls onto the plate. Return the frying pan to the tripod and slide the frittata from the plate back into the frying pan so the uncooked side is down. Continue cooking for 1 or 2 minutes until the egg sets. Slide the frittata out of the frying pan onto the serving plate, and shovel the embers back into the fireplace. Cut into wedges and serve immediately, or let cool and cut just before serving.

INGREDIENTS
(Serves 4)

Herb Filling

½ cup (45 g) finely chopped fresh herbs such as parsley, dill, basil, or thyme

½ teaspoon salt

Greens Filling

½ to 1 cup (65 to 150 g) boiled or sautéed mixed chopped greens such as kale, mustard, and radicchio, seasoned to taste with salt

Leftovers Filling

½ to 1 cup (75 to 175 g) finely chopped mixed leftovers such as roasted and grilled vegetables and roasted chicken

6 eggs

Salt

Fondue Moitie–Moitie

BASIC METHOD

Hearthside Tripod

EQUIPMENT

2-quart (2-l)
    heavy saucepan,
    preferably terra-cotta
    or enameled iron

Tripod

Shovel

PRIMARY VENUE

Hearth

ALTERNATE VENUES

Barbecue

Campfire

MOST OF SWITZERLAND IS SO RUGGED that it would seem impossible to make the nation prosperous, and yet Switzerland is one of the most prosperous nations in the world. Rather than fight one another over scarce mountain meadows, all the people of the mountains became Swiss and, in one of the great stories of human perseverance toward a rational goal, created an affluent country for themselves despite adverse topography, multiple religions, and multiple languages.

Swiss alpine farmers are able to raise cows and not much else. They store the fat of the summer in the form of huge hard cheeses for winter consumption. Even now, the life of these farmers is a hard one. A glance at the terrain from a passing train is enough to make the most jaded observer marvel at the physical stamina of the people who work the land.

There are two simple, but famous, Swiss dishes centered on hot cheese and the hearth. One is raclette, the name of both the dish and the cheese, and the other is fondue. Raclette, a deeply flavored, even pungent cheese, is made in huge rounds. An open round is pushed before the fire, and as the cheese melts, it is scraped onto a plate of boiled potatoes. If you make raclette, buy as large a piece of the cheese as possible—several pounds at a minimum. Ask to have the piece cut as a block and not as a pie-shaped wedge. Gherkins, and sometimes cured ham, are served as accompaniments.

Fondue is a pot of melted cheese that is eaten by dipping pieces of bread into it. It makes an informal meal for friends and family around the hearth. In Switzerland, there are many versions of cheese fondue. This version is called *moitie-moitie*, half-and-half, which indicates that you use equal quantities of two cheeses. While city practice calls for special forks and cutting the bread into cubes, fondue tastes better when eaten the country way—everyone in front of the fire dipping shards of bread torn from a large loaf into a pot of cheese silhouetted against a roaring fire.

The Fire: A mature fire with gentle to moderate flames.

Mix together the cheeses and cornstarch in a bowl and set aside. Rub the saucepan with the garlic clove and mince the clove finely. Add the wine, kirsch, and minced garlic to the saucepan. On the hearth, place the pan on the tripod where a gentle side heat will fall on one side. Shovel a thick layer of embers underneath to bring the liquid to a simmer or even a boil. Continue heating for a few minutes to burn off the alcohol.

Add a handful of cheese to the hot wine mixture. Stir until the cheese is mostly melted. Add another handful, and stir until mostly melted. Continue in this way until all the cheese is utilized. Add additional embers under the pan as needed. Be cautious, however, as the cheese must never simmer or boil.

When the cheese is fully melted, the fondue is ready to serve along with the bread. If serving on the hearth, place the pot on the tripod close to where you are sitting on the floor, shovel the old embers back into the fireplace, and shovel a scant shovelful of embers underneath the fondue, just enough to keep the cheese melted. As people eat, add embers under the pan as necessary to keep the cheese hot, but don't let the cheese simmer or boil. If you serve the fondue at the table, set the pan over votive candles, an alcohol lamp, or sterno. Before sitting down to eat, shovel the embers back into the fireplace.

INGREDIENTS
(Serves 6)

1 pound (450 g) well-aged Gruyère cheese, cut into small cubes

1 pound (450 g) Vacherin Fribourgeois, Emmentaler, or Appenzeller cheese, cut into small cubes

1 tablespoon cornstarch

1 clove garlic

1 1/2 cups (350 ml) dry white wine

1/4 cup (60 ml) kirsch

1 or 2 long loaves lightly stale coarse country bread with a thick crust, 2 to 3 pounds (1 to 1.5 kg), cut in half lengthwise and further divided, as appropriate, into 6 servings

A plume of smoke soared up suddenly from her father's chimney, the sight of which made her heart ache. The aspect of the interior, when she reached it, made her heart ache more. Her mother, who had just come down stairs, turned to greet her from the fireplace, where she was kindling barked-oak twigs under the breakfast kettle.

THOMAS HARDY, *Tess of the d'Urbervilles*

GRAINS

Polenta

BASIC METHOD

Hearthside Tripod

EQUIPMENT

3- to 4-quart (3- to 4-l)
   unlined copper
   polenta pot
   or any heavy
   saucepan with lid

Tripod

Shovel

PRIMARY VENUE

Hearth

ALTERNATE VENUE

Campfire

*I used to call the fire at home, her books, for she was always full of fancies
. . . when she sat looking at it.*

CHARLES DICKENS, *Our Mutual Friend*

*An heirloom corn from
Trento, Italy, grown for polenta*

IN LATIN, *polenta* means "gruel." In Roman times, the gruel was most often made with barley. For the last few hundred years, corn has been the dominant, but by no means only, Italian polenta grain. But whatever the grain, up until the first decades of the twentieth century, polenta was the staple food of the northern Italian countryside, and it was the culinary emblem of northern Italian poverty. Many fled a polenta flavored with the tears of desperation for the promise of a more nutritious and varied diet in New York City.

Polenta was a world unto itself—the drone that in bad times played alone, and that in good times played under a rich layer of culinary improvisation. As with other staples in this book, it is always as an outsider that we make our visit. We visit the world of polenta in the same way we visit the world's poorest countries—with ready money to buy a cold, imported beer when the heat and dust get to us, and with a ticket and passport out. In a sense, ironically, no matter how far away we travel in the physical world, or how deeply we delve into peasant cuisine, we never really get there.

Times have changed. Northern Italy is now one of the richest places in the world. Polenta is no longer the meal; it is now an occasional part of a meal, and has acquired enough status to be served in fashionable restaurants. Polenta was born over the open fire. This is where the pot was stirred by the woman of the hourse. I am struck by how often American Italian cookbooks speak of stirring polenta as an onerous task. In practice, it does not have to be constant. Cooked in a thick, unlined copper polenta pan, even at a boil over high heat, polenta requires no more than an occasional stirring to keep it from burning. I think that the traditional requirement for constant stirring had to do with something other than the food itself. It provided an opportunity for busy country women to be alone before the fire. Stirring was a relief from farm work, a time when children could be made to stay away. Time moves differently on the hearth. The flames, and the stories written in them, are the cook's companion. Even now, in our lives, stirring polenta on the hearth can mean a time of repose.

Stirring polenta is also the gift of the cook to those who eat. It is a prayer to the family that transforms the ordinary into the sacred. Something exists so deeply ancient about hearth-cooked polenta that it brushes up against the rituals of prayer and burnt offerings that, in Homer and the Old Testament, transform meals into occasions of spirituality. By bringing the polenta pot back to the fire, making it the focus of the meal, and letting the stirring itself take on meaning, you rediscover in polenta a hint of its previous centrality.

PART OF OUR CONTEMPORARY ATTRACTION TO POLENTA is the attraction of literary imagination—our dream of the country cottage. When we order polenta in a restaurant, we reach, with great expectation, for something that, in fact, cannot be bought. No matter how good the polenta, it is not possible to buy the mythic element that sits at the heart of the grain, which is the giving that was inherent in the meal of porridge served to children in an impoverished household.

On your hearth, you can bring polenta back in its full richness—for one night, for many nights—in the form of a story told as fairytales ought to be told, safely before a warm fire with the promise, afterward, of a comfortable bed. Polenta poured onto a board in the center of the table, piled with Sautéed Greens (page 141), circled with Grilled Quail (page 77), and eaten before the fire is a meal fit for royalty.

Golden or whole grain? The polenta of contemporary commerce is a refined meal made from dried yellow corn. There is no bran. Like grits, commercial polenta meal is made from the germ. It was not always so. In the Italian countryside, polenta was ground by each family from the corn they grew. This corn was not always yellow, and the polenta was whole grain, that is, the bran was included in the porridge. The orange corn illustrated on page 88 is an heirloom variety formerly used for polenta around the city of Trento, in northwestern Italy.

Whole-grain polenta is a revelation. It has a richness of color, texture, and flavor that sets it apart from the polenta of commerce. All those peasant-derived dishes—polenta with greens, polenta with mushrooms, polenta with sausage—come alive when made with whole-grain polenta, its deep flavor blending with the deep flavor of the sauces.

FOR LESS THAN THE PRICE OF THIS BOOK, you can buy a simple hand grinder and grind your own polenta. If you have a vegetable garden, and live where the summers are hot, grow the American nineteenth-century heirloom variety known as Bloody Butcher. Otherwise, buy ears of "ornamental" corn. These are edible varieties of previous centuries. When using a hand grinder, grind the corn twice, and sift out the larger pieces of bran. Although Bloody Butcher is colored red it makes blue-tinted polenta. Whole-grain polenta will always reward you in flavor and color for the work you put into it. However, if grinding your own corn is impractical, buy polenta at the grocery store and make it anyway. Polenta, whatever the flour used, is one of the great traditional foods of the open hearth.

Finally, there is the polenta pot. The traditional pot, the *paiolo*, is made of thick unlined copper. The *paiolo* has advantages over pots made of other materials. Even over continuous high heat, polenta doesn't burn when cooked in unlined copper. The *paiolo* is also easy to clean: soak in water after use and the polenta stuck to the sides peels away. Scrub the inside of the pot bright with a paste of salt and vinegar before each use. Copper oxides adversely affect taste.

 The Fire: A mature fire with gentle to moderate flames.

There is no single correct consistency for polenta. It can be made thin, like a gruel, or so thick that a spoon can stand up in it. Even as the polenta cooks, water can be added to make it looser, and polenta can be added to make it thicker. The ratio in this recipe, 4 parts water to 1 part cornmeal, creates a thick porridge. Start there, and then, in the future, make adjustments to suit your taste. Polenta can be enriched by substituting cow's, goat's, or sheep's milk for the water.

Pour the lightly salted water into the saucepan, cover, and place on the tripod so the pan sits within 4 to 6 inches (10 to 15 cm) of the fire. Push embers against the base of the pan where it is nearest the flames. In 20 to 25 minutes, the water nearest the heat will simmer. Lift the pan and shovel a thick layer of embers under and around the tripod. Replace the pan. In 3 to 5 minutes, the water will boil. When the water comes to a boil, remove the lid and add the polenta in a thin stream.

Stir often. You may let the heat die down under the pan, but maintain a simmer on the side nearest the flames. A small wooden stool for sitting while stirring is helpful. If you don't stir continuously, and the polenta gets hard or lumpy, add water and use a whisk to make it smooth again. Polenta is flexible. As long as you don't burn it, you can't hurt it. It always sticks to the hot side of the pan, but don't take this as a sign that it is done! Polenta is ready when it is firm, tastes tender, and pulls away from the sides of the pan, usually in 30 to 45 minutes. When done, remove the pan from the fire, return the embers to the fireplace, and taste for salt.

Serving the polenta is part of the dish itself. In a poor country house, polenta was often poured onto the center of the table. I suggest pouring it onto an oiled wooden plank. Turn the pan over onto the plank and then lift, releasing a cloud of steam. Use a spatula to finish scraping out the polenta pan. Put toppings—sauce, greens, grilled meats—on the polenta, and let everyone serve themselves.

INGREDIENTS
(Serves 4 to 8)

2 cups (275 g)
    polenta cornmeal
2 quarts (2 l)
    water, lightly salted
Salt

Grilled Polenta

BASIC METHOD
Hearthside Grilling

EQUIPMENT
Grill
Shovel

PRIMARY VENUE
Hearth

ALTERNATE VENUES
Barbecue
Campfire

INGREDIENTS
(Serves 4 to 8)

1 recipe cooked
polenta from Polenta
(page 91)

Traditionally, it was the leftover polenta that was grilled. However, grilled polenta is so good that, in America and elsewhere, a tradition has developed of making polenta expressly for the purpose of grilling it. Grilled polenta can be served as is or with a sauce. Grated cheese—Parmesan or a pecorino would be used in northern Italy—and herbs—thyme, sage, rosemary—can be stirred into the polenta before it is poured onto a slab to cool.

 The Fire: A mature fire with gentle to moderate flames.

Pour the cooked polenta onto an oiled marble counter or baking sheet. Spread it evenly; it should be about 1 inch (2.5 cm) thick at the center, and a little thinner toward the edges. When the polenta is cool, cut it into slabs of desired size for grilling. The polenta can be set aside at this point for grilling later.

Place the clean grill on the hearth near the fire. Shovel an even layer of embers underneath to create gentle to moderate heat. When the grill is hot, brush it with oil. Lay the polenta slabs on the grill and grill, turning once, until the polenta is hot all the way through and lightly browned on both sides, 10 to 15 minutes. Replenish the embers as needed, a sprinkling at a time. When done, transfer the polenta to a serving plate, return the embers to the fireplace, and serve the polenta.

Polenta Toppings

Porcino mushrooms

POLENTA HAS MANAGED TO SURVIVE even the deadening effects of restaurants' white plates, white tablecloths, and careful candles. Polenta's original service—dumped out of the copper pan onto the center of a wooden dining table—was much rougher. Whatever enrichments there were—grated cheese, greens, a ragout of wild mushrooms, a bit of meat—were placed in the middle of the steaming porridge, which was then attacked by the family. Polenta, particularly that ground from whole corn, marries well with other flavors. Many of the recipes in this book are spectacular over polenta, soft or grilled, but if you choose to visit polenta often, the polenta and the fire itself will be your guides.

Verona radicchio

 The Fire: Consult individual recipes.

Make 1 recipe polenta from Polenta (page 91) or Grilled Polenta (page 92) and serve with one or more of the following toppings. While it is best to make the polenta at the same time you prepare the topping, polenta can be prepared an hour or two in advance. To do so, increase the water to at least 5 parts water to 1 part cornmeal because polenta thickens as it cools. Re-heat on the hearth by placing the polenta pot on a tripod pushed near the fire. Whisk the polenta and add water as necessary until the polenta is once again smooth. Once it is smooth, stir as needed to distribute the heat until the polenta is hot.

Roasted onion

Cheese: Sprinkle with Parmesan or other hard northern Italian cheese—the whole family of pecorinos (sheep's milk cheeses) is appropriate. Start with 2 tablespoons per person and serve a bowl of grated cheese on the side.

Ember-roasted vegetables: Vegetables cooked on embers (page 136) bring their distinctive flavor to polenta. Onions are an outstanding choice, finely chopped or minced. Plan on half an onion per person. See Roasted Onions (page 22).

Greens: Plan on ⅓ pound (150 g) greens per person. These go well with grilled meats and poultry. My favorite combination on polenta is sautéed kale with grilled quail. See Sautéed Greens (page 141) and Grilled Quail (page 77).

Grilled meats: Any grilled meats—particularly those with strong flavors such as sausage and quail—are good. Many Italians are crazy about pigeons, what we call squab, and polenta with grilled squab is an authentic combination. Whatever the choice of meat, small quantities are appropriate, about ¼ pound (100 g) per person. The meal is the polenta, not the meat. See Grilled Sausage (page 118) and Grilled Quail (page 77).

Mushrooms: It would have been a desperate northern Italian farm family that did not have a large supply of dried porcino mushrooms for the winter. For four to six people, soak 4 to 6 ounces (100 to 175 g) dried porcini in a bowl with hot water just to cover. When they are soft, remove from the water and chop; reserve the water. Mince 1 yellow onion and 4 cloves garlic. In a saucepan on the hearth, combine 2 tablespoons olive oil, the onion, and the garlic, and season with salt; sauté slowly until the onion is translucent, about 15 minutes. Add the chopped mushrooms; the mushroom water, less the sediment at the bottom of the cup; and 1 cup (240 ml) light stock or water, and simmer slowly until the liquid is nearly evaporated. Take off the heat and stir in ⅓ cup (40 g) grated hard cheese such as Parmesan and ¼ cup (15 g) chopped fresh flat-leaf parsley. Serve the mushrooms over the polenta. A sauté of fresh mushrooms is always welcome on polenta as well. Plan on ⅓ pound (150 g) fresh mushrooms per person. See also Grilled Porcini (page 146).

Stew or broth: Leftover stew or the broth from boiling chicken or meats makes an excellent polenta topping. See Chicken in a Pot (page 60), A French Daube (page 106), Pot-au-Feu (page 114), or Pot Roast (page 122) for recipes that are likely to result in leftovers that would be good spooned over polenta.

Chicory: Variegata
Castelfranco di Lusia

Whole Grains

FIRE. WINTER'S GRAY LIGHT. DEEP QUIET. The poetry of the hearth is the poetry of stillness. A friend of mine says, by way of reproach: "But, William, you think everything cooked on the hearth tastes better," which I do, even a cup of tea, even a bowl of boiled grains.

Sit by the hearth with no electric lights and no music and watch a pot of grains cooking in the glow of the fire. There is little that is more beautiful, at least to me, than this yellow light falling on the side of a pot silhouetted against flames. Let evening settle in and time slow down.

When the dish is done, remain sitting within the compass of the hearth and eat the grains from a bowl with a spoon. Some people complain, "But it's too dark! I can't see anything!" to which I reply that the darkness makes a focus of the light. It centers taste. It concentrates thoughts. It leavens conversation.

Whole grains make a fine one-pot meal when simplicity is what is best; they also work well as a side dish to accompany grilled meat. I often serve grains enriched with deeply flavored greens, salt, and olive oil, which is the recipe that follows.

 The Fire: A mature fire with gentle to moderate flames.

Place the covered saucepan 4 to 6 inches (10 to 15 cm) from the fire, either on the hearth or set beside the fire within the firebox. If the pan is sitting on the hearth, at your discretion, use the shovel to push embers against the base of the pan where it is nearest the flames. If it is sitting within the firebox, you may ring the pan with embers. When the water nearest the flames begins to simmer, about 15 minutes, uncover, add the grains, and re-cover. Add water if it is absorbed by the grains before they are done and stir occasionally, particularly toward the end of the cooking, to prevent burning. Grains are done when they are soft and you can easily bite the grain in half, about 1½ hours at a slow simmer. When the grains are done, stir in the greens. When they have wilted, remove the pan from the hearth, drain, then transfer to a serving bowl, season with salt, add the olive oil, and serve.

BASIC METHOD
Pot Beside the Fire

EQUIPMENT
Saucepan
Shovel

PRIMARY VENUE
Hearth

ALTERNATE VENUES
Barbecue
Campfire
Bread Oven

INGREDIENTS
(Serves 4 as a main dish, 8 as a side dish)

6 cups (1.5 l) water

2 cups (350 g) whole grains such as spelt, wheat berries, rye, or barley

½ cup (40 g) finely chopped tender greens such as mustard, broccoli, rabe, or young kale

1 teaspoon salt

4 tablespoons olive oil

Porridge

BASIC METHOD
Boiling

EQUIPMENT
Saucepan
Tripod
Shovel

PRIMARY VENUE
Hearth

ALTERNATE VENUE
Campfire

How the deuce am I to keep up my position in the world upon such a pitiful pittance? I can't change my habits. I must have my comforts. I wasn't brought up on porridge, like MacWhirter. . . .

WILLIAM MAKEPEACE THACKERAY, *Vanity Fair*

"Please, sir, I want some more."

CHARLES DICKENS, *Oliver Twist*

OATMEAL PORRIDGE WAS THE DINNER OF POVERTY in nineteenth-century Britain. Our upwardly mobile friend in *Vanity Fair* was willing to do anything to avoid descending the social ladder to a meal of the poorest of the poor. Even worse than porridge was thinned porridge, gruel, the food of Oliver Twist's workhouse. In England, porridge was so associated with poverty that it never made it onto the dinner table of affluent farmers or the urban middle class. Unlike the Italians, the English did not have a tradition of enriching porridge with cheese, greens, or meats that was strong enough to carry over into a more affluent life. In England, porridge, in whatever form, was a food to run away from, and millions did, to America, or to a completely different middle-class cuisine. *Mrs. Beeton's Every-day Cookery and Housekeeping Book* (1865 edition, with sixteen hundred recipes) doesn't include an entry for porridge.

The American view of porridge is heavily influenced by British preju- dice. Breakfast, yes. Dinner, no. Officially, our dinner table is porridge free. Fortunately, though, for the sake of our dining pleasure, the contradictions and small hypocrisies of food prejudice are rarely allowed to stand in the way of a good meal. Under the names "grits" and "polenta," we are happy to eat corn porridge, and while the name "rice porridge" isn't likely to sell many entrées at a restaurant, under the Italian name "risotto," we eat with great pleasure.

Porridge is so easy to make on the hearth, and, as one of the first cooked foods, has such a long hearthside tradition, that I feel it is important to find a porridge that one likes. The grain itself is not important.

In England, porridge largely meant oatmeal, and since porridge largely means oatmeal to us, I include here a recipe for steel-cut oats that brings our beloved breakfast porridge to the dinner table.

INGREDIENTS
(Serves 4 to 6)

3 cups (725 ml) water

1 cup (75 g) steel-cut oats

1 cup (75 g) finely chopped greens such as kale or mustard

¼ cup (25 g) grated hard cheese such as Parmesan or an aged farm- house Cheddar

Salt

 The Fire: A mature fire with gentle to moderate flames.

Pour the water into the saucepan, cover, and place on the tripod so the saucepan sits within 4 to 6 inches (10 to 15 cm) of the fire. Push embers against the base of the saucepan where it is nearest the flames. In 10 to 12 minutes, the water nearest the heat will simmer. Lift the saucepan and shovel a thick layer of embers under and around the tripod. Replace the saucepan. In 2 to 3 minutes, the water will boil. Remove the lid and add the oats in a thin stream. Stir as needed to keep lumps from forming and recover the pot. Let the embers under the pot die down, but maintain the simmer on the side of the pot nearest the flames. Stir occasionally, particularly towards the end of the cooking, to prevent burning. When the porridge is tender, 30 to 45 minutes, stir in the greens and cheese. When the greens have wilted, take the pan off the heat and shovel the embers back into the fireplace. Taste the oatmeal, season with salt, and serve.

And they shall eat the flesh in that night, roast with fire,
and unleavened bread; and with bitter herbs they shall eat it.

Eat not of it raw, nor sodden at all with water, but roast with
fire; his head with his legs, and with the purtenance thereof.

And ye shall let nothing of it remain until the morning; and that
which remaineth of it until the morning ye shall burn with fire.

Exodus 12:8

RED MEAT

Brisket Baked in Ash

BASIC METHOD
Ash Baking

EQUIPMENT
Shovel
Long-handled fork

PRIMARY VENUE
Firebox

ALTERNATE VENUES
Barbecue
Campfire

I DISCOVERED THIS RECIPE in *Cold Mountain,* by Charles Frazier. I knew there was some risk in following a recipe from a novel, but the book gives the impression of being so accurately imagined that I assumed the core concept would be viable, and it is. Brisket encased in a sugar-salt-pepper rub, laid on hot ashes, piled with more hot ashes, and then cooked under a roaring fire bakes to perfection in forty-five minutes. In his novel, Frazier writes, "The spices had formed a crust around the brisket, and Ruby put it on a stump and sliced it thin across the grain. . . ." In my experience, the spice crust picks up ash and must be rinsed under running water before serving.

My first experiment with ash-baked brisket was such a complete success that it immediately became my favorite roast. My friends ate an unreasonable amount of the meat, and I found myself mysteriously famished. With the excuse that I needed another bite to "confirm the flavor," I ate slice after slice.

The brisket comes from the embers pink in the middle. The flavor carries a hint of smoke and a hint of something else, something one cannot quite identify but that brings with it a reminder that the fireplace is the firepit brought indoors. In *Cold Mountain,* the meat is eaten under the open sky, with Mars rising above Jonas Ridge. From within our dining rooms we cannot see the stars, but we can find in the embers themselves, and through the flavor of the meat, our own red star rising in the form of the fire god of the hearth, the vision of good things pulled from the heart of the flame.

The Fire: At least 4 inches (10 cm) of ash in which to bury the brisket, a mature fire with a substantial bed of embers to begin the baking, and a fire of moderate to high flames burning on top of the meat while it bakes in the ashes.

Pound the peppercorns in a mortar until coarsely ground. In a bowl, mix together the ground peppercorns, sugar, salt, and chile pepper flakes. Rub the meat with this mixture and let it sit for 2 hours at room temperature. Just before baking, dry the surface of the brisket by dusting liberally with flour.

Use the shovel to dig a trench in a bed of ash large enough to place the meat. Line the trench with a thick layer of embers and cover with ½ inch (1 cm) of ash. Lay the meat in the trench, cover with 1 inch (2.5 cm) of ash, and pile with a substantial bed of embers. Finally, build a hot fire on top. Through creating the hottest environment one can for the meat, one creates predictable conditions for baking.

Use the long-handled fork to remove the meat from the fireplace in exactly 45 minutes. The brisket is usually well done in the thinnest portion and rare to medium-rare in the thickest portion. Dust off as much ash as you can, and bring the meat to the kitchen. While still hot, rinse under the tap with warm water until all the ash is removed. Place on a serving plate. Let rest for a few minutes and serve.

Note: The only time I would remove the meat sooner than 45 minutes is if the brisket were a thin one with no fat and I had a clue, such as smell, that the meat was done.

INGREDIENTS
(Serves 8 to 12)

2 tablespoons peppercorns

6 tablespoons (90 g) sugar

6 tablespoons (90 g) salt

2 tablespoons chile pepper flakes

1 beef brisket from the thick end of the cut and with a layer of fat on both sides, 6 pounds (2.75 kg)

Flour for dusting

Peppercorns

Grilled Stuffed Chops

BASIC METHOD

Hearthside Grilling

EQUIPMENT

10-inch (25-cm) frying
    pan with lid

Tripod

Shovel

Grill

PRIMARY VENUE

Firebox

ALTERNATE VENUES

Barbecue

Campfire

O N MANY NIGHTS, the perfect hearthside preparation for chops—beef, lamb, pork, venison, wild boar—is simply salt and a grill. On the other hand, grilling offers many opportunities for experimentation. With different combinations and proportions of salt, spices, and herbs, you can create a wide variety of flavors on even the smallest grill. Stuffing introduces color, flavor, and texture to each slice of meat. Thicker chops are easier to stuff than thinner ones, but as long as you can cut a chop in half horizontally, it can be stuffed. Stuffing is also appropriate for boned poultry pieces such as chicken breasts or thighs, and for slices at least one and one-half inches (4 cm) thick cut from roasts such as pork loins.

 The Fire: A mature fire with moderate to high flames to pull smoke up the chimney while grilling.

To make the stuffing: Place the frying pan on the tripod and shovel embers underneath to create moderate heat. Add the oil, onion, and ½ teaspoon of the salt and sauté slowly, letting the heat fall to gentle, until the onions are translucent, 10 to 15 minutes. Add the greens, the remaining salt, and a small amount of water to help the vegetables cook. Cover, increase the heat under the pan to high, and cook until the vegetables have wilted and are tender, removing the lid to stir as necessary. This will take 5 to 10 minutes. When done, remove the vegetables from the pan to a plate. When cool, press the vegetables against a sieve to remove excess water, place on a chopping block, and finely chop.

To stuff chops or pieces from a roast: If there is a bone, create a pocket by cutting horizontally through the meat to the bone, leaving the meat attached at the bone like pages attached to the spine of a book. If there is no bone, cut all the way through the meat to separate the halves completely. Fill with a layer of stuffing at least ½ inch (1 cm) thick. Sew up the meat along the perimeter with needle and thread. Rub with olive oil and salt.

To stuff poultry: Boned poultry pieces are often most easily stuffed by sandwiching the stuffing between 2 separate layers of meat, for example between the separated halves of a chicken breast. Add enough stuffing to form a layer at least ½ inch (1 cm) thick. Tie the meat together with kitchen string and rub with olive oil and salt.

Grilling: Place the clean grill on the hearth close to the fire. Shovel an even layer of embers underneath to create moderate heat. When the grill is hot, brush with olive oil and lay down the meat or poultry. Throughout the cooking, add embers, a sprinkling at a time, to maintain the desired temperature. If, after a few minutes, the meat is not cooking enough, add more embers; otherwise, do not add embers until the meat is turned. Most stuffed meats or poultry will cook in 10 to 15 minutes with a single turn. When cooked to your preference, remove to a serving platter, return the embers to the fireplace, and serve.

INGREDIENTS
(Serves 4)

Mixed Green Stuffing

3 tablespoons olive oil

½ yellow onion, minced

1 teaspoon salt

¾ pound (350 g) mixed greens such as kale, chicory, radicchio, and mustard, coarsely chopped

4 thick chops, or four 1¾- inch (4-cm) slices of boneless pork roast, or 2 to 4 boned chicken breasts

Olive oil

Salt

Chicory: Variegata
Castelfranco di Lusia

Russian kale   Verona radicchio   Treviso radicchio

Irish Stew

BASIC METHOD
Dutch Oven

EQUIPMENT
5-quart (5-l) Dutch oven
   with legs
Shovel
Pot hook

PRIMARY VENUE
Hearth

ALTERNATE VENUES
Campfire
Bread Oven

Sage

ALTHOUGH RARE, hearth cooking is still practiced in the Irish countryside. The common fuel is peat, which is slow burning. The Emerald Island is green, damp, and far north, and until recently, a large portion of the population was rural and poor. Irish stew, a mainstay of American pub cookery, was neither the nightly fare of the typical Irish farmer, nor the meat-dominated stew of the Irish-American restaurant. The poverty out of which this recipe grew is evident by the cut of meat—goat or lamb neck—and by the relative importance of the vegetables.

Irish Stew should cook at a bare simmer. To preserve as much moisture as possible, it is often prepared with the lid of the Dutch oven sealed with a stiff paste of flour and water. When the stew reaches its peak of flavor, the meat is tender and, although the flavors have melded, each ingredient still retains its character. Even if the pot is sealed, the escaping aroma lets you know when the stew is done.

Eaten in front of the hearth in a room illuminated by a kerosene lantern, all quiet except for the sound of the fire, this Sunday stew of hardworking Irish farmers, served along with soda farl (Irish Soda Bread, page 170), and Guinness, sets your cares aside.

The Fire: A mature fire with gentle to moderate flames.

Oil the bottom of the Dutch oven. Start with a layer of potatoes, then one of onions, then one of meat. Sprinkle with a little of the salt and pepper and several sage leaves. Repeat the layers until the ingredients are used up, ending with a layer of potatoes and seasoning. Add the water and cover the Dutch oven.

Place the Dutch oven on the hearth where it will receive moderate side heat from the fire, usually 6 to 8 inches (15 to 20 cm) back from the edge of the firebox. Begin by shoveling a thick layer of embers underneath the Dutch oven to create high heat. When the stew is simmering, both from underneath and on the side nearest the fire, let the embers underneath die down to a gentle heat. At this point, you can seal the lid with a flour paste to limit evaporation. Mix the flour and water in a bowl to form a stiff but sticky dough. Roll out the dough into a "snake" 1 inch (2.5 cm) in diameter. Bring the dough to the hearth, lift the lid of the Dutch oven, line the oven lip with the dough, and replace the lid. Add an occasional sprinkling of embers under the stew to maintain an even, low temperature.

After 1 hour, mound embers on the lid, replenishing them as needed to maintain moderate to high heat. The stew is done when the meat and potatoes are tender, the flavors begin to blend, and a wonderful smell begins to rise from the pot. This should take 2 to 2½ hours. When you think the stew is done, use the pot hook to lift the lid, breaking the dough seal if necessary. If the top of the stew is not brown when the stew is done, replace all of the embers on the lid with a fresh pile that is as deep and

hot as you can make it. The top should brown in 5 to 10 minutes. When the stew is done, shovel the embers back into the fireplace. The stew may be served as soon as it is ready, or reheated later on the hearth.

INGREDIENTS
(Serves 6 to 8)

3 pounds (1.5 kg) potatoes, peeled and thinly sliced

1 pound (450 g) yellow onions, thinly sliced into rings

2 pounds (1 kg) goat or lamb neck, divided into cutlets and trimmed of skin and fat

2 teaspoons salt

½ teaspoon pepper

Fresh or dried sage leaves

3 cups (725 ml) water

Optional Flour Paste

3½ cups (450 g) flour and 1¼ cups (300 ml) water to make a dough to seal the lid

A French Daube

BASIC METHOD
Dutch Oven

EQUIPMENT
Saucepan with lid
7-quart (7-l) Dutch
   oven with legs
   or terra-cotta bean
   pot with tripod
Shovel

PRIMARY VENUE
Hearth

ALTERNATE VENUES
Campfire
Bread Oven

STEWING IN YOUR OWN JUICES when you are angry is a terrible condition, but it's the state you want your stew to be in for a long time. Slowly, slowly, let the stew, well, stew. An unhurried cooking by the side of the fire is the way of the French daube, and the strength of the open hearth.

In the past, when daubes were more often made with the meat of an old farm animal, or with game, they were started at night by surrounding the *daubière*, or Dutch oven, in the hot ashes of a banked fire. In the morning, the daube was pulled from the ashes, the fire was rekindled, and the stew continued cooking on the hearth until the meat was tender. Store-bought meat does not need such long cooking. When using meat from the market, start the pot around noon and cook slowly for six hours. By dinnertime, the daube will have become that thick blend of flavors that is the hallmark of the perfect stew. A handful of dried wild mushrooms enhances the flavor of the overall dish and highlights the warm tonalities of fire and earth that make stews a welcome winter meal.

Any single list of ingredients for a country stew is, by the nature of country stews, arbitrary. French daubes developed specific regional traits reflecting the crops and preferences of particular places. This daube recipe follows the broad Burgundian custom of marinating beef in wine, then cooking the meat in the marinade along with vegetables. It does not, however, trace its origins to any particular handful of Burgundian soil.

Cuts of meat that include fat and connective tissue are ideal for stews. The slow cooking that is at the heart of daube technique—don't let it boil, let it simmer barely—renders out the fat and turns connective tissues gelatinous.

Serve the daube along with boiled potatoes—in the fall use boiled chestnuts—Sautéed Greens (page 141), and bread. There are thousands of published recipes for European pot roasts and stews. Ultimately, all the recipes derive from fireplace cookery. As you gain experience, you will find it is easy to readapt recipes to the open hearth. The flavor of pot roasts and stews can be enhanced by larding the meat with garlic and herbs.

The Fire: A mature fire with gentle to moderate flames, started 8 to 9 hours before serving dinner.

One to two days before cooking: Remove the meat from the shank, cutting it into fairly large pieces (in chunks of at least 1.5 inches/3.75 cm). Separate the ribs. In a bowl, toss the meat with the salt and pepper. Add the onion, garlic, carrots, and 1 bouquet garni and mix well. Pour in the red wine to cover, then cover the bowl and refrigerate.

On the cooking day, 8 to 9 hours before serving: Remove the bowl holding the meat and vegetables from the refrigerator. Discard the bouquet garni; let the meat and vegetables come to room temperature.

In the covered saucepan bring the water to a boil as described on page 257. This will take 30 to 40 minutes. Once the water is boiling, add the calf's foot and simmer, covered, for 15 minutes. Remove the pan from the hearth, drain and rinse the foot in cold water. Set aside.

Line the bottom of the Dutch oven with the piece of fat back, skin-side up. Scoop out the meat and vegetables from their marinade and add to the Dutch oven along with the calf's foot, the remaining bouquet garni, and the mushrooms. Cover with the marinade and top with the lid.

Six hours before serving: Place the Dutch oven on the hearth where it will receive gentle side heat from the fire, usually 6 to 8 inches (15 to 20 cm) back from the edge of the firebox. Begin by shoveling a thick layer of embers underneath the Dutch oven to create high heat. When the daube is simmering both from underneath and on the side nearest the fire, let the embers underneath die out. At this point, you can seal the lid with a flour paste to limit evaporation. Mix the flour and water in a bowl to form a stiff but sticky dough. Roll out the dough into a "snake" 1 inch (2.5 cm) in diameter. Bring the dough to the hearth, lift the lid of the Dutch oven, line the oven lip with the dough, and replace the lid. If the lid has a lip, fill with water. The cooking temperature is correct if you see steam rising from the water. The temperature on the side of the Dutch oven nearest the flames should be about 250°F (120°C) and the underside of the Dutch oven should be about 160°F (70°C). After 6 hours, remove the Dutch oven from the hearth, and shovel the embers back into the fireplace. Uncover the Dutch oven, removing the lid carefully if you have filled it with water and/or have used a flour-water seal. Skim off any fat from the surface of the daube and discard it before serving the stew.

INGREDIENTS
(Serves 6 to 8)

3 pounds (1.5 kg) beef shank

3 pounds (1.5 kg) short ribs

1 tablespoon salt

½ teaspoon pepper

1 yellow onion, thinly sliced

1 head garlic, halved

1 pound (500 g) carrots, peeled and cut into thirds

2 bouquets garnis of 6 parsley sprigs, 2 thyme sprigs, 1 bay leaf, and 1 celery stalk, halved, each tied together with kitchen string

4 cups (1 l) red wine

2 quarts (2 l) water

1 pound (450 g) calf's or small pig's foot, halved lengthwise

1-pound (450-g) piece fat back, fresh or lightly salted

½ ounce (15 g) dried porcino mushrooms

Optional Flour Paste

3½ cups (450 g) flour and 1¼ cups (300 ml) water to make a dough to seal the lid

Roasted Leg of Lamb

BASIC METHOD

Spit Roasting,
   String Roasting, or
   Roasting on a Stand

EQUIPMENT

See equipment list
   for selected
   roasting method

PRIMARY VENUE

Hearth

ALTERNATE VENUES

Campfire

Bread Oven

Garlic

Rosemary

Lifting her skirt at the knee with two fingers and pulling it up to her ankle, she held out her foot, in its black high-topped shoe, towards the flames, over the lamb turning on the spit.

GUSTAVE FLAUBERT, *Madam Bovary*

NOTHING APPEARS IN A NOVEL BY CHANCE. Of the many meats that might have been roasting on the spit over which Emma warmed her feet—chicken, duck, rabbit, pork—Flaubert chose a sheep, the allegorical animal of sacrifice. In the Old Testament, Isaac sacrifices a sheep in place of his son. Far more playfully, in *The Hobbit*, trolls satisfy themselves with a little "toasted sheep leg" while waiting around for an even more tasty villager. In Christian symbolism, the parishioners themselves are sheep, as is written, "The Lord is our Shepherd. . . ." And so it goes, through literature, religion, cuisine—deep into culture itself—lambs and sheep are entwined in allegorical meaning.

"Toasted sheep leg" and, more specifically, toasted leg of lamb, is a delicacy that crosses continents, cuisines, and religions. Made golden before an open fire, lamb is one of the great flavors of the open hearth. The recipe I give here is based on my mother's. I have taken her recipe to where I think she would have taken it had she discovered the magic of fire. Through long marinating and a hot fire, my recipe fuses garlic, rosemary, olive oil, and salt to the delicate flavor of the meat. This rosemary-studded lamb makes a beautiful image either turning on the spit or hanging from a looped string in the manner of *gigot à la ficelle*, the French Provençal specialty. On the serving plate, the presentation is striking. Once tasted, the flavor is memorable. Serve with Vegetables in Drippings (page 140), Sautéed Greens (page 141), salad, a full-bodied red wine, and Baked Apples (page 204) for dessert.

The Fire: A mature fire with moderate to high flames, and a substantial bed of embers.

The day before roasting: Place the boned leg of lamb in a roasting pan. Use a thin, sharp knife, to pierce the roast with 15 to 24 holes each about 1 1/2 inches (3.75 cm) deep. Fill each hole with a sliver of garlic, a pinch of salt, and olive oil.

To make the marinade: In a mortar, pound the garlic and salt to form a rough paste. Add the rosemary leaves and pound until they are well bruised. Add the olive oil and pound to mix well. Rub the lamb with the marinade. Cover the pan with a towel and place in the refrigerator for 24 hours.

2 hours before roasting: Remove the lamb from the refrigerator and bring it to room temperature. Re-form the meat into its original shape and tie securely with kitchen string. Don't be concerned if your tying job doesn't look professional.

For the second larding: Using a metal skewer, pierce the lamb by running the skewer through the short dimension, exiting the opposite side. Insert a rosemary branch into the hole so that it protrudes from both sides of the meat. Repeat, inserting as many rosemary branches as look good, usually 12 to 24, in any pattern that appeals to you. If the rosemary is too flimsy to feed all the way through the meat, do the best you can to create the illusion of the branches reaching all the way through. When all of the branches are larded into the lamb, trim them to within 1 inch (2.5 cm) of the lamb itself.

To roast the leg: Insert the skewers if string roasting (page 62), or the spit if spit roasting (page 127). If you are going to cook Vegetables in Drippings, see page 140. Otherwise, place the drip pan with 1 cup (240 ml) of water on the hearth where it will catch the drippings. Set up the equipment around the hearth as required for your selected roasting method.

When the fire is ready, bring the lamb to the hearth and set it up on the string, spit, or stand. This lamb does not need basting if roasted in less than 1 hour. If basting, brush with olive oil and any excess marinade. If roasting from a string, flip the lamb at least once to ensure even roasting. (See page 64 for details.) The lamb should be served rare—140°F (60°C)—and will take 50 minutes to 1 hour before an intensely hot fire, and about 1 1/2 hours before a more moderate fire. If roasting on a stand set back 12 inches (25 cm) from the fire and turned every 30 minutes, the lamb will cook in 2 to 2 1/2 hours. When done, remove the lamb from the hearth to a serving platter and let rest for 10 minutes before serving.

INGREDIENTS
(Serves 8 to 15)

1 leg of lamb,
    4 to 6 pounds
    (1.75 to 2.75 kg),
    boned and untied

First Larding
1/2 head garlic,
    cloves separated,
    peeled, and slivered

Salt

Olive oil

Marinade
1/2 head garlic,
    cloves separated
    and peeled

1 tablespoon salt

3 tablespoons fresh
    rosemary leaves

3/4 cup (180 ml)
    olive oil

Second Larding
12 to 24 sturdy
    rosemary branches,
    each about 8 inches
    (20 cm) long

Roasts, Plain and Elaborate

BASIC METHOD

String Roasting,
    Spit Roasting, or
    Roasting on a Stand

EQUIPMENT

See equipment list
    for selected
    roasting method

PRIMARY VENUE

Hearth

ALTERNATE VENUES

Campfire

Bread Oven

"Who knows, Partridge, but the loveliest creature in the universe may have her eyes now fixed on that very moon which I behold at this instant?" "Very likely, sir," answered Partridge; "and if my eyes were fixed on a good sirloin of roast beef, the devil might take the moon and her horns into the bargain."

HENRY FIELDING, *The History of Tom Jones, a Foundling*

WHAT IS THERE TO SAY? If you are one of those people who loves a roast—and you know who you are—then a fine roast is the star of your table. For that ultimate roast—the perfect combination of flavor and crust—there is only one place to cook it, and that is on the open hearth. The concept is simple: meat is placed on the edge of the hearth—just where the hearth ends and the ash begins—and turned in the heat radiating out of the fireplace. Whether it is turned by a mechanical spit or a loop of string hanging from the ceiling, or sits on a stand and you turn it with a fork as needed, the results are the same: a roast that looks beautiful and tastes wonderful.

How to get started? Review the three basic roasting methods, String Roasting (page 62), Spit Roasting (page 127), and Roasting on a Stand (page 124), to determine which system is most practical for your situation. For many of you, string roasting or roasting on a stand will be the best choice. Compared with spit roasting, both systems are cheap and quick to set up, and flexible to operate.

The basic roast: Bring the meat to room temperature. If you wish to lard the roast (directions follow), do it now. Whether the roast is larded or not, rub it thoroughly with olive oil and season with salt. In a small bowl, mix together the 1/4 cup (60 ml) olive oil and the 1 teaspoon salt for the basting sauce. For specific roasting instructions, see String Roasting (page 62), Roasting on a Stand (page 124), or Spit Roasting (page 127).

The larded roast: Larding is when you insert something into the meat. Traditionally, meats were larded with extra fat to give additional moisture and flavor. Game such as venison is often lean, and it roasts dry unless larded with fat. If you are interested in creating a roast that is larded with fat, consult a standard reference such as the *Joy* *of Cooking* in the United States and Canada, or Delia Smith's *Complete Cookery Course* in England. Larding, however, is not limited to fat. Vegetables and herbs can also be larded into meat, with exceptional results.

Larding with vegetables: This method creates beautiful patterns within the meat, and is most effective with boned roasts. Bring a small saucepan to a boil with enough water to cover the vegetables as described on page 257. Once the water is boiling, add the beans, re-cover, and simmer until the beans are tender but still have a little crunch, 3 to 5 minutes. Remove from the heat, drain, and immediately immerse the beans in cold water.

Working in the direction of the grain, typically the long dimension of the roast, use a metal skewer to pierce the roast by running the skewer all the way through, exiting the opposite side. Make about 12 holes. Working one hole at a time, use your index finger to enlarge the hole at each end and then stuff each hole with a bean. If the bean is still a little crunchy, you should be able to force it in. If the bean is not long enough to go all the way through, then stuff a bean in from each end and trim the beans flush with the meat. The vegetables form a pattern, so as you are making the holes, think about the pattern you'd like to see on the plate when you carve the meat. A circle near the perimeter is a simple and pleasing pattern. Carrots can be sliced and used like beans. Use your imagination to extend this concept to include vegetables of different colors, such as squashes and potatoes. After larding, prepare the roast as directed for the basic roast.

Larding with spices or herbs: This is a method that introduces additional flavor deep into the meat. Mix the salt and ground cumin or the finely minced herbs with salt in a bowl. Working in the direction of the grain, typically the long dimension of the roast, use a thick metal skewer to pierce the roast by running the skewer all the way through, exiting the opposite side. Make about 12 holes in a pattern that will distribute the flavoring evenly and also look good in cross-section when the meat is served. Working one hole at a time, use your index finger to enlarge the hole at each end and then stuff each hole with the salt-cumin or the salt-herb mixture. If your finger cannot reach to the middle of the roast, use the handle of a wooden spoon as a pusher. Fill the hole with olive oil and repeat, until all the holes are larded. After larding, prepare the roast as described for the basic roast.

INGREDIENTS
(Serves 6)

Basic Roast

1 4-pound (1.75 kg) boned roast such as leg of lamb, rolled pork loin, rolled sirloin rump, haunch of venison, or wild boar

¼ cup (60 ml) olive oil, plus more for rubbing

1 teaspoon salt, plus more for rubbing

Larding with Vegetables

24 fairly mature green beans

Larding with Spices or Herbs

2 tablespoons salt and 4 tablespoons ground cumin, or 2 tablespoons salt and 8 tablespoons finely chopped thyme or sage sprigs

Olive oil

Lamb Kebab

BASIC METHOD
Hearthside Grilling

EQUIPMENT
Metal or wooden
  skewers
Grill or 2 common
  red bricks
Shovel

PRIMARY VENUE
Hearth

ALTERNATE VENUES
Barbecue
Campfire

I dined on what they call "robber steak"—bits of bacon, onion, and beef, seasoned with red pepper, and strung on sticks and roasted over the fire.

BRAM STOKER, *Dracula*

PERHAPS THERE IS SOMETHING atavistically pleasurable about kebabs, a deep memory of nomadic life that makes this meal the one that I find most quieting: skewered lamb, salt, flat bread. Grilling kebabs by the light of the fire, flat breads piled high, one could be nearly anywhere from North Africa through Arabia, or deep into Central Asia, now, or thousands of years ago. Few foods are simpler to make, and few give such pleasure for so little work.

Lamb is the kebab meat of choice; its fatty flesh lends itself to grilling in small pieces. The meat that can be separated from the fat and sinew of the cheaper cuts—lamb shank, lamb neck—makes the tastiest kebabs. This is partly because these cuts are inherently flavorful and also because by the time the meat has been prepared for the skewers, it is in small, irregular pieces—much smaller than bite-sized—and they readily pick up flavor from grilling. Premium cuts, such as leg of lamb or large loin lamb chops, can also be used and require far less trimming. When buying the meat, take the weight of the bones into account.

Flat breads are the traditional accompaniment, but any bread with character is appropriate. Part of me wants to say that kebabs have become a food of the world and that you should feel free to treat them as such and serve them with any sauce you like, but for this recipe I am looking to the source of lamb kebabs for inspiration. Serve them with only one condiment, a bowl of salt—preferably a salt still gray with impurities—bread, beer or red wine, and salad.

INGREDIENTS
(Serves 4 to 6)

1½ pounds (750 g) lamb

2 bunches of rosemary or thyme sprigs, or a handful of dried rosemary or thyme, soaked in water

Gray sea salt or other coarse sea salt

 The Fire: A mature fire with moderate to high flames to pull smoke up the chimney while grilling.

Cut the meat into pieces that are more or less the same size, ranging from ¼ to ½ inch (6 mm to 1 cm) on a side. As much as possible, work with the structure of the meat, discarding as much fat and sinew as you can. Thread the prepared meat onto skewers.

Place the clean grill on the hearth near the fire, or put 2 bricks parallel to each other and pointing toward the fire, each of them resting on its broadest face, and positioned so they can be spanned by the skewers. Shovel an even layer of embers underneath the grill or between the bricks to create moderate to high heat. Lay down the skewers. Turn the skewers as the meat cooks, adding the fresh herbs to the embers to create light smoke toward the end of the cooking time. The smallest pieces of meat will cook in 3 to 5 minutes, larger pieces in 8 to 10 minutes. Lamb is best when eaten rare. When done, transfer the kebabs to a platter and return the embers to the fireplace. Serve with a bowl of sea salt.

Pot-au-Feu

THE POT-AU-FEU is a boiled, actually a gently simmered, meal that holds the imagination of the French people in a way that few meals do. The "fire pot" is the emblem of rural prosperity—the mythic Sunday dinner—a national sign of tradition and contentment, the very signature of the good country life. This fabulous culinary creation is complete, as so many fabulous culinary creations are, only with a certain ritual—the manner in which the food is cooked, the way in which the food is presented, and the order in which it is eaten.

For the full realization of its potential as both a celebration and a great meal, the pot-au-feu requires at least the number of diners you'd expect a traditional farm family to serve for Sunday dinner. It is a fall and winter meal, and in a farm setting, ingredients typically change from one week to the next, although root vegetables are always an important component.

The pot-au-feu is a two-course meal. The first course is a light, sweet, clean-flavored bouillon served over lightly toasted bread that may, at the discretion of each diner, be lightly enriched with a spoonful of red wine. The main course consists of simmered meats, vegetables, boiled cabbage, and marrowbones. This recipe serves between fifteen and twenty people. When I make it, I line up tables diagonally from one corner of my dining room to the other, with half the guests sitting on benches from the backyard picnic table. The more crowded the room, and the bigger the pot-au-feu, the better.

Serve it with bread and wine. For dessert, I recommend something light, like Steamed Custard (page 208) or Clafouti (page 194), along with fresh fruit and a small shot of strong coffee.

The Fire: A mature fire with gentle to moderate flames to maintain the pot-au-feu at a simmer for several hours, and embers to prepare the toast, cabbage, and marrowbones.

Cooking the pot-au-feu is not difficult, but there are many steps. It is helpful to think of the preparation in terms of distinct phases, which is how I have presented the recipe. The total cooking time is approximately 6 hours. If your fireplace is equipped with a crane, use it for cooking the bouillon and the main pot-au-feu, but keep the pot well to the side of the fire so the water doesn't boil.

First phase (3 hours; bouillon): Place the oxtails, vegetables, herbs, and peppercorns in the 8-quart (8-l) stockpot. Add water to cover by 1 inch (2.5 cm)—2½ to 3 quarts (2.5 to 3 l)—and cover. Place the 2 bricks on the hearth parallel to each other and perpendicular to the fireplace opening so that the bricks' leading edges are touching the ash of the fireplace. Place the pot over the bricks so that a portion of the pot sits within 4 to 6 inches (10 to 15 cm) of the fire. Push embers against the base of the pot where it is within the firebox. Do not put embers under the pot. Maintain the fire so the pot simmers on the side closest to the flames. Cook at a low simmer for 3 hours, skimming as necessary.

(continued)

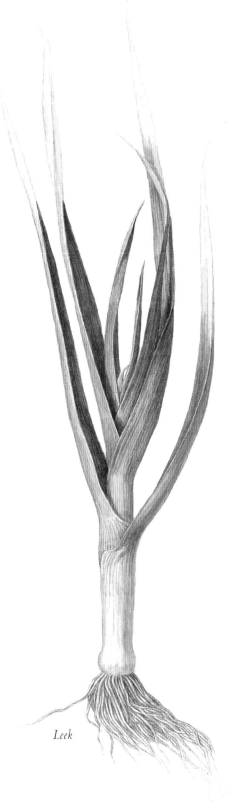

Leek

INGREDIENTS
(Serves 15 to 20)

First Phase (Bouillon)

4 pounds (1.75 kg) oxtails

2 yellow onions, each studded with 2 whole cloves

1 parsnip, peeled

2 large carrots, peeled

1 celery stalk

1 head garlic, halved

3 bay leaves

6 thyme sprigs

1 small bunch flat-leaf parsley

10 peppercorns

Second Phase (Meat)

3 pounds (1.5 kg) beef shank

3 pounds (1.5 kg) beef chuck

3 pounds (1.5 kg) short ribs

All the bouillon from the recipe, above

Water

Pot-au-Feu
(continued)

INGREDIENTS
(continued)

Third Phase

1 chicken,
4 to 5 pounds
(1.75 to 2.25 kg)

Bouquet garni of
6 flat-leaf parsley
sprigs, 2 thyme sprigs,
1 bay leaf, and
1 celery stalk (halved)
tied together with
kitchen string

Any 3 of the following
vegetables: turnips,
parsnips, carrots,
and potatoes, peeled
(depending on size,
plan on 1 to 3 of
each kind per person)

2½ pounds (1.5 kg)
small leeks, white
parts only, tied in
several bundles

Salt

Toast, Cabbage,
Marrowbones

30 to 40 slices bread

1 medium head cabbage,
cut into 8 wedges

Beef marrowbones,
cut into 15 to 20
pieces, each 1 inch
(2.5 cm) long

Condiments

Cornichons, mustard,
coarse salt, and reduced
tomato sauce (optional)

Second phase (1½ hours; meat): Take the stockpot from the hearth to the kitchen. Remove the oxtails and set aside. Strain the bouillon and discard the contents of the sieve. Spoon off as much fat as possible. Place the beef shank, chuck, and short ribs in the 20-quart (20-l) stockpot. Put the pot on the hearth near the fire as you did the pot for the bouillon. Adjust the bricks, if necessary, to ensure the pot's stability. Pour the bouillon over the meats and add water as needed to cover by 1 inch (2.5 cm). Bring to a slow simmer on the side of the pot nearest the fire, skimming as necessary. Maintain the simmer for 1½ hours. During this period prepare the bread, vegetables, and marrowbones for cooking during the next phase.

Third phase (1½ hours; completing the pot-au-feu): Let the covered pot continue to simmer on the side closest to the flames for an additional 1½ hours. While you are working with the main pot-au-feu, prepare the toast, cabbage, and marrowbones (see directions below). Immediately add to the pot-au-feu the reserved oxtails, the whole chicken, and the bouquet garni. After 30 minutes, begin adding the vegetables, adding the potatoes first since they cook the longest. Add the leeks last, about 30 minutes before serving. As you add ingredients, add water as needed to cover. When the last of the vegetables are tender, season with salt. Assuming the toast, cabbage, and marrowbones, are now finished, the pot-au-feu is ready to be served.

To prepare the toast, cabbage, and marrowbones: If your fireplace is large enough, you can do all of these steps in front of the fire. If your fireplace is small, like mine, the stockpot will monopolize all the space on the hearth and you will have to do this cooking in the kitchen. If you are preparing on the hearth, shovel the embers back into the fireplace when you are finished with each preparation.

To prepare the toast, place the clean grill on the hearth. Shovel an even layer of embers underneath to create gentle to moderate heat. Lay the bread on the grill, turning once, until both sides are light brown, adding additional embers as needed. When done, set the toast aside. (If there is no room on your hearth, grill on a barbecue, or toast the bread in the broiler.)

To prepare the cabbage, begin as soon as you begin the third phase. Fill a 4-quart (4-l) saucepan three-fourths full of lightly salted water, cover, and place on the tripod set on the hearth so the pan sits within 4 to 6 inches (10 to 15 cm) of the flames. Push embers against the base of the pot nearest the flames. When the water nearest the flames approaches a simmer, lift the saucepan and shovel a thick layer of embers under and around the tripod. Replace the saucepan. In 8 minutes the water will boil. Add the cabbage wedges and simmer, covered, until the cabbage is tender, about 15 minutes. Remove the wedges from the water and set aside.

Skim 6 tablespoons of fat from the pot-au-feu and reserve it. Place the frying pan on the hearthside tripod. Add the cabbage, the reserved fat, and 1/2 cup (250 ml) bouillon from the pot-au-feu. Cover, and shovel embers underneath the tripod to create high heat. Once the cabbage begins to simmer, let the heat fall to moderate, and then continue simmering for 20 minutes. When done, set aside and keep warm near the fire.

Bay leaves

To prepare the marrowbones, bring the other covered 4-quart (4-l) saucepan three-fourths full of lightly salted water to a boil, following the procedure described for the cabbage. When the water is boiling, add the bones and simmer for 15 to 20 minutes, skimming as needed. When done, remove the saucepan to the kitchen, drain, and set aside, keeping them warm on the hearth.

To serve the pot-au-feu: An assistant is helpful. Seat the guests. Remove the stockpot from the hearth. Remove all of the ingredients except the bouillon from the pot onto platters. Use 1 platter for each type of meat and at least 2 platters or bowls for the vegetables. Place the marrowbones and the cabbage on separate serving dishes. Cut the cabbage wedges in half. Set all the food by the fire to keep it warm. Reserve the toast.

Thyme

Next, use a spoon to skim any fat from the surface of the bouillon. Complete the skimming by laying a paper towel flat on the surface of the soup to soak up any remaining fat. Repeat a few times, if necessary, until the bouillon is free of surface fat. Season with salt one last time. The bouillon may be served informally from the stockpot or more formally strained into a tureen. Ladle into bowls over toast, 1 piece per bowl. Put a bottle of red wine on the table so that each diner may enrich his or her bowl of soup with a tablespoon of wine.

After the soup course, carve the meat and serve the rest of the meal along with the recommended condiments. Serve the remaining toast along with the marrowbones. Provide small spoons or knives for scooping out the marrow to spread on the toast.

Grilled Sausage

BASIC METHOD
Hearthside Grilling

EQUIPMENT
Long-handled fork
    or grill and shovel

PRIMARY VENUE
Hearth

ALTERNATE VENUES
Barbecue
Campfire

INGREDIENTS
(Serves 6)

6 to 12 sausages,
    depending on size
    of sausages and
    appetites of diners
Mustard (optional)

But when she noticed that she was lying on a bed of heather with a furry mantle over her, and saw a cheery fire crackling (as if newly lit) on a stone hearth and, further off, morning sunlight coming in through the cave's mouth, she remembered all the happy truth. They had had a delightful supper, all crowded into that cave, in spite of being so sleepy before it was properly over. She had a vague impression of Dwarfs crowding round the fire with frying pans rather bigger than themselves, and the hissing, and delicious smell of sausages, and more, and more, and more sausages. And not wretched sausages half full of bread and Soya Bean either, but real meaty, spicy ones, fat and piping hot and burst and just the tiniest bit burnt. And great mugs of frothy chocolate, and roast potatoes and roast chestnuts, and baked apples with raisins stuck in where the cores had been, and then ices just to freshen you up after all the hot things.

C. S. LEWIS, *The Silver Chair*

J ILL EARNED HER FABULOUS SAUSAGE meal, no fillers, and "just the tiniest bit burnt," by risking her life in a grand quest for a lost Prince. While it is unlikely that any of my readers have been to Narnia and quested through the lands of giants and evil witches, many of us after a winter's day of less adventurous pursuits—hiking, skiing, clearing a snowbound path, or, in my snowless part of the world, searching for mushrooms in the forest—will feel, if not quite as proud as Jill after she found the lost Prince, at least as hungry as Jill, and as thankful for a fire-roasted dinner.

As a hearth-cooked meal, the Dwarfs' dinner speaks for itself—a welcome feast for a hungry English child. Had Narnia's associations been more northern Italian, C. S. Lewis might have had the Dwarfs cook a slightly different meal—sausages, "the tiniest bit burnt," of course, but with polenta replacing the potatoes. Of course, the chestnuts, which suggest that Jill was in Narnia in late fall or early winter, are welcome whatever the cuisine. Modify the Dwarfs' menu to make it more suitable for adults by serving ale or wine in lieu of hot chocolate, and either Baked Apples (page 204) or an ice, but not both, for dessert.

My only substantive quibble with the Dwarfs' cooking is over the idea of pan roasting the sausages. Pan roasting does work, of course, but grilling creates a more flavorful sausage. If you're cooking for one to three people, the sausages can easily be roasted at the end of a fork, in the manner of toast or marshmallows. If cooking for more than three, set up a grill on the hearth and grill the sausages over embers pulled from the fire.

 The Fire: A mature fire with moderate to high flames.

Roasting on a fork: Place a sausage on the end of the long-handled fork. Roast it in front of, but not over, the fire. At first, roast the sausage slowly so the heat penetrates to the center before the skin browns. When the sausage is hot inside, which you can tell because it will begin to swell, hold the sausage closer to the fire and brown the skin. When one side is browned, remove the sausage from the fork, turn it 180 degrees, put it back on the fork, and cook the other side until it is also lightly browned and "the tiniest bit burnt." Remove from the fork to a serving plate.

Roasting on a grill: Place a clean grill on the hearth near the fire. Shovel an even layer of embers underneath to create moderate heat. When the grill is hot, begin cooking the sausages. Turn as each side is lightly browned and "the tiniest bit burnt." Maintain a hot fire in the fireplace to pull smoke up the chimney. The sausages are done when they are full, plump, and seemingly ready to burst. Remove them from the grill to a platter and return the embers to the fireplace.

Long-handled fork

Grilled Strips of Meat

BASIC METHOD
Hearthside Grilling

EQUIPMENT
Grill
Shovel

PRIMARY VENUE
Hearth

ALTERNATE VENUES
Barbecue
Campfire

INGREDIENTS
(Serves 4 to 6)

¾ pound (350 g)
   boneless chicken,
   pork, lamb, or beef,
   cut into strips ⅛ to
   ¼ inch (3 to 6 mm)
   thick

¾ teaspoon salt

¼ cup (60 ml)
   olive oil, plus oil for
   brushing on grill

1 generous tablespoon
   finely chopped fresh
   herbs such as thyme
   or flat-leaf parsley

MY FATHER often called my mother just before leaving work to let her know that he was bringing company home. My mother had many strategies for these last-minute guests. One was to cut up meat into strips—"People," she said, "eat less when meat is sliced thinly."

Thinly sliced meat goes further, is easy to make taste good, and cooks quickly, making it an excellent choice for instant dinners. The only prerequisite is that there are enough embers to rake out of the fireplace onto the hearth to start grilling. Thinly sliced meats respond quickly to marinating, and easily take on a hint of smoke. If sliced finely enough, meat grills in two to four minutes, and may not even need to be turned. With different sauces, flavored oils, or butters, the meat takes on the flavor of different cuisines—American (barbecue sauce), Thai (fish sauce), Moroccan (harissa), French (tarragon butter). But it is always delicious served with the simplest sauce of all: a sprinkling of salt and fresh herbs.

 The Fire: A mature fire with moderate to high flames to pull smoke up the chimney while grilling.

Toss the sliced meat in a bowl with the salt and the olive oil. Place the clean grill on the hearth near the fire. Shovel embers under the grill to create moderate to high heat. When the grill is hot, brush it with olive oil and lay the strips of meat on it. The meat cooks quickly and may not require turning. When the meat is done, usually in 2 to 4 minutes, use a fork to transfer it to a serving plate and return the embers to the fireplace. Sprinkle the meat with the herbs and serve.

Lamb Shanks on Embers

THE SAMBURU, A TRIBE IN NORTHERN KENYA, divide up their slaughtered animals according to the sex and age of the recipients. Boys get one part of the sheep, girls another. Warriors get one part, old men another. The elder women receive the shanks along with other cuts. As soon as they receive them, they roast the shanks on embers. Because they are the first cut separated from the sheep carcass, and because they cook in a few minutes, they are the first snack the women enjoy after the slaughter.

Letina Letua, a Samburu friend and guide during my stay in northern Kenya, says that the Samburu are like the Jews—a people of milk and honey. I imagine that the life of the Samburu shares similarities with that of the ancient Jews, one primary culinary difference being that the Samburu drink the blood of their animals.

Jews have long made lamb shanks an important part of the Passover ritual. Roasting lamb shanks on the embers deepens the celebration by using a method that reaches back in time to when Passover was celebrated by herders in the desert. In fact, the primary ingredients for the ritual Passover plate—roast lamb shank, roasted eggs, and matzo—are foods that were originally cooked on an open fire, and each picks up meaning and flavor from being returned to the hearth.

 The Fire: A mature fire with gentle flames.

Remove the shanks from the refrigerator and let them come to room temperature. If they are damp, pat them dry and dust with flour. Use the shovel to spread embers beside the fire. Allow a thin layer of ash to form or sprinkle with ash—just enough so that the meat does not burn on contact.

Use the tongs to place the shanks on the embers 12 to 15 inches (30 to 35 cm) from the fire. To keep the meat from burning, turn the shanks from time to time and adjust their distance from the fire as necessary. Lamb shanks are best when still a little pink at the center. Aim for a cooking time of 15 to 20 minutes. Remove the shanks to a platter that already holds a bowl of coarse gray salt and serve.

BASIC METHOD
Ember Baking

EQUIPMENT
Shovel
Long-handled tongs

PRIMARY VENUE
Firebox

ALTERNATE VENUES
Barbecue
Campfire

INGREDIENTS
(Serves 4)

4 lamb shanks, about 1 pound (450 g) each
Flour, if needed
Coarse sea salt

Samburu tribeswoman, daughter of Elizabeth, Likisn Manyatta, Keyna

Pot Roast

BASIC METHOD

Dutch Oven

EQUIPMENT

7-quart (7-l) Dutch oven
    with legs or large,
    straight-sided terra-
    cotta cooking pot
    with a tripod
Shovel

PRIMARY VENUE

Hearth

ALTERNATE VENUES

Campfire
Bread Oven

M Y MOTHER'S pot roast was one of the mainstays of our family table. Richly aromatic, the smell of the roast announced a fabulous dinner long before we sat down to eat.

Pot roast is timeless. For as long as there have been pots, large pieces of meat have been cooked in them. Pot roasts look to steaming or a slow simmer to render fat and to make the meat tender. Historically, cooking in pots has been seen as more civilized than roasting over an open fire. To this day, in nomadic cultures, the cooking pot is one of the few material possessions of a family, and thus an object of great importance. I grew up in a household with a truckload of possessions, including a substantial inventory of kitchen utensils. However, the only pot that I distinctly remember is an iron pot with a glass lid in which my mother cooked her pot roast.

Terra-cotta pots are the ideal containers for cooking roasts because ceramic flattens out the warming and cooling cycles of the fire. But if you do not have a terra-cotta pot, a metal Dutch oven, stockpot, or any other pot that will hold the ingredients will serve the purpose.

The roast I present, here, my mother's recipe, is simmered slowly. Start in the afternoon for the evening meal, or, since the flavors of pot roasts often become more pronounced from resting and reheating, cook the roast on the evening fire for the next day. Store-bought meat will be tender in two to three hours; game may take longer. This simmered pot roast yields fork-tender, wine-deepened meat along with an array of vegetables that are perfectly tender when served.

The Fire: A steady mature fire with gentle to moderate flames.

Place the Dutch oven on the hearth near the fire and shovel a thick layer of embers underneath to create high heat. Pat the meat dry and rub with salt. Add the oil to the pan. When the oil is hot, but not smoking, add the meat. Sear it on both sides, remove it to a bowl, and shovel the embers back into the fireplace. Put the thyme and bay leaves in the bottom of the Dutch oven and add the meat. Place the garlic heads on top of the meat, add the wine, and cover.

Place the Dutch oven on the hearth where it will receive moderate side heat from the fire, usually 4 to 6 inches (10 to 15 cm) back from the edge of the firebox. Begin by shoveling a thick layer of embers underneath the Dutch oven to create high heat. When the roast is simmering, both from underneath and on the side nearest the fire, let the embers underneath die out. Throughout the 2½-hour cooking time, the pot should simmer on the side nearest the flames. After the meat has simmered for 1½ hours, add the carrots and parsnips. They should cook for about 1 hour. The pot roast is done when the vegetables and the meat are both tender. Move the Dutch oven away from the fire and shovel the embers back into the fireplace. If you are going to serve the pot roast immediately, remove the meat to one bowl and the vegetables to another. Pour the juices over the meat. Keeping both bowls warm by the hearth, let the meat rest for 10 minutes, then transfer it to a serving platter and surround with the vegetables. Spoon off the fat from the juices, transfer the juices to a pitcher, and serve. Alternatively, leave the meat and vegetables in the bowls, let cool, cover, and refrigerate. The next day, before reheating, remove the solidified fat, return all the meat and juices to the Dutch oven, followed by the vegetables, and reheat on the hearth before serving.

INGREDIENTS
(Serves 6 to 12)

4 pounds (1.75 kg) beef chuck or stewing meat of choice, including lamb, pork or game

1 tablespoon salt

4 tablespoons olive oil

1 bunch thyme

2 bay leaves

4 heads garlic, unpeeled, but with top cut off

2 cups (500 ml) red wine

1 pound (450 g) carrots, peeled

1 pound (450 g) parsnips, peeled and halved or quartered to match diameter of carrots

BASIC METHOD
Radiant Heat

EQUIPMENT
Grill
Drip pan
Meat fork
Basting brush

French meat fork, circa 1740 (details of shaft and tine, right)

Roasting on a Stand

THIS IS THE METHOD THAT YOU CAN USE to roast meat on the hearth whether you are roasting at home on your own fireplace, at a friend's house, or in a rented cabin. It requires no specialized equipment and effectively no set-up. The principle is simple: meat sits on a stand some distance from the fire and is turned with a fork by the cook to keep it from burning. This is the roasting method often described by Homer in *The Iliad* and *The Odyssey.* This method lends itself to improvisation. A stand for the meat can be anything from an over-turned frying pan, to a grill set up on bricks, to a piece of aluminum foil. The meat can sit on the hearth in front of the fire or beside the fire within the firebox. I describe two cooking methods. One requires turning the meat often before a searingly hot fire, while in the other method the meat cooks slowly and thus requires less attention from the cook. Both methods produce exceptional results. Review the section for Radiant Heat (page 264) for information that will help you control cooking speed.

 The Fire: A mature fire with moderate to high flames.

Quarter-turn roasting: In this method, the meat sits on a stand placed close to a very hot fire. Because the meat is close to the fire, it must be turned every few minutes to prevent the meat from charring. This method creates a roast that is identical in appearance with one that is spit or string roasted. It will have a beautiful crust and will be evenly roasted. This method is most appropriate for the most symmetrical roasts and well-trussed rabbits.

Prepare the roast according to the recipe and then place the clean grill on the hearth near a hot fire. Set the roast on the edge of the grill 6 to 8 inches (15 to 20 cm) from the fire over a drip pan filled with 1 cup (250 ml) water. The fire should be so hot you can't hold your hand near the meat for longer than 10 seconds. Every 3 to 4 minutes, use a meat fork to turn the meat a quarter-turn. Baste each time you turn the meat with a basting sauce made from the oil and salt. If the meat begins to char, move it farther away from the flames, but keep in mind that small changes in distance mean significant changes in temperature. One to 2 inches (2.5 to 5 cm) farther away from the fire can mean a significant reduction in the amount of heat falling on the surface of the meat. The meat is done when the inte-

---

PRIMARY VENUE
Hearth

ALTERNATE VENUE
Campfire

INGREDIENTS
Roasts
Rabbits
Birds of all sizes

Basting Sauce
¼ cup (60 ml) olive oil
1 teaspoon salt

RECIPES USING THIS METHOD INCLUDE:
Roasted Chicken, 70
Roasted Duck, 73
Roasted Leg of Lamb, 108
Roasts, Plain and Elaborate, 110

rior temperature is appropriate for the cut. If the roast is not cooked enough in the middle when you need to eat, carve the cooked outer pieces and continue roasting the balance. If, for whatever reason, something comes up and you cannot turn the meat every 3 to 4 minutes, move it back farther from the fire. It will still cook, though more slowly, and there will be no risk of burning it.

Half-turn to third-turn roasting: In this method, the meat cooks farther away from the fire. It therefore cooks more slowly and does not run the risk of burning. Rather than cooking at 350° to 375°F (175° to 190°C), one is cooking at 250° to 275°F (120° to 135°C). Prepare the roast according to the recipe and place the clean grill on the hearth near a moderate fire. Set the roast toward the center or back of the grill 10 to 12 inches (25 to 30 cm) from the fire over a drip pan filled with 1 cup (250 ml) water. Use the meat fork to rotate the meat one-third turn at your leisure. Adjust the temperature by moving the meat closer to or farther away from the fire. There really are no rules. I find a half-turn every 30 minutes is usually effective. Baste often with the basting sauce of oil and salt. A leg of lamb will take about 2½ hours. With 30 minutes on a side, expect the meat to be medium-rare to well done. If ever the roast is not cooked enough in the middle when you need to eat, carve the cooked outer pieces and continue roasting the remainder.

Note on birds and poultry: *Birds and poultry, no matter how tightly trussed, are never as symmetrical as a roast and are not so easily turned the precise amount one wants. Therefore, birds and poultry are more effectively roasted when they are held by a stand in a vertical position. Stands that hold roasts vertically can be purchased, or one can be improvised by bending two or three wire hangers into a conical shape, like a conifer tree. The bird should be able to rest upright and yet be stable so you can turn the base as needed. The base should sit in a pan to catch drippings.*

Once you have purchased or devised a stand for a bird—for example, a stand for a chicken—prepare the chicken according to the recipe and roast it quickly or slowly as described above.

Spit Roasting

ILLUMINATED MEDIEVAL MANUSCRIPTS present many examples of spit roasting before a fire. The one idea that comes across from these early images is that roasting is best when done before an intensely hot fire. Of the three roasting methods described in this book—string roasting, spit roasting, and roasting on a stand—spit roasting is the method in which the heat of the fire can be pushed the hottest. High heat produces exquisite golden crusts and the most flavorful roasts. See page 266 and also the List of Suppliers, page 278, for information on buying a mechanical spit.

 The Fire: A mature fire with moderate to high flames combined with a substantial bed of embers to radiate a significant amount of heat onto the hearth.

After preparing the roasts, poultry, or birds according to one of the suggested recipes, truss them with string so they are as compact and symmetrical as possible. Thread the meat onto the spit, lock in place, and test for balance. If the meat is not perfectly balanced, rethread the meat. You should be able to turn the spit in your hands and feel that the meat turns smoothly and evenly.

Set up the spit mechanism, whether clockwork or electric, to one side of the fireplace where it is shielded from the heat. Place the stand that will hold the other end of the spit on the opposite side of the fireplace. Set the drip pan on the hearth under where the meat will turn. Bring the spit to the hearth, and attach one end to the motor and the other to the stand. The spit should be positioned parallel to the fire, as close as possible to the fire while still being over the hearth, and about 13 inches (33 cm) above the hearth. Adjust the position of the drip pan and start the meat turning.

Refer back to individual recipes for details about basting. As a rule, when using a mechanical spit, I advise roasting before an intensely hot fire so the air at the edge of the hearth is the equivalent of an oven set to 375° to 450°F (190° to 230°C). Cooking this hot, however, is not a requirement. Find a cooking temperature that matches your personal style. Add wood, including kindling, as needed to maintain the heat and add water to the drip pan as needed to prevent the drippings from burning.

When the meat is done, remove the spit from the hearth, and the meat from the spit. Let the meat rest for 10 minutes before serving. If you want to use the drippings, skim and pour into a small pitcher to serve with the meat.

EQUIPMENT
Mechanical Spit
Drip pan
Shovel

PRIMARY VENUE
Hearth

ALTERNATE VENUE
Campfire

RECIPES USING THIS
METHOD INCLUDE:
Roasted Chicken, 70
Roasted Duck, 73
Roasted Leg of Lamb, 108
Roasts, Plain and Elaborate, 110

Philippe's Veal Roast

P HILIPPE IRRMAN MAINTAINS A MIRACLE in the heart of Paris: a working kitchen fireplace. His fireplace is part of a dream of fire where fire has been all but extinguished. It is also part of a larger dream, that of creating harmony within the many discontinuities of modern life. Philippe's collection of culinary objects is both magnificent and extensive. In its totality, ranging from the pots and pans of the open hearth to the smallest storage container, his *batterie de cuisine* describes a poetry of domestic life that has been all but forgotten.

Until I met Philippe, I had never known anyone else who cooked on a fireplace as a matter of routine. It was, then, a great surprise to discover that our imaginations were differently engaged. Almost exclusively, his foods are invisibly transformed by fire. His flavors are created in an alchemist's retort, his open fire producing results that taste as if they came from an oven. Philippe's hearth envelops visitors in the protective warmth of the farmhouse kitchen. By contrast, my greatest pleasure is to create food so directly shocked by the intensity of a roaring fire, and the touch of glowing embers, that when we taste it, we feel ourselves to be under a star-studded sky protected only by a nomad's fire, a beacon of warmth and safety in an arid wilderness.

Philippe's roast is a simple one that highlights clean flavors. He uses veal, small white onions, carrots—carrots to die for—and potatoes. The choice of vegetables is not important—leeks could replace onions, turnips the potatoes. What does count is the quality of the ingredients. The dry heat that builds up within the Dutch oven intensifies flavors; the more flavorful the vegetables are to begin with, the more remarkable the plate will be when served. The skill is in bringing the roast and the vegetables to the point of peak flavor at the same moment. Once Philippe sees the vegetables are beginning to cook, he checks them frequently, and serves the roast the moment they are done. Serve with Clafouti (page 194) for dessert.

 The Fire: A mature fire with gentle to moderate flames.

Remove the veal roast from the refrigerator. Rub the roast with olive oil, salt, and pepper. Let the meat come to room temperature. Put 8 tablespoons (120 ml) olive oil, the thyme, bay leaves, and the roast in the Dutch oven.

Place the Dutch oven on the hearth where it will receive moderate to high side heat from the fire, usually 3 to 5 inches (7 to 12 cm) back from the edge of the firebox. Begin by shoveling a thick layer of embers underneath the Dutch oven to create high heat. Lightly sear the veal on all sides. Cover the Dutch oven and allow the embers underneath to die out.

When the roast's internal temperature begins to rise, usually after about 30 minutes, add the vegetables. Replace the lid and mound embers on it to create high heat. Maintain high heat on the lid by replenishing the embers as needed. After the vegetables begin cooking, check often by using a pot hook to lift the lid. The veal is done at 140° to 145°F (60° to 63°C). The vegetables are done when you can pierce them with a fork, usually in 20 to 35 minutes. If the roast isn't also done, transfer the vegetables to a platter and continue cooking the roast. Otherwise, move the Dutch oven away from the fire and shovel the embers back into the fireplace. Transfer the roast and vegetables to a serving platter, let the meat rest for a few minutes, and serve.

INGREDIENTS
(Serves 6 to 8)

1 boned veal roast, 2½ pounds (1.25 kg)

Olive oil

Salt

Pepper

8 sprigs thyme

2 bay leaves

1½ pounds (750 g) boiling onions, leeks, or onions, trimmed and peeled as necessary

1 pound (450 g) small carrots or parsnips, peeled

1 pound (450 g) small potatoes or turnips, peeled

Pot hook

Here was one quartered upon me half a year, who had
the conscience to take up one of my best beds, though he hardly
spent a shilling a day in the house, and suffered his men
to roast cabbages at the kitchen fire, because I would not give
them a dinner on a Sunday.

HENRY FIELDING, *The History of Tom Jones, a Foundling*

VEGETABLES

Potato Tureen

BASIC METHOD
Dutch Oven

EQUIPMENT
5-quart (5-l) Dutch oven
  with legs
Shovel
Pot hook

PRIMARY VENUE
Hearth

ALTERNATE VENUES
Campfire
Bread Oven

Jerusalem artichoke

THIS IS ONE OF THE MOST FLEXIBLE and delicious meals you can make. It lends itself to last-minute production and can usually be improvised from pantry, garden, or refrigerator staples. In northern Europe, where potatoes are among the main crops of subsistence farmers, potato tureens are everyday dishes. If these tureens were not part of your childhood, you may find the plainness of their ingredients deceiving: the ingredients, and the fire baking, create a dish of melded flavors that, though seldom flashy, has its own kind of intensity—an intensity that passes into memory as longing.

The potato kugel, known in America as a Jewish dish, is common to a huge swath of central Europe. Although potato tureens differ from place to place—some, for example, are commonly made with cheese, while others never are—the basic concept is the same. Potatoes are layered with onions and sometimes other ingredients—wild mushrooms, herbs, greens, smoked fat—and then everything is moistened with liquid, which can be anything from a truffle-laced cream to a light stock to water to milk. The tureen is then baked in a Dutch oven on the hearth, in a terra-cotta pot buried in the embers, or, in northern Europe, in a bread oven.

If Jerusalem artichokes are in season, use at least a few of them in this dish. Even a small quantity contributes sweetness and earthiness. Winter black truffles are especially good with potatoes. Even if you only have one truffle, follow the instructions here for macerating it with cream and then add it to

A 17th-century brass French Dutch oven

the tureen. You will sit down to a memorable dish. Do not add more liquid than the recipe indicates. Too much liquid changes the texture completely.

 The Fire: A mature fire with gentle to moderate flames.

Oil the sides and bottom of the Dutch oven. Using one-third of the potatoes (or the potatoes and Jerusalem artichokes), place a layer of potatoes in the bottom of the pot. Sprinkle with salt and follow with a layer of the onion, parsley, thyme, sage, and cheese. Repeat the layers until all of the ingredients are used up, ending with a layer of potatoes. Pour the cream over the ingredients and cover the pot.

Place the Dutch oven on the hearth where it will receive moderate side heat from the fire, usually 4 to 6 inches (10 to 15 cm) back from the edge of the firebox. Begin by shoveling embers underneath the Dutch oven to create moderate heat and shovel embers onto the lid to create high heat. Let the embers underneath cool a little, refresh them as needed, a sprinkling at a time, to maintain gentle heat under the oven while maintaining moderate to high heat on the lid. After 20 minutes, use a pot hook to lift the lid and check the progress. Adjust the temperature according to what you see. The total cooking time should be between 30 and 40 minutes. About 10 minutes before you think the tureen will be done, replace all the embers on the lid with a substantial pile of fresh embers in order to brown the top. When the tureen is done, shovel all the embers back into the fireplace, and serve the tureen.

Mushroom variation: Thinly slice 2 pounds (1 kg) fresh porcino mushrooms, or soak 3½ ounces (90 g) dried porcino mushrooms in warm water until rehydrated and drain. Distribute the mushrooms in each layer along with the onion and herbs.

Truffle variation: Two days in advance, rinse 2 ounces (50 g) fresh European black winter truffles or 3 to 4 ounces (75 to 100 g) fresh Chinese or European black summer truffles to remove any remaining dirt. Finely shave, or grate, into 1 cup (250 ml) heavy cream. Store for 2 days in the refrigerator. The long maceration in cream is an absolute requirement for the successful use of the truffles.

Just before baking, assemble the tureen as directed, ending with a layer of potatoes. If you have additional truffles, include some finely shaved, or grated, truffle on each potato layer. Use the truffle-laced cream in place of the plain cream called for in the recipe. See pages 276–277 for information on buying, storing, and handling fresh truffles.

INGREDIENTS
(Serves 4 to 6)

Olive Oil

2 pounds (1 kg) potatoes, or 1½ pounds (725 g) potatoes and ½ pound (225 g) Jerusalem artichokes, peeled and thinly sliced

Salt

1 large yellow onion, thinly sliced

12 flat-leaf parsley sprigs

4 thyme sprigs, or 1½ teaspoons dried thyme

4 sage sprigs, or 1½ teaspoons dried sage

4 to 6 ounces (100 to 150 g) fresh goat cheese, crumbled

1 cup (250 ml) heavy cream

Grilled Vegetables

BASIC METHOD
Hearthside Grilling

EQUIPMENT
Grill
Shovel

PRIMARY VENUE
Hearth

ALTERNATE VENUES
Barbecue
Campfire

Onions

T HE MARRIAGE OF OIL, salt, browning from contact with the grill, and a light smoking from the embers is what makes grilled vegetables memorable. Whenever practical, cut the vegetables—at least in half—so the oil and salt can fully penetrate the flesh. Given a choice, select younger specimens, rather than mature ones.

Serve grilled vegetables dressed with a light vinaigrette for a first course, as the core of a vegetarian meal, or as an accompaniment to meat, fish, or poultry. As a rule, most vegetables are best cooked over cool to moderate embers and benefit from an occasional basting with olive oil. The equivalent of a one-pot meal can be made by grilling vegetables alongside sausage, poultry, or chops. If serving fish, grill the vegetables first, and follow with the fish.

The Fire: A mature fire with gentle flames, and if basting the vegetables with oil while grilling, moderate to high flames to pull smoke up the chimney.

Brush the following vegetables with olive oil and sprinkle with salt just before placing them on the grill:

Parboiled asparagus

Halved Japanese eggplants

Zucchini

Globe eggplants sliced ¼ inch (6 mm) thick

Whole baby leeks or halved or quartered mature leeks (white parts only)

Whole green onions

Whole small zucchini or summer squashes (ideally, with flowers still attached) or larger summer squashes halved or sliced

Mushrooms purchased in the market are often a little dry, so before treating them to oil and salt for grilling, soak them in a bowl of lightly salted water for an hour, and let them drain for an hour on a towel (see pages 146 and 148 for other grilled mushrooms).

Shucked whole ears of corn and *whole or halved tomatoes* are grilled without oil or salt.

Place the clean grill on the hearth close to the fire. Shovel embers underneath to create gentle heat. When the grill is hot, brush it with olive oil and lay down the prepared vegetables. Over the space of a few minutes, add additional embers, a sprinkling at a time, until you can hear or see the vegetables cooking. From this point on, add embers only to maintain the desired temperature. If you see the vegetables drying out while cooking, brush them with olive oil. Use a fork or spatula to turn the vegetables as required. The vegetables are done when they are tender. To test, pierce them with a knife. Remove the vegetables from the grill, and return the embers to the fireplace. Burned sections, if any, such as the outer leaf of a leek, should be trimmed off before serving.

Ember-Roasted Vegetables

BASIC METHOD

Ember Roasting

EQUIPMENT

Shovel

Long-handled tongs

PRIMARY VENUE

Firebox

ALTERNATE VENUES

Barbecue

Campfire

INGREDIENTS

See individual recipes

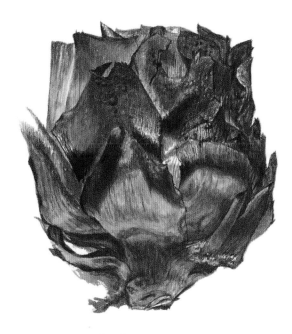

I F THERE IS A SINGLE reason to embrace the open hearth, it is for the richness of flavor that ember roasting brings to vegetables. Between the vegetables presented here and those treated elsewhere in this book, you will have a significant repertoire of ember-roasted vegetables from which to build your own experiments. Many of these vegetables are excellent as appetizers, and others can be served as a first course or they can be incorporated into another dish. A mix of finely diced roasted onions or roasted artichoke hearts, for example, makes a fantastic pasta sauce and puréed ember-roasted parsnips are a superb sauce for grilled meat.

The first time you make the more extreme preparations, and I count burying artichokes and cabbage in embers as extreme preparations, do so when you are not under pressure to make dinner for company. Charring the skins of the vegetables is a required part of many of the recipes that follow. In all cases, the parts that burn are scraped or cut away before serving. What one loses through charring, one gains in flavor: sweetness, a hint of smoke, and, overall, a subtle but distinctive change in the vegetable itself.

Since we usually speak of roasting peppers, but of baking potatoes, even when the cooking method is the same, I sometimes refer to "ember roasting" and at other times to "ember baking." Both terms refer to the same method and may be used interchangeably.

The Fire: A mature fire that has produced a substantive bed of embers is appropriate for most of the vegetables. If cooking only a few vegetables, any mature fire will work. If cooking a substantial number—a dozen peppers or artichokes—a concerted effort to create embers may be needed. Many of the vegetables require gentle to moderate flames in addition to embers.

Hardwoods create hotter and longer-lasting embers than softwoods, making them the best choice for ember roasting or baking. Control the temperature of embers by fanning them to make them hotter and by letting them sit or by dusting them with ash to make them cooler. Unless otherwise stated, these recipes assume that you have used a shovel to create a flat bed of embers within the firebox 6 to 12 inches (15 to 30 cm) from the fire on which to roast the vegetables.

Artichokes: Ember roasting is a classic preparation for artichokes in several Mediterranean regions, including areas of southern Italy and Spain. Select medium to large artichokes. Cut off the top quarter of each artichoke and fan the leaves open, including those around the choke. The stem helps stabilize the artichoke in the embers, so trim the stem to between 2 and 3 inches (5 and 7 cm). Spread the leaves to create space, distribute half a dozen pieces of slivered garlic between the leaves, pushing them down toward the heart, along with leaves of fresh oregano, thyme, or sage. Sprinkle with salt and fill the artichoke with olive oil, being sure to get oil deep into the heart. Set aside, being careful not to spill the oil. Use the shovel to make a trench in a deep bed of intensely hot embers. With the long-handled tongs, place the artichokes in the trench and push hot embers against the sides of the artichokes so they sit one-third buried in the embers. The bed of embers should be just shy of a heat so intense that it is difficult to perform these actions. Turn the artichokes as needed to promote even cooking, but if the embers are as hot as described, turning will not be necessary. When the outer leaves are burned, and the entire head has changed color from bright to dull green—about 20 minutes for a medium-large artichoke—remove the artichokes from the embers. Let cool, remove the burned outer leaves, and serve.

(continued)

Long-handled tongs

Ember-Roasted Vegetables
(continued)

Leek

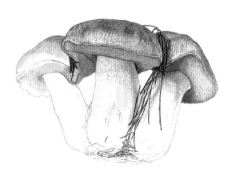

Porcini

Beets: Ember-roasted beets produce the most concentrated beet flavor of any method for cooking beets. Follow the instructions for Roasted Onions (page 22). Remove the beets from the embers when they can be pierced easily with a fork, usually 40 minutes to 1 hour. When cool enough to handle, scrape off the burned outer layer, quarter, and serve as a side dish. Serve them thinly sliced in a light vinaigrette as an appetizer.

Cabbage: Cabbages emerge from the embers transformed—suffused with a light smoky flavor among other changes to their taste. Use the shovel to half-bury small heads of cabbage—I emphasize small heads—in a hot deep bed of embers. Use the long-handled tongs to turn once. The outer leaves will char. The cabbage is done when a fork easily penetrates to the center, usually 15 to 30 minutes. Remove from the heat with the tongs or shovel, trim off the burned leaves, quarter, and serve.

Carrots and parsnips: After a day in the mountains of China collecting truffles, my friend and I were invited to dinner at the house of the truffle collector. The meal itself was not as memorable as the preparations: five cooking fires laid out on the floor in a room without a chimney. On one of the fires, our truffle guide roasted carrots on the embers. To roast carrots, select medium-large carrots. Roast them unpeeled on embers that are covered with a light layer of ash, and turn them often. Expect a little blistering and a few spots of charring. Carrots are done when they can be pierced with a fork, usually 20 to 40 minutes. Scrape off the blisters and any char before serving. Roast small parsnips in the same manner. Large parsnips, however, are best baked in hot ash.

Corn: Grilled corn is an international street food. I have eaten many versions in many places: under a baobab tree in Tanzania, in the middle of a dusty, cacophonous street in Yemen, amid a line of food sellers in one of China's newly built cities, by the Seine in Paris, in a formal park in Mexico. In all cases, the corn was less sweet than American sweet corn and instead much closer to the corn we feed animals. For this ember-roasting recipe from Yemen, use shucked mature ears of corn, ones that may even be a little dried out. Dust a bed of embers with ash—the corn should not touch hot embers—and roast, turning frequently. Corn is done when it is hot, but for this recipe continue roasting until at least some of the kernels on all sides of the corn are a caramel color, usually 10 to 15 minutes. Serve as is, or, before serving, follow the Mexican method of dipping in lightly salted water.

Garlic: See Baked Garlic (page 28).

Leeks: Use whole thick leeks. Trim off the roots and green leaves. Place on a bed of moderately hot embers lightly dusted with ash. Turn every 2 to 3 minutes. Leeks are done when they can be easily pierced with a fork, 10 to 20 minutes depending on the thickness of the leek. The outer leaves will become golden and may have to be trimmed away. Serve whole or quartered.

Mushrooms: Many of the indigenous peoples of Mexico roast the Mexican version of *Amanita caesarea,* Italy's favorite mushroom, by lowering the mushroom by its stalk onto embers. The method is well suited to the more flavorful gilled mushrooms including matsutake *(Armillaria matsutake* or *A. ponderosa)* and the giant parasol mushroom *(Lepiota procera).* The commercial portobello mushroom *(A. bisporis, var.)* can also be cooked directly on embers. Portobellos are sometimes dehydrated from their time spent in the market. I therefore advise soaking portobellos in a bowl of lightly salted water for 2 to 4 hours and then letting the mushrooms dry on a towel for 1 hour before cooking them on embers.

Roasted red pepper

To cook gilled mushrooms on embers, clean them as you normally would. However, since the stalk is used as a handle, do not trim it off. Lower the mushroom by its stalk onto embers lightly covered with ash. Sprinkle the gills with salt. To promote even cooking, use the upturned stem to give the mushroom a one-quarter turn every 2 to 3 minutes and move it slightly so it is not always sitting in the same spot. As the mushroom cooks, it becomes damp with steam. You may also see water boiling between the gills. When the gills are cooked, the mushroom is done, usually 6 to 12 minutes. Remove from the heat, cut off the stem, and serve the cap while it is hot. The stem is often good eating. Cook the stem by laying it down on the embers, turning it as needed.

Onions: See Roasted Onions (page 22).

Peppers: See Roasted Red Peppers (page 24).

Potatoes: See Ember-Baked Potatoes (page 154).

Verona radicchio

Radicchio: This bitter chicory lives for ember roasting. The heads are often small—watch them closely so they don't burn up. Use the long-handled tongs to nestle the radicchio heads in hot embers and turn them often. When soft all the way through, usually 8 to 10 minutes, remove the burned outer leaves, quarter, sprinkle with salt and a fruity olive oil, and serve. I particularly recommend roasted radicchio as a side dish for a main dish that can benefit from a strong contrasting flavor, such as for roast duck. If you grow your own, pick the head just above the crown and the plant will continue to produce leaves that are excellent braised.

Roasted onion

Vegetables in Drippings

BASIC METHOD
Hearthside Tripod

EQUIPMENT
Frying pan or other
    shallow pan
Shovel
Tripod

PRIMARY VENUE
Hearth

ALTERNATE VENUES
Campfire
Bread Oven

INGREDIENTS
(Serves 4 to 6)

1½ pounds (725 g)
    potatoes, peeled
    and sliced ½ inch
    (1 cm) thick

1 yellow onion, diced

1 head garlic, cloves
    separated and
    peeled but left whole

Neck and organs
    from bird, if
    roasting poultry

1 cup (250 ml) water

Spider

PARISIANS ARE FORTUNATE. They don't need to cook their own dinners to sit down to a great meal in their own dining rooms. After work, walking back home from the metro stop, they inevitably pass a butcher shop selling freshly roasted chickens along with potatoes and pearl onions cooked in the drippings. Roots and tubers—carrots, parsnips, turnips, potatoes, Jerusalem artichokes, kohlrabi (a brassica I think of as an honorary root vegetable)—are particularly good when cooked under roasting meat or birds. Robust greens—collards, kale, cabbage—are all spectacular cooked in drippings as well.

When roasting a domestic duck (page 72), I suggest putting sliced potatoes in the drip pan and then, toward the end of the cooking, boiling off the water and frying the potatoes in the fat. Potatoes fried in duck fat is an example of a preparation that I would describe as "too delicious." Don't make it a daily habit.

 The Fire: Whatever fire is specified for the roasting meat.

Set a frying pan that is large enough to comfortably fit the ingredients on the tripod placed on the edge of the hearth directly under where the meat will roast. Start the meat or poultry roasting, either on a spit or hanging from a string. The roasting meat or poultry should clear the pan by 3 inches (7.5 cm).

Add the vegetables, neck and organs (if using), and the water to the pan, and shovel a thick layer of embers underneath the pan to create high heat. Let the embers cool a little; refresh them as needed, a sprinkling at a time, to maintain gentle to moderate heat under the pan until the contents are cooked to your satisfaction. Stir as needed to ensure even cooking. Since many meats are roasted before an intensely hot fire, embers will be very close to, and even touching, the drip pan on the side nearest the flames. The leading edge of the pan may be over 600°F (315°C), so be attentive to burning fats. Retain a little water in the pan until the very end, when you may boil off the water to brown the vegetables. If the vegetables are done before the meat, push them away from the hot side of the pan to keep them warm while the meat continues cooking. As a rule, there is no need to salt the vegetables because of the salt in the drippings.

Sautéed Greens

CABBAGE AND OTHER STRONG-flavored greens—kales and mustards—along with greens that are a little bitter—mature lettuce plants and various chicories—deliver the classic flavors of wintertime vegetables. They refresh whatever they accompany—a plate of grilled meat, a long-simmered stew, a pot of baked beans. As I became more deeply involved with developing a hearth cuisine, I simultaneously began developing my kitchen garden. Living in the preternatural spring of Northern California, I specialize in long-lived greens and grow a garden that is a bit like a meadow.

Russian kale

If you don't have a garden in which to graze for greens, use the grocery store as if it were your garden. Instead of buying a single variety of green, buy two or three, and use them in combination. Radicchio is a reliable source of bitterness. Robust salad greens, like frisée and romaine, are excellent cooked. In addition, the refrigerator often provides foraging opportunities. Cabbage, celery, some parsley, and other green odds and ends typically lurk in the bottom of many refrigerators. Take some of this and that, chop them, and sauté them on the hearth for a taste of spring, even as snow drapes the trees and the sky hangs leaden and cold.

 The Fire: A mature fire with gentle to moderate flames.

Put the frying pan on the tripod placed on the hearth where a gentle side heat will fall on the pan. Shovel a thick layer of embers underneath the pan to create high heat. Add the vegetables, the olive oil, and a sprinkling of salt. If the greens are not wet from washing, add a generous ¼ cup (60 ml) water. When the greens start cooking, stir and cover until they wilt and are tender, 5 to 8 minutes. Remove the lid and refresh embers underneath the pan to maintain high heat. Continue to stir as needed to prevent scorching until all the water has evaporated. Remove the pan from the hearth and shovel the embers back into the firebox. Season the greens with salt and transfer them to a serving bowl.

BASIC METHOD
Hearthside Tripod

EQUIPMENT
Large frying pan
   with lid
Tripod
Shovel

PRIMARY VENUE
Hearth

ALTERNATE VENUES
Barbecue
Campfire

INGREDIENTS
(Serves 4 to 6)

12 oz (350 g)
   chopped mixed
   greens (7 cups),
   including at least
   one bitter green
   such as radicchio
   or dandelion

3 tablespoons
   (45 ml) olive oil

Salt

Truffles under Embers

BURIED UNDERGROUND, even under a foot of rock, the scent of the European black winter truffle *(Tuber melanosporum)* is strong enough for a dog to find. When truffle collectors enter a café with even a small handful of truffles in a pocket, the scent fills the room. Against one's nose, truffles are pungent; at a distance, their smell is light, attractive, attracting. I cannot think of a food analogy. At its core is a smell that we cannot smell—the intangible smell within the smell that draws us to our love. Rather than make you hungry, like other food smells, it fills you with the desire to smell again.

Unfortunately, this tantalizing smell is difficult to capture as taste. As a food, on the dinner plate, whether cooked or raw, black truffles have many flavors, including the flavor "none." You can eat lots of truffle, and, but for its blackness, not know it. To make truffle the extraordinary ingredient that it is, you must give it time. The way to capture the black truffle's sweet evanescence is to transfer it into something else, slowly, over a period of days. Over time, fat absorbs the aspect of truffle smell that tastes sweet. And since the sweetness is more the sweetness of a deep, lingering kiss than that of a frosted cake, no matter how many times you taste, you want to taste again.

Shave, or finely grate, two ounces (30 g) of freshly washed truffle into one cup (250 ml) of heavy cream. Put the truffled cream in a container, close the lid, and place in the refrigerator for two days. Use this cream along with freshly shaved truffle on pasta. Two other simple, traditional, and incredibly delicious truffle recipes are truffled omelet and truffled fried eggs. For either preparation, infuse the eggs in their shells with the taste of truffle by sealing them along with a few truffles in a refrigerated container for two days before use. At the same time, infuse a little unsalted butter with shaved truffle for use when cooking the eggs. When the eggs are cooked, shave fresh truffle over them just before serving, or, even better, finish with a small amount of the truffle butter.

Winter is the season for *T. melanosporum.* Long ago, in the rocky and comparatively unfertile truffle region of Provence, winter was not a time of plenty. Country people prepared truffles in the simplest way. They roasted them in the ashes and ate them with their fingers. Enough romance remains attached to *truffes sous la cendre* for the recipe to be included in many French cookbooks. Modern versions of the recipe invariably call for wrapping the truffles in foil or oiled paper, often with a piece of lard. The original method of baking directly in ash produces a distinctly cleaner taste and richer texture, and so that is the method I provide here.

Truffles are expensive. Unless you are in France during truffle season in the area where they are hunted, you are unlikely to be able to afford the pound (450 g) of truffles that is ideal for making a fully truffled meal. If you have only a couple of truffles, you will get the most flavor from them by using them in the Potato Tureen (page 132) or with eggs. But if you have many truffles, bake a handful in the ashes.

Truffles, like many luxuries, are inextricably woven into a cloth of myth and mystification. Everyone knows the name "truffle," but few know the thing itself. Truffles have become, at heart, a literary food entangled in a fantasy of wealth, champagne, linen, silver, and sparkling women. The truffle can stand for wealth and ostentatious display, but it can also stand for simple pleasures. My own sense of truffle is expressed through a fantasy of a truffle hunter at home in an isolated stone house perched on a steep slope in

Provence around the turn of the twentieth century. I imagine a man alone with his olives, dogs, and a small herd of goats. During the truffle season, he goes with his dogs to hunt for truffles, scrambling among stones and oaks. But truffles are difficult to find, and prices are variable.

INGREDIENTS

3 to 5 black winter truffles per person, each ¾ to 1 inch (2 to 2.5 cm) in diameter

He doesn't always have enough tubers to make the trip into town worthwhile. And so, in the quiet of the evening, sitting in front of his fire of oak and olive wood, he roasts truffles in the embers—tiny, black, golden potatoes—and eats them out of hand.

Ash cakes, roasted truffles, and a bottle of wine—a meal that helps you find your way through winter's gray.

 The Fire: A mature fire with gentle flames, and a solid base of ash across the fireplace floor.

Before you begin, see pages 276–277 for information on truffle species, and on buying, storing, and handling fresh truffles.

If the truffles still have dirt on them, clean them under running water with a soft brush. Pat them dry and dust with flour to keep ash from sticking to the dampness. Use the shovel to make a well in warm ash. Put the truffles in the well, cover with a 1-inch (2.5-cm) layer of ash, and pile with a thick layer of embers. Bake the truffles for 10 minutes under high heat. Remove them from the embers, brush off the ash, and serve the truffles while they are still warm. They should be eaten out of hand like potatoes baked in embers (page 154).

Sweet Potato Casserole

Tего HIS IS A SOUTHERN DISH— and it's soul food—although for most Americans it is eaten only once a year, as one of the ritual plates of the Thanksgiving table. There are so many versions of this casserole, and so many of them are much-loved, long-practiced family recipes, that introducing my own mother's recipe makes me fear I may make some readers unhappy enough to declare, "Why, that's not sweet potato casserole!"

This recipe is lean—it doesn't have butter in it—and as with much of my mother's cooking, sugar is kept to a minimum. These potatoes are sweet enough to lift your spirits, while still leaving room for dessert. As a dish incorporating sugar served alongside the main course, it points back to a time when sweets were not necessarily reserved for the end of the meal.

 The Fire: A mature fire with gentle to moderate flames.

Put the potatoes, sugar, and water in the Dutch oven and cover. Place the Dutch oven on the hearth where it will receive moderate side heat from the fire, usually 4 to 6 inches (10 to 15 cm) back from the edge of the firebox. Begin by shoveling embers underneath the Dutch oven to create high heat. Let the embers underneath cool a little, then refresh them as needed, a sprinkling at a time, to maintain the potatoes at a simmer. Lift the lid and stir once or twice to mix the potatoes. When they are soft, 20 to 30 minutes, remove the lid and boil away the water. Shovel all the embers back into the fireplace and serve the sweet potatoes hot.

BASIC METHOD
Dutch Oven

EQUIPMENT
5-quart (5-l) Dutch oven with legs
Shovel

PRIMARY VENUE
Hearth

ALTERNATE VENUES
Campfire
Bread Oven

INGREDIENTS
(Serves 8 to 10)

4 pounds (1.75 kg) sweet potatoes, peeled and sliced ½ inch (1 cm) thick

½ cup (100 g) firmly packed turbinado or light brown sugar

1 cup (250 ml) water

Grilled Porcini

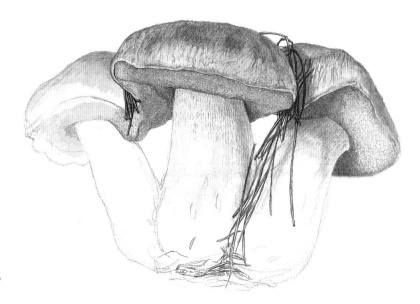

BASIC METHOD
Hearthside Grilling

EQUIPMENT
Grill
Shovel

PRIMARY VENUE
Hearth

ALTERNATE VENUES
Barbecue
Campfire

I N ITALY THEY ARE CALLED PORCINI, in France, *cèpes*. Russians call them *belyie griby*, Lithuanians *baravykai*, Poles *prawdziwki*, Slovenians *globanje*, and Germans *Steinpilze*. Whatever the local name, *Boletus edulis* is The Mushroom to the vast majority of European mushroom collectors in the same sense that Irene Adler is The Woman to Sherlock Holmes. I do not exaggerate. Once, on a visit to Slovenia, after having collected two baskets of mushrooms, my Slovenian friend and I returned home to his flat. The baskets were overflowing, and the selection was varied and fabulous. Anton's wife called from another room, "Did you find any mushrooms?" My friend called out, "Two!" And indeed, among the bountiful harvest we did have two small *globanje*.

What to do with a porcino treasure? If the mushroom is young, in perfect condition, with white pores and without worms, follow the Italian practice: slice it wafer thin and eat it raw as a salad with a little salt and your best olive oil. If a little more mature, but the pores are still firm, grill the cap. More mature specimens are best for sauces and stews, with the oldest reserved for drying.

The secret to grilling mushrooms—whether those with gills on the underside of the cap, or those with pores, like porcini—is slow cooking. Browning or charring the cap may create bitter flavors. Grilling the porcini caps slowly with salt and olive oil deepens and sweetens their flavor, and develops the porcini's famed texture, at once solid and buttery.

In southern Europe, the most flavorful porcini grow under chestnut trees. For those of us with inherently less flavorful specimens, a little work at the grill can go a long way. Grilling mushroom caps over chestnut leaves imparts flavor to the mushrooms, reduces the chance of burning, and makes a beautiful presentation. If chestnut trees are rare in your area, then when you find a tree, pick a couple dozen leaves and dry them for later use.

A last fact—think of it as a bit of brave cookbook verité—porcini often come inhabited by a fair number of little white worms, actually larvae. Italians, who are otherwise larvae phobic, choose to overlook these fungal visitors, even in their grilled caps. Unless the infestation is extreme—never eat rotten mushrooms—my advice is to do the same.

 The Fire: A mature fire with gentle flames to produce a steady supply of embers.

If you have collected the mushrooms in the wild, clean each mushroom in the field as much as possible. In the kitchen, rinse each cap under running water, keeping the pores dry. After rinsing, trim away any parts that are still dirty or that are discolored. Place the mushrooms, stem-sides up, on a cutting board and cut off the stems flush with the pores, reserving the stems for drying. Insert 6 to 8 garlic slivers into the pores of each cap and rub the smooth part of each cap with olive oil. If you have dried chestnut leaves, rehydrate them in hot water to cover for several minutes.

Place the clean grill on the hearth far enough from the fire that the mushrooms will not cook from the fire's side heat. Brush the grill with olive oil. Place each cap, pores-side up, directly on the grill, or, if you have chestnut leaves, on a layer of the leaves. Sprinkle the pores with salt and olive oil. While you don't want to flood the pores entirely with oil, be generous, pouring in a zigzag pattern to cover 50 to 75 percent of the cap. Start the cooking slowly by shoveling a thin layer of embers under the grill to create gentle heat. Wait a couple of minutes before adding more. Continue adding embers under the grill as necessary, but always keep the heat gentle. Aim to cook the caps in 20 to 40 minutes without browning. Use a fork or spatula to turn once or twice, as needed. Do not be in a rush to remove the mushrooms from the grill. They are best when they are tender and have stewed a while in their own juices. When done, return the embers to the fireplace, transfer the mushrooms to a serving plate, cut into sections, and serve.

INGREDIENTS
(Serves 8 to 16 as an appetizer, 4 to 6 as a first course)

4 porcino or other bolete mushrooms, each weighing no more than ½ pound (225 g)

2 to 4 cloves garlic, slivered

Olive oil

Fresh or dried chestnut leaves (optional)

Salt

Grilled Saffron Milk Caps

BASIC METHOD
Hearthside Grilling

EQUIPMENT
Grill
Shovel

PRIMARY VENUE
Hearth

ALTERNATE VENUE
Campfire

L ACTARIUS DELICIOSUS, the beautiful saffron milk cap, and its close relatives, including the gorgeous red milk cap *(L. sanguifluus)*, are favorite mushrooms of Spain and the Mediterranean regions of France and Italy. The popularity of the genus in Europe is longstanding: a painting of the fungus on a wall in Pompeii is the oldest surviving representation of a mushroom in Western art. These mushrooms are traditionally grilled gill-sides up over embers. The gills are sprinkled with salt, liberally dressed with olive oil, and dotted with chopped garlic and parsley. Piles of the spectacular orange-and-green-stained mushrooms are sold in farmers' markets during the fall, with related species intermingled.

The secret to grilling these mushrooms, and, in fact, to grilling most mushroom caps, is slow cooking. After adding oil and salt—slowly, slowly, with no browning—let the heat of the embers work its way up through the caps to stew the mushrooms in their own juices. Toward the end of the cooking period, begin drying them out, transforming the caps into the focused essence of themselves. You can hardly grill too slowly. This recipe, from an Umbrian hearth, takes an hour. You will find that it is a cooking method tolerant of distraction, however, since the grilling is mostly on the cool side of gentle. Serve the mushrooms as an appetizer.

The Fire: A mature fire with gentle flames to produce embers for the hour-long grilling.

INGREDIENTS

(Serves 4)

12 young saffron
    milk caps

Salt

Olive oil

6 cloves garlic, finely
    minced

Finely minced fresh
    flat-leaf parsley

Clean the mushrooms—they may be washed in water—and trim stems to approximately ¾ inch (2 cm). Place the clean grill on the hearth far enough from the fire (about 8 inches/20 cm) that the mushrooms will not cook from side heat from the edge of the firebox. Brush the grill with olive oil. Using the stems as a handle, place the mushrooms, gill-sides up, on the grill. Sprinkle the gills with salt and a liberal dose of olive oil. Place some minced garlic on each upturned cap and sprinkle with a generous amount of the parsley.

Start the cooking slowly by shoveling a sprinkling of embers under the grill. After about 5 minutes, you should begin to see some evidence of cooking. Add another sprinkling of embers. After about 10 minutes, the gills will be flooded with water. If they aren't, increase the heat. After 15 to 20 minutes, water should begin to form on the end of the cut stems; the gills will still be flooded with water. Add oil to any mushrooms that seem dry. You may increase the heat slightly with additional sprinklings of embers.

After 40 minutes, raise the temperature so the water at the end of the stalks, and between the gills, boils. Open-hearth grilling can be very precise. Add embers under any mushrooms that are not boiling. Maintain the temperature so the mushrooms cook thoroughly—5 to 10 minutes—and then let the embers die down. Continue cooking more slowly, adding embers as needed to keep the mushrooms on the cusp between cooking and not cooking. After about 1 hour, the mushrooms will have changed color—they will no longer be a fresh orange—and they will be slightly shriveled at the edge of the cap. There should be no browning or charring. Remove the mushrooms from the grill to a serving plate and return the embers to the fireplace. Dribble the mushrooms with an aromatic olive oil and serve warm.

Mushroom Stew

One of her greatest pleasures in summer was the very Russian sport of hodit' po gribï (looking for mushrooms). Fried in butter and thickened with sour cream, her delicious finds appeared regularly on the dinner table.

VLADIMIR NABOKOV, *Speak, Memory: An Autobiography Revisited*

BASIC METHOD
Hearthside Tripod

EQUIPMENT
10-inch (25-cm)
    frying pan with lid
Tripod
Shovel

PRIMARY VENUE
Hearth

ALTERNATE VENUE
Campfire

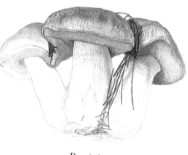
Porcini

MUSHROOMS ARE A GIFT of the forest. On the luckiest of days, they spread out between the trees like meadow flowers—yellow, red, russet, white, blue, gray. Whether you are out on one of these days, or on a day on which the mushrooms are hiding, every hunt has the feel of a treasure hunt—of searching for jewels on the forest floor.

There are, as everyone knows, mushrooms that can hurt you. In a way, these are the most beautiful mushrooms of all. Their beauty is made deeper by the same quality that attracts us to cliffs and towers, that gives an edge to the exuberance felt while driving too fast on a bright spring day along a winding road. Hold the death cap (*Amanita phalloides*) in your hands to feel the allure of danger.

Identifying mushrooms is not difficult. The average shopper in a grocery store routinely displays the skills needed to identify wild mushrooms. Anyone who can tell a parsnip from a carrot, a white boiling potato from a red one, a navel orange from a Valencia, can easily learn to identify which mushrooms to avoid. You are in the forest, you pick a mushroom that looks beautiful, but you have some doubt? Always follow the one overriding rule of mushroom collecting: In case of doubt, throw it out.

Every mushroom hunt is actually two hunts. The first is the forest hunt. The second is the hunt relived in the kitchen as you sort and clean your collection. In the field, take care to clean

Puffball

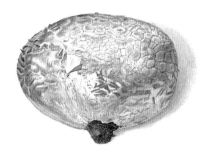

each mushroom and keep it intact in the basket. Collect as many kinds of mushrooms as you know from as many different habitats as possible. In the kitchen, the holding of each mushroom evokes the memory of where it was found, so the more varied the basket, the more pleasurable this second hunt, and almost secondarily, the more varied the flavors and textures of the stew.

Russula sp.

Of all the mushroom stews I've eaten with mushroom collectors in Europe, the one that I find the most consistently delicious is the one made with sour cream and dill in the far north. It is the dish Nabokov describes his mother making. In Lithuania, typical for much of this region, mushroom stew is eaten with plain boiled potatoes and vodka, a combination that well serves the mushroom collector on what passes for a summer day at 55 degrees north latitude.

 The Fire: A mature fire with gentle to moderate flames.

The cleaner you bring home mushrooms from the forest, the better. As you pick them, trim all dirt from the stem and use a small paintbrush to clean leaves, dirt, and sand from the cap. In your kitchen, trim further as necessary, cutting away any areas that are infested with a significant number of larvae. If the mushrooms are still dirty, brush clean under running water or in a bowl of water. When the mushrooms are clean, thinly slice them and set aside.

Place the frying pan with the butter, onion, and salt on the hearthside tripod and shovel embers underneath to create gentle heat. Slowly sauté the onions until they are translucent, about 15 minutes. Add the mushrooms and half the sour cream and cover the pan. Adding embers, cook gently over moderate heat until the mushrooms begin to give off their water. Remove the lid and continue to cook, stirring often, until all of the water has evaporated, usually 20 to 30 minutes. When cooking wild mushrooms it is best, as a general rule, to cook them thoroughly. Add the balance of the sour cream and the dill. Stir and cook until the dill begins to wilt. Season with salt. Remove from the heat, shovel the embers back into the fireplace, and serve the mushrooms.

INGREDIENTS
(Serves 6 to 8)

2 pounds (1 kg) mixed mushrooms if gathering in the wild, or 1 pound (450 g) each mixed portobello and cremini mushrooms and mixed oyster, shiitake, and other mushrooms of choice if purchasing

2 tablespoons (30 g) unsalted butter

1 large or 2 medium yellow onions, minced

1½ teaspoons salt

¼ cup (60 ml) sour cream

1 bunch dill, finely chopped

Fava Beans

FAVA BEANS ARE OFTEN GROWN to be "turned under." Rich in nitrogen, the plants are a legendary "green manure." From the perspective of most Americans, peering into the cuisines of England and southern Europe, fava beans—English broad beans—are an exotic mention, as fresh ones are absent from most American markets. The surest way to get fresh fava beans is to grow them. In mild climates, they can be grown twelve months a year. Where summers are hot, plant an early-maturing variety in spring and late summer.

This recipe makes fava bean converts of anyone who is not already a fan. It has even turned several of my friends into small-scale fava bean farmers. The hearth is the ideal place to prepare the recipe because it requires even, high heat—something easy to achieve with embers under the frying pan, but impossible to achieve on a standard kitchen stove. Cookbook authors often suggest peeling the tough skin from around each bean before cooking. My method of preparing mature favas requires that the skin be left in place. I cook them so hot that the skins begin to brown, which is the secret of the recipe. At my house, everyone eats favas with their fingers, squeezing the beans out of their skins into their mouths. The beans should taste a little salty.

 The Fire: A mature fire with a solid reservoir of embers to ensure that the beans cook hot and fast.

Put the frying pan on the tripod placed on the hearth near the fire. Shovel a thick layer of embers underneath to create high heat and keep the heat high throughout the cooking. Add the olive oil. When it is hot, but before it begins smoking, add the fava beans, sage, and salt. Stir to mix thoroughly. When the beans start cooking, add the water and bring to a rapid boil. When the water has evaporated, the beans should be soft and the outer skins of at least a few will have split open. If the favas aren't ready, add another 1 cup (250 ml) water and boil down again. When the water has evaporated, finish by stirring continuously over high heat. The favas are done when they are soft and a fair number of beans are lightly browned. The whole process takes 5 to 8 minutes. Transfer the favas to a platter, shovel the embers back into the fireplace, and serve the favas.

INGREDIENTS
(Serves 4 to 6)

4 tablespoons (60 ml) olive oil

4 pounds (1.75 kg) mature fava beans, shelled (about 3 cups/500 g)

1 bunch sage

3/4 teaspoon salt

1 cup (250 ml) water, or as needed

Ember-Baked Potatoes

BASIC METHOD

Ember Baking or
    Ash Baking

EQUIPMENT

Long-handled tongs,
    fork, or potato rake

Shovel

PRIMARY VENUE

Firebox

ALTERNATE VENUES

Barbecue

Campfire

Bread Oven

During the Maytime storms, when streams of water gushed noisily past the blurred windows, threatening to flood their last refuge, the lovers would light the stove and bake potatoes. The potatoes steamed, and the charred skins blackened their fingers. There was laughter in the basement, and in the garden the trees would shed broken twigs and white clusters of flowers after the rain.

MIKHAIL BULGAKOV, *The Master and Margarita*

EVERYONE WHO TASTES THESE potatoes smiles. The meat of ember-baked potatoes is suffused with a mysterious sweetness that comes from having burnt at least part of the outer skin. The taste is so delicious that one is loath to dilute it—not even with the reassuring flavor of butter or sour cream. This is not, however, a potato for a formal dinner. Eaten out of hand, the charred potato blackens the diner's fingers. In the spirit of the hearth, and, at least once, as a favor to yourself, make these potatoes in a room illuminated only by firelight. Eat them in front of the flames, sitting on the floor if there is no table. There may be times when the fire dies down and you cannot clearly see your hands. That's all right. Let the shadows come in from the walls. In this dim light, faces and hands pull away from time, dress is obscured, and we become potato eaters in our hut, or by our campfire, bathed in the warmth and glow of the hearth fire, the source of life itself.

I also include here a recipe for baking potatoes in hot ashes. Ash baking was common enough in nineteenth-century England for there to be a specialized tool, a curved hook, for raking potatoes out of the fireplace. Ash-baked potatoes are not always charred, however, so they usually taste more like potatoes baked in the oven.

The Fire: A mature fire, moderate to high flames, a substantial bed of embers for ember baking, and a deep bed of hot ash for ash baking.

To bake on embers: Pierce each potato with a knife or fork so it won't explode in the fire. Use the shovel to spread embers beside the fire and use the shovel and/or long-handled tongs to nestle the potatoes into the embers 4 to 8 inches (10 to 20 cm) from the flames. The embers contribute to the cooking, but the primary cooking comes from the potatoes' proximity to the flames. The correct distance from the flames is the distance that chars the outer skin, but also gives heat time to penetrate to the center. Turn approximately every 15 minutes to promote even cooking. It is desirable to have at least one side charred to a depth of 1/8 inch (3 mm). Medium potatoes cook in 45 minutes, whole large potatoes take about 1 hour. Test from time to time by piercing with a sharp knife or fork and adjust the potatoes' distance from the fire as needed. When done, the potato should be soft inside and a fork should easily pierce to the center. Remove the potatoes from the fireplace with the long-handled tongs. Let cool long enough for any glowing spots to cool and serve. These potatoes are excellent eaten as they are—without salt, oil, or herbs.

To bake in ash: Pierce each potato with a knife or fork so it won't explode in the fire. If there is not already a bed of hot ash, use the shovel to stir embers into a pile of ash to create a 50-50 mix of embers to ash. Bury the potatoes in the hot ash and cover with embers. Dig out a potato in 30 minutes to check its progress. If it is cooking too slowly, pile additional embers on top to speed up the cooking. The potatoes are ready when they can be pierced easily with a knife. Dig up the potatoes with the shovel and serve with salt, olive oil, and a sprinkling of herbs.

INGREDIENTS
(Serves 4 to 6)

For Ember Baking
4 large or 8 medium russet potatoes

For Ash Baking
16 to 24 small or 8 medium russet potatoes

Salt

Olive oil, butter, or sour cream

Finely chopped fresh chives, thyme, or flat-leaf parsley

The Highest gave understanding unto the five men, and they wrote the wonderful visions of the night that were told, which they knew not: and they sat forty days, and they wrote in the day, and at night they ate bread.

2 Esdras 14:42

BREADS

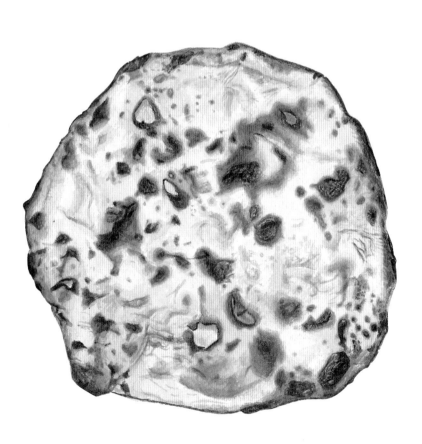

Ash Cakes

His wife was called up—for it was now about midnight—a fire was made, some Indian meal was soon mixed with salt and water, and an ash cake was baked in a hurry to relieve my hunger.

FREDERICK DOUGLASS, *My Bondage and My Freedom*

BASIC METHOD
Ash Baking

EQUIPMENT
Shovel
Long-handled
tongs

PRIMARY VENUE
Firebox

ALTERNATE VENUES
Barbecue
Campfire

*California live oak
(Quercus agrifolia)*

ASH CAKE IS THE BREAD OF ancient Mesopotamia. It is the bread of soldiers when supply lines break down, of slaves, fugitives, shepherds, wanderers, and pioneers. Ash cake is the bread anyone who has nothing can make, a bread of extreme simplicity: a flat cake about the size of a saucer and about as thick as a finger, baked under the ashes and piled with hot embers. Whether made with grain, corn, pulses, or starchy nuts such as acorns or chestnuts, ash cakes are crisp at the edges, moist inside, and invariably delicious. They are the accompaniment to simple hearth-baked meals—ones that rely on a single pot, an impromptu grill, and the embers themselves.

When you make ash cakes from spelt, emmer, barley, and other ancient grains, you make a food that is very close to the first grain breads. Boil acorns until the bitterness is washed away, grind the meat, and, in the palm of your hand, shape the meat into small, thin cakes to create a bread of ancient Greece. Use freshly ground corn, the Indian meal of Frederick Douglass's narrative, to make a bread that was vital to colonial America, the American slave, and pioneers on their westward expansion. The Lu, who live in the Himalayan foothills of Yunnan, China, make ash cakes from buckwheat, and the descendants of the Maya make them from ground *nixtamal,* corn that has been softened in lime water.

As for the question, "Won't the bread taste of ash?" The answer is "no." As long as the dough is firm, and the outside is dusted with flour, the ash is easily brushed off the baked bread. Ash cakes are ashless.

 The Fire: A mature fire, gentle to moderate flames, and at least 4 inches (10 cm) of ash across the fireplace floor.

Unless the fire has been burning all day, 1 hour before baking, stir embers into a bed of ash using an equal amount of each.

Select one of the breads to make. To make wheat breads, place the flour in a bowl and stir in the salt. Make a well in the center, add the water, and mix all the ingredients together with a spoon or with your hands until the mixture forms a homogenous dough. The dough should be fairly stiff. Turn it out onto a floured work surface. Knead until the dough is smooth and elastic, about 3 minutes, and let the dough rest for 10 to 20 minutes before proceeding to form the breads. To make nonwheat breads, mix the dough as described above, but only include salt if the recipe calls for it. These breads, however, do not require kneading. As soon as the dough is mixed, it can be formed into breads. If making the cornbread, boil the water as described on page 257 and let the dough rest for 2 hours before forming the breads.

To form the breads, divide the dough into 7 to 9 balls. Either work each ball of dough between your hands or roll it out on a well-floured work surface into a disk about the thickness of a finger, 1/2 inch (1 cm). When divided into the same number of pieces, each of these recipes produces breads of a slightly different size. Dust the finished breads with flour so they are dry to the touch.

To the side of the fire, use the shovel to dig a trench in the ashes large enough for all the cakes. Lay down the disks of dough, cover with a layer of ash 1/2 inch (1 cm) thick, and pile with a thick layer of embers. Bake the breads for 20 minutes under high heat. Remove the cakes with the long-handled tongs, brush off the ash, and serve the cakes while they are still warm.

Note: American colonial and pioneer practice included baking ash cakes between leaves, often corn husks or cabbage leaves. If using dried corn husks, soak them in warm water to soften before folding them around the cakes. If using cabbage leaves, lay the disk of dough between 2 leaves, fold the leaves around the dough, and proceed to bake the cakes as described above.

INGREDIENTS
(Most of the recipes make about seven 4-ounce/100-g or nine 3-ounce/75-g breads)

White Flour

3 1/2 cups (450 g) unbleached white flour

1 1/2 teaspoons salt

1 1/2 cups (350 ml) water

Semolina Flour

3 cups (450 g) fine semolina flour

1 teaspoon salt

1 cup (250 ml) water

Cornmeal

3 1/4 cups (450 g) cornmeal

1 teaspoon salt

2 cups (480 ml) boiling water

Cabbage leaves or corn husks (optional)

Masa Harina

4 1/4 cups (450 g) masa harina

2 3/4 cups (650 ml) water

Corn husks (optional)

Chestnut Flour

4 3/4 cups (450 g) chestnut flour

1 cup (250 ml) water

Spider Corn Bread

BASIC METHOD
Hearthside Tripod

EQUIPMENT
10-inch (25-cm) spider
    or iron frying pan on
    a tripod or a 5-quart
    (5-l) Dutch oven with
    legs
Small saucepan
Lid (optional)
Shovel
Pot hook (optional)

PRIMARY VENUE
Hearth

ALTERNATE VENUES
Campfire
Bread Oven

C ORN BREAD REMAINS THE REGIONAL BREAD of the American South. There are many varieties and, between the hearthside griddle, frying pan, and Dutch oven, one can make them all. The recipe I include here calls for hearthside baking in a spider, a three-legged frying pan, or a Dutch oven. Early American settlers, subsistence farmers, and cowboys made bread out of the corn they grew, or out of the cornmeal sold at the local store—yellow, white, or red, fine or coarsely ground. They didn't have the luxury, or curse, of choice. In keeping with a spirit of improvisation, I advise that you choose whatever cornmeal you have on hand for this bread. If, however, you have a fanatic's love for corn bread, you will find that fresh, somewhat irregularly ground meal makes the best-flavored bread. With an inexpensive hand grinder, and colorful "ornamental corn," one can make the corn bread of the eighteenth- and nineteenth-century American country hearth. If you have a summer garden, and live where summers are hot, grow the heirloom corn "Bloody Butcher" to dry and grind into meal. It only takes a few ears to make one cup (150 g) of meal, so this is an eminently practical project.

While sugar has crept into most modern recipes, corn bread without sugar has a more distinctive flavor. This recipe is taken from a late-nineteenth-century source. It is easily modified to create an ever-varied dinner or appetizer bread. Follow the lead of the cooks who developed the innovative Southwest cuisine by adding flavorings—dried herbs, caramelized minced onions, diced cooked bacon, diced roasted chile, puréed squash—to create breads that can be thoughtfully integrated into whatever meal you are serving.

The Fire: *A mature fire with gentle to moderate flames.*

Butter the sides of the spider or other pan and line the bottom with parchment paper or oiled brown paper. Set the pan aside.

Melt the butter in a small saucepan pushed into the embers and bring the pan to where the bread will be prepared. Break the eggs into a bowl, mix well, and whisk in the buttermilk, the melted butter, cornmeal, baking soda, and salt. Add additional liquid as needed to form a thick pourable batter.

Place the spider on the hearth where the side heat will not significantly affect the cooking. Pour the batter into the pan. If you are using a pan made of cast iron or other heavy metal, shovel a thick bed of embers underneath to create high heat. If the pan is not made of a thick metal, create a bed of embers that is gentle to moderate. If the surface of the bread becomes a mass of bubbles in 5 to 10 minutes, the bread will probably bake completely on that first load of embers. If it takes longer for bubbles to cover the surface—you will see them forming first along the edges— you will need to add embers. Remember, however, that once the bottom crust has set, it becomes susceptible to burning, so when you add embers, add them a sprinkling at a time, just enough to maintain the pan's temperature at that of a slow oven—225° to 250°F (101° to 120°C).

The bread is ready when a knife inserted into the center comes out clean and it has pulled away from the side nearest the fire, depending on thickness, 20 to 40 minutes. At this point, you can remove it from the hearth, shovel the embers back into the fireplace, and turn the bread out onto a cake rack to cool, or you can proceed to the optional next step.

This step browns the bread, cooks it further, and makes it more distinctive. Shovel the embers from under the corn bread. Place a lid over the corn bread and pile it with embers. The optimal distance between the bread and the lid is 2 inches (5 cm). After 3 minutes, use a pot hook to lift the lid. Check the progress, dump the old embers into the fireplace, and replace them with fresh embers. Check again in 3 minutes and continue checking and replacing embers until the bread is a uniform golden brown. When done, transfer to a rack to cool.

INGREDIENTS

(Serves 4 to 6 as a dinner bread, 8 to 12 as an appetizer bread)

1 tablespoon butter

2 eggs

2 cups (475 ml) buttermilk

2 cups (275 g) cornmeal

1 teaspoon baking soda

1 teaspoon salt

Flat Bread

And the people took their dough before it was leavened, their kneading troughs being bound up in their clothes upon their shoulders.

Exodus 12:34

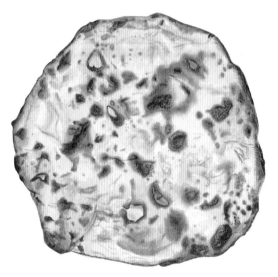

I STILL FIND IT INCREDIBLE. Flat breads baked on embers! Yet, the method is simple and reliable and produces a spectacular array of delicious breads from North Africa, the Middle East, central Asia, and the Indian subcontinent. Ember-baked breads are the equal of those produced in bread ovens, but they require no equipment beyond a fireplace shovel and long-handled tongs. In fact, nomads, refugees—the Jews of Exodus—and experienced fireplace cooks bake flat breads on the embers using their fingers.

Baking flat breads naturally divides into two phases. In the first phase, the bread is baked to the point where the dough sets. In the second, this partially cooked bread, exposed to intense heat, puffs up into a ball and is browned. Counterintuitively, baking on embers poses the problem that the dough snuffs out the embers, not that ash sticks to the dough or that the breads burn. Because raw dough quickly snuffs out the embers, baking start to finish on embers is practical only for batches of four to eight breads. For more than eight breads I always start baking on a griddle.

In India, hundreds of millions of women bake flat breads every day. They begin baking chapati or roti on a griddle called a *tava*, and finish them on a bed of embers or propped one to two inches (2.5 to 5 cm) from the flames of a wood fire. If working on a gas stove, they finish the breads by placing them directly on the burner. Indian woman usually bake two breads at once—one is on the griddle while the other is being exposed to high heat. Cooks in Indian restaurants, however, often bake a batch of breads to the first stage, and then wait to finish them off on embers or beside flames as orders are placed. It is this method that I describe in my recipe.

Flat breads are easy to vary, and they are instantly gratifying. They may be made from leavened or unleavened dough; flavored with oils, herbs, onions, or spices and even thinly stuffed. Semolina flour makes perfect pita bread; finely sifted whole wheat is the flour used for chapati. Modern matzo is made with white flour; thoroughly prick the thinly rolled unleavened dough with a fork before baking.

Serve flat breads warm, if possible. They are excellent offered along with appetizers, and as the bread accompaniment to Lamb Kebab (page 112) or Ember-Baked Fish (page 48). Whenever possible, save the dramatic second step, when the breads puff up on the embers, for when your guests are watching. Flat breads are also a good choice for baking on campfires.

The Fire: If baking the breads from start to finish on the embers, start with the deepest and hottest bed of embers you can muster, the product of a long-burning hardwood fire. If baking the breads first on a griddle and finishing them on embers, you need a mature fire with a reasonable quantity of embers to heat the griddle, and later a bed of embers to finish the baking.

Mix together the flour and salt in a large bowl. (If using seawater, add it with the water.) Make a well in the center, add the water, and mix first with a spoon and then with your hands until the dough is homogeneous. Turn it out onto a floured work surface, wash your hands free of flour, and while your hands are still wet, begin kneading the dough, adding water 1 tablespoon at a time if necessary to form a firm, but soft dough. If your hands become sticky, rinse them free of dough and continue kneading until the dough is elastic and satiny, 3 to 5 minutes.

Divide the dough into 12 equal pieces. Roll each piece in the palm of your hand to form a perfect ball. Dust with flour and place on a well-floured work surface. With the flat of your fingers, press the ball into a disk. Sprinkle with flour and use a rolling pin to thin the disk further, both rotating the dough slightly as you roll and flipping it over as necessary. Always keep the dough floured to prevent sticking. Thinner breads taste different from thicker ones, so experiment to decide which you like. I'd

INGREDIENTS

(Makes twelve 7-inch/ 18-cm breads)

3 1/2 cups (450 g) unbleached white or whole-wheat pastry flour

1 1/2 teaspoons salt, or a small amount of seawater

1 1/2 cups (350 ml) water

Flat Bread
(continued)

start with a thinness of about ⅛ inch (3 mm). As a rule, ember baking is more successful with the thinnest breads. Dust each finished disk liberally with flour and stack the disks on a well-floured plate.

The first baking: This step can be done on a griddle or on the embers.

If doing it on a griddle, place the griddle on the tripod positioned so the fire's side heat will not affect the baking. Shovel an even layer of embers underneath to create a hot griddle (400°F/200°C). See page 261 for advice on judging griddle temperature. When the griddle is hot, lay down a disk of dough. When the first side has set, 15 to 20 seconds for a bread ⅛ inch (3 mm) thick, flip the bread and cook on the second side for 15 to 20 seconds. The bread should be set but not browned. Thicker breads may take longer and may also require a lower temperature to ensure they set but don't color. When the bread is done, transfer it to a plate and continue baking until all the disks are done, stacking them as they are ready. Replenish the embers as needed to maintain the griddle's temperature.

If doing it on the embers, working inside the firebox, use the shovel to create a flat bed of embers. Let the embers sit for 1 minute and then lightly toss 1 disk onto the embers. The procedure for baking the breads is then exactly the same as for baking on a griddle as described above. Flip the breads as needed to set the dough, but don't brown the breads. Because dough placed directly on embers smothers the embers, they will quickly cool. It will take an increasingly longer time to bake each bread, so refresh the embers as needed to maintain a reasonable cooking time. Set each bread aside when done.

The second baking: This step is done on embers. In the firebox, use the shovel to create a deep bed of embers wide enough for 1 or 2 breads. Immediately, while the embers are still glowing, place a precooked bread onto the embers. Within a few seconds it should begin to puff up. Flip to the second side with the long-handled tongs or, as Indian bakers do, with your fingers. Within a few seconds, the bread, which began puffing up on the first side, should puff into a ball. If it doesn't, it usually means the embers are not hot enough. Once the bread has become spherical, give it a few seconds to cook and either remove it from the heat to a stack of cooked breads or continue flipping the bread back and forth until both sides are the color you prefer. The second baking should always go quickly, so keep up the temperature of the embers as needed by stirring them, adding fresh embers, and/or by fanning them with bellows. As you stack the finished breads, press them flat, but be careful not to get burned on the steam trapped inside. Serve warm.

Crumpets and English Muffins

. . . he yet hoped to see the day when crumpets should be toasted in her lowly cabins, and muffin bells should ring in her rich green valleys.

CHARLES DICKENS, *Nicolas Nickleby*

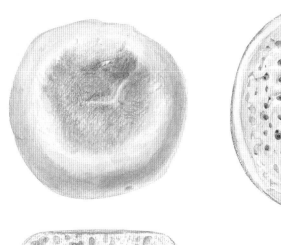

English muffin

Crumpet

BASIC METHOD
Hearthside Griddle

EQUIPMENT
1-quart (1-l) saucepan

Griddle

Tripod

Shovel

6 crumpet rings,
   3¾ inches (9.75 cm)
   in diameter by
   ⅝ inch (1.75 cm)
   high

6 English muffin rings,
   3¼ inches
   (8 cm) in diameter
   by 1½ inches (4 cm)
   high (optional)

PRIMARY VENUE
Hearth

ALTERNATE VENUE
Campfire

CRUMPETS AND MUFFINS ARE THE TWO GREAT BREADS of nineteenth-century English literature. They form the core of a literary dream of contentment: crumpets, muffins, a parlor fire, a toasting fork, butter, jam, and a bottomless cup of tea.

Like many foods that have a long tradition behind them, neither crumpets nor muffins can be linked to a single definitive recipe. There are, however, distinctive features that make them singularly themselves. They are both griddle-baked hearth breads firmly entrenched in eighteenth-century England. They are both yeast-leavened breads, but because they predate the invention of commercial yeast, they were originally leavened with a wild yeast starter or with beer barm, the yeasty sediment left after beer ferments. In addition to flour, water, yeast, and salt, both breads may include milk and

eggs, and the muffins a little butter, but neither bread is ever so enriched that it strays into the realm of cake.

Crumpets and muffins straddle the line between pancake and bread. Crumpets are thick pancakes that are made by pouring batter into a ring. Anyone who has made American pancakes is familiar with the bubbles that rise to the surface when the batter first flows onto the griddle. In the case of crumpets, it is the baking into place of the pathways these bubbles take that gives the breads their characteristic honeycomb texture. Thicken crumpet batter to the point you can roll it out and you have muffin dough.

These two breads share a curious feature. They are never eaten untoasted. They should be thought of as breads that are cooked twice: once on the griddle and the second time before the fire on the end of a toasting fork. These breads have long been an integral part of the highly ritualized English parlor tea, and each comes with its own toasting customs. Crumpets are toasted before the fire whole with the bottom side first, and the top side, the one with the holes, second. They are served piping hot so butter, which by tradition is spread with a lavish hand, quickly melts and fills the holes. Muffins are split through the middle with a fork—not cut with a knife—and the rough inner sides are held before the fire. They are also served buttered and hot. Both crumpets and muffins are served with jam and, of course, tea.

Beer barm is heavily hopped and intensely bitter. The amount of barm called for in the crumpet recipe leavens the dough in a reasonable amount of time and gives it a pleasant taste. Five gallons (20 l) of homemade beer yields approximately two cups (500 ml) barm. Pastry flour is closer to the soft-wheat flours used for bread making in eighteenth-century England, and, together with the barm, creates the perfect crumpet. If you have neither crumpet nor muffin rings, use standard tuna cans with both ends removed.

The Fire: A mature fire with gentle to moderate flames.

Two Crumpet Recipes

Modern crumpet recipe: In a small bowl, dissolve the yeast in the warm water. At the same time, warm the milk in a saucepan pushed beside the fire. When the yeast is dissolved, put the yeast mixture in a large bowl. Add the warm milk, the flour, a beaten egg, and the salt. Whisk to remove lumps until you achieve a batter the consistency of heavy cream. Cover and let stand for 4 to 5 hours—2 hours at room temperature and the balance in a warm place (78°F/25°C). The batter is ready to bake when it is a mass of bubbles. Butter the crumpet rings and dust with flour. Set aside.

Eighteenth-century crumpet recipe: Follow the instructions for modern crumpets with these changes: omit the yeast, warm the water and milk together, add the beer barm when you add the beaten egg, and don't add the salt until just before you bake the crumpets. If the beer barm is fresh, the recipe will work as written. If the beer barm is not fresh, the batter may need to sit in a warm place for much longer. For example, batter made with barm that is 2 weeks old may take 24 hours resting in a warm place before the dough is sufficiently fermented to bake.

English Muffin Recipe

In a small bowl, dissolve the yeast in the 1 cup (250 ml) warm water. When the yeast is dissolved, put the yeast mixture into a large bowl and add the remaining water, the flour, and salt. Mix with a spoon or with your hands until the dough is homogeneous. Turn it out onto a floured work surface, wash your hands free of flour, and, while your hands are still wet, knead the dough until it is soft and elastic, about 3 minutes. If necessary, add additional water, 1 tablespoon at a time, to soften the dough. If your hands become sticky before the dough is ready, rinse them in water and continue kneading.

Place the muffin dough in a bowl, cover with a cloth, and let the dough rise for 4 to 5 hours—2 hours at room temperature and the balance in a warm place (78°F/25°C) until it doubles in bulk. Punch down the dough and remove it from the bowl. On a floured work surface, roll out the dough ¾ inch (2 cm) thick. Using a muffin ring, cut out rounds. Alternatively, divide the dough into 12 equal portions, shape each portion into a ball, and press out into a round 3¼ inches (8 cm) in diameter and ¾ inch (2 cm) thick. Cover the rounds with a floured cloth and place in a warm place until they begin to rise, about 30 minutes. If baking in muffin rings, butter the rings and dust with flour.

(continued)

INGREDIENTS

(Each recipe makes 12 breads)

Crumpets

1 teaspoon active dry yeast, or 2 tablespoons fresh beer barm

1 cup (250 ml) water, warmed to 110°F/43°C

1 cup (250 ml) milk, warmed

2 cups (275 g) slightly mounded unbleached white bread flour

1 egg

½ teaspoon salt

English Muffins

1 teaspoon active dry yeast

1 cup (250 ml) water, warmed to 110°F/43°C, plus ½ cup (125 ml) cool water

3½ cups (450 g) flour

1 teaspoon salt

To cook the crumpets and muffins: Place the griddle on the tripod positioned on the hearth so that the fire's side heat will not affect the baking. Shovel a thin layer of embers underneath. Over a period of a few minutes, as the griddle heats, add additional embers to bring the griddle up to a moderate heat for muffins—350°F (180°C)—and up to 400°F (200°C) for crumpets. For the moderate griddle, a finger dipped in water and then touched to the surface releases a drop of water that sizzles and breaks up into several sizzling drops before quickly evaporating; for the hotter griddle, it is the same, but faster. If the drop of water seems to explode when it touches the griddle, the surface is too hot. Throughout the cooking, add embers, a sprinkling at a time, to maintain the griddle at the appropriate temperature. You may use an infrared thermometer to measure the temperature directly.

If cooking crumpets, lightly oil the griddle. Place as many prepared rings as will fit on the griddle comfortably and pour the batter into the rings to a depth of ½ inch (1 cm). The top of each crumpet should be a mass of small bubbles that soon break open to become holes as the crumpet cooks. Once the holes form, you should be able to see down through the holes, almost to the griddle. When the top is set, 4 to 6 minutes, detach from the rings, turn, and bake until the second side is lightly golden, 1 to 2 minutes. Crumpets may be served warm or let them cool on a wire rack.

If cooking muffins, lightly oil the griddle. Place the muffins on the griddle in the prepared muffin rings or freestanding. When you judge the muffins have baked a little more than halfway through, 7 to 10 minutes, turn and bake on the second side. The muffins are done when both sides are lightly browned, 15 to 20 minutes. Remove and let cool on a wire rack before serving.

Note: *If bubbles fail to form on the surface of the crumpets, or if the bubbles form and then close in, this usually means that the crumpet batter is not sufficiently fermented. Let the batter sit in a warm place for a while longer and try again.*

Cheese Waffles

STRANGE WAYS THE WORKING OF CUSTOM. From Phnom Penh where waffles are a street food, to North America where they are eaten at breakfast, to Scandinavia and Belgium—the centers of European waffledom—waffles are invariably a sweet batter cake. There is absolutely no reason for this to be so. Minus the sugar, and with the addition of grated cheese and herbs, the modern sweet waffle becomes a quickly made savory bread. Savory waffles were a common street food in medieval Europe. The recipe I include here, which is flavored with cheese and is based on a French source, makes a terrific appetizer bread. Use a waffle or wafer iron designed for use on the stovetop, or an antique iron designed for hearth cooking. The stovetop Scandinavian iron that makes heart-shaped waffles works well.

 The Fire: A mature fire with gentle to moderate flames.

Break the eggs into a bowl and beat until blended. Stir in the flour, cheese, and wine to form a thick batter.

Set the tripod on the hearth and shovel embers underneath to create high heat. Place the iron over the tripod and heat both sides until they are the temperature of a hot griddle—400°F (200°C). A finger dipped in water and then touched to the iron releases a drop of water that sizzles and breaks up into several sizzling drops that almost immediately evaporate. If the drop of water seems to explode when it touches the iron, however, the iron is too hot.

Once the iron is hot, start baking by determining which of the iron's 2 plates is coolest and place that side down on the tripod. Open the iron, lightly oil both plates, and place a spoonful of batter in the center. Close the iron. Bake until the waffle is browned on both sides, 2 to 3 minutes. Remove from the iron and place on a rack to cool. The ideal rhythm is to cook the waffle for 2 to 3 minutes, and then to reverse the iron so the top plate—now the cooler plate—is on the tripod over the embers. After the first 2 waffles, oiling the iron should not be necessary. Replenish embers as needed and continue until all of the waffles are baked.

BASIC METHOD
Hearthside Griddle

EQUIPMENT
Shallow waffle iron
  or wafer iron
Tripod
Shovel

PRIMARY VENUE
Hearth

ALTERNATE VENUES
Barbecue
Campfire
Bread Oven

INGREDIENTS
(Makes 6 waffles with
2 tablespoons of bat-
ter, and 12 wafers with
1 tablespoon of batter)

4 eggs
1 cup (120 g) all-
  purpose flour,
  or whole-wheat
  pastry flour
¼ pound (100 g)
  hard cheese such as
  Parmesan, grated
⅓ cup (80 ml) white
  wine
Vegetable oil, for
  oiling the iron

Irish Soda Bread

I RELAND IS A COUNTRY WITH FEW TREES, but lots of peat. Peat burns slowly, making it a poor fuel for bread ovens; therefore, Irish staple breads tend to be either griddle cakes or Dutch-oven breads. Soda breads are "quick" breads, leavened by the chemical reaction between soda and acid, here provided by buttermilk, rather than by yeast. They are the bread of choice for Irish stew and are light, clean flavored, easy to mix, and easy to bake—a bread that goes together on the spur of the moment. The griddle-baked farl form—a farl is any bread baked in quarters—is the shape I prefer, both for dinner and for tea. Served with butter and jam, a farl warm from the griddle is hard to beat on a cold, misty day. The key to its successful baking is embodied in a single word: slow. Gradually build up the heat under the griddle as the bread begins to bake, and aim for twenty minutes on each side.

Because the ingredients for soda bread are so few, the quality of the loaf is dependent on the flour. The more freshly ground, and the more coarsely ground, the more satisfied you will be with the results. Currants or raisins, one cup (175 g) per one pound (450 g) of flour, turn a savory loaf into a sweet breakfast bread or a tea cake.

The Fire: A mature fire with gentle to moderate flames.

Stir together the flour, salt, and baking soda in a bowl. Make a well in the center, add the buttermilk, and mix all the ingredients together with a spoon. As soon as the ingredients are roughly combined, turn the mixture out onto a floured work surface and knead a few times to form a homogeneous dough. If baking on a griddle, roll or press into a disk 1 inch (2.5 cm) thick. If baking in a Dutch oven, make the dough thicker, 1½ inches (4 cm). Cut the disk into quarters.

To bake on a griddle: Place the griddle on the tripod positioned so the fire's side heat will not affect the baking. Shovel a thin layer of embers underneath. Over a period of a few minutes, as the griddle heats, add additional embers to bring the griddle up to a gentle heat of 225° to 250°F (110° to 120°C). It is ready if a finger dipped in water and then touched to the griddle leaves a black mark before the water fully evaporates. Lightly oil the griddle and lay down the farl. Bake for 20 minutes on the first side and turn and bake for an additional 20 minutes. Throughout the baking, add embers, a sprinkling at a time, to maintain the griddle at a gentle heat. You may use an infrared thermometer to measure the temperature directly. The farl is ready when a knife inserted into the center of the bread comes out clean and the surface is light brown. Serve warm or let cool on a wire rack. Return the embers to the fireplace.

To bake in a Dutch oven: Butter the Dutch oven and line the bottom with buttered parchment paper. Lay down the farl and cover. Place the Dutch oven on the hearth where it will receive gentle to moderate side heat from the fire, usually 5 to 8 inches (12 to 20 cm) back from the edge of the firebox. Begin by shoveling embers underneath the Dutch oven to create moderate heat and shovel embers onto the lid to create high heat. Let the embers underneath cool to gentle, then refresh them as needed, a sprinkling at a time, to maintain a very gentle heat under the oven, while maintaining moderate to high heat on the lid. Taking into account the side heat, maintain an overall temperature of the Dutch oven at gentle to moderate. After 20 minutes, use a pot hook to lift the lid and check the progress. Adjust the temperature according to what you see. Total cooking time should be about 40 minutes. The farl is done when a knife inserted into the center of the bread comes out clean. Serve warm or let cool on a wire rack. Return the embers to the fireplace.

INGREDIENTS
(Serves 4 to 6)

3½ cups (450 g) coarsely ground whole-wheat flour

½ teaspoon salt

½ teaspoon baking soda

2 cups (475 ml) buttermilk

Les Galettes de Sarasin

SOFT, THIN BATTER BREADS cooked on a pan or griddle are extremely versatile foods. As any visitor to Paris knows, the French crêpe is a common street food. You want dessert, but your companion wants dinner? No problem—one crêpe is spread with sugar, the other with ham. Crêpes are the proto-typical peasant food. They cook quickly with little fuel and can be as simple or as complex as the pantry or the budget allows. Even in their simplest form of flour, water, salt, and a few wild greens, crêpes make up one of the meals of rural poverty that, in an irony of our times, costs a fortune in a Manhattan restaurant.

Brittany is the home of the buckwheat crêpe, *ur galetezenn gwinizh-du* in Breton, long a staple of the local diet. In the past, farmers returning from the fields knew that a bowl of fermenting *galette* batter was always waiting, ready to be made into the large, thin pancakes that formed the core of the meal.

A blazing fire, a wind-whipped storm as evening wends its way into night, *galettes,* and hard cider—this is the combination that can pull your spirit to the rough and rocky coast of northern France, to a night when storm-driven waves pounded hard against the shore and the flames of the open hearth offered the only promise of warmth and comfort.

Buckwheat contributes flavor, texture, and color to *galettes,* giving them the strength of character to stand on their own. Stack *galettes* on the table to be used like bread, serving them alongside strong-flavored meats—roasted duck or lamb—or a rich bean soup. They hold up well to fillings of deeply flavored greens like dandelion, kale, and chicory. They also make a fine breakfast or dessert with honey or jam.

The Fire: A mature fire with gentle to moderate flames.

Prepare the batter 2 hours before baking. Mix the flour and salt together in a bowl. Add the water, and whisk until you have a batter the consistency of heavy cream. Cover with a cloth and set aside. Stir just before baking and adjust with more water or flour as necessary to achieve a cream-like consistency. Transfer the batter to a pitcher.

To cook the galettes: Place the griddle on the tripod positioned on the hearth so the fire's side heat will not affect the baking. Lightly oil the griddle. Shovel an even layer of embers underneath. The griddle is ready when the oil starts smoking. From this point on, add embers, a sprinkling at a time, as necessary to maintain the griddle's temperature.

Pour the batter from the pitcher onto the griddle in a spiral pattern, working from the center out. *Galettes* are thin, not just because the batter is thin, but because once they are on the griddle, you must spread them out with a *rouable* or the back of a wide wooden spoon. Work quickly because the batter sets within seconds.

Cook until the top is well set and the underside is lightly browned, 1 to 3 minutes. Slip the long, thin spatula under the *galette*, flip it, and cook briefly on the second side. After the first 2 or 3 *galettes*, oiling the griddle should not be necessary. As the *galettes* are finished, stack them and cover with a cloth to keep warm. Serve the *galettes* as soon as all the batter has been used. Return the embers to the fireplace.

INGREDIENTS

(Makes about eighteen 8-inch/20-cm galettes)

3 cups (450 g) buckwheat flour

1/2 teaspoon salt

4 cups (1 l) water

Vegetable oil, for oiling griddle

Chicories

Tile-Baked Breads

BASIC METHOD

Tile Baking

EQUIPMENT

10 tiles

6 common red bricks
or a baking stand
(see page 177)

Long-handled tongs

Shovel

PRIMARY VENUES

Firebox
and Hearth

ALTERNATE VENUES

Barbecue

Campfire

INGREDIENTS

(Most of the recipes
will yield a dozen
3-inch/7.5-cm breads)

Simit dough, 178

English Muffins dough,
165

Flat Bread dough, 162

Ash Cakes dough, 158

Fresh or dried chestnut
or walnut leaves or
fresh cabbage leaves
(optional)

THERE ARE NO NEW WAYS TO BAKE BREAD. There are only ancient ways to be rediscovered. Thirty-six hundred years ago, Babylonians baked breads sandwiched between patterned hot tiles. Until the middle of the twentieth century, this was also the method for baking the staple breads of the Modenese Apennines, the mountains that rise behind Modena in northern Italy. Every morning, terra-cotta tiles made glowing in the fireplace were pulled onto the hearth to cool. They were then stacked with dough sandwiched between them to bake *crescentine*, the local breads of the open hearth.

The *crescentine* of the early twentieth century were made with stone-ground flour. Aside from this single constant, recipes varied. Farmers at different elevations grew different types of wheat, some of which had very different baking qualities. Whether breads were baked unleavened or were leavened with yeast or a sour starter depended on the grain and the cook's style. Aromatic leaves such as chestnut and oak were often placed between the dough and the tiles to moderate the heat and to impart flavor to the bread. After baking, *crescentine* were often baked a second time on embers, at which point they puffed up into a ball and browned.

As the northern Italian countryside became wealthier, and as the fabric of subsistence farms gave way to the current suburban model of country life, *crescentine*, like so many other foods, lost a substantial portion of their previous richness and variety. The *crescentine* of today are not as complex as those of even the mid-twentieth century. It is up to us, enthusiasts of the open hearth, to re-invigorate the tradition.

The first step is to make the tiles, or *tigelle* as they are known in this area of the Apennines. Fortunately, this couldn't be simpler. The only skill required is the skill of a child making mud pies. Full instructions are included in the sidebar at right.

What makes tile-baked breads distinctive is the crust that develops by baking under weight. Experiment creating breads with different flours—unbleached white, whole-wheat pastry, semolina, and the Italian farro flours of spelt, emmer, and einkhorn. Tile-baked breads are part of an ancient tradition, but one with virtually no written record. Be imaginative. Also consider doughs filled with herbs and breads baked with fillings.

In practice, tile baking can get intense—the fire is hot and you have to work quickly. You can approximate the effect of heating the tiles in the fireplace by heating them in the oven to 550°F/285°C. These breads are not as visually interesting as those baked on tiles heated in the fireplace. However, to help develop confidence in baking with tiles, I suggest heating them at least once in the oven. Finish them on the embers as described in the recipe instructions.

Eat *crescentine* while they are warm. In the Modenese Apennines, they are often cut in half and served with *pesto lardo*, pork fat pounded with garlic and rosemary and salted to taste.

MAKING THE TILES

The way tigelle *are made in the Modenese Apennines is by baking limestone in the fireplace under a hot fire for 12 hours.*

When the stone is cool, it is broken into pieces with a hammer and then pulverized into sand, which is added to the clay in the proportion of 1 part limestone to 2 parts clay. The stone makes the clay more refractory, but in my experience, both clay dug from the ground and clay purchased in the art supply store make excellent bread-baking tiles.

Purchase a 25-pound (11-kg) bag of low-fire clay from an art supply store. Form into patties 4¼ inches (10 cm) in diameter and one-finger thick.

Let the tigelle *dry for at least a week, and then further dry the tiles by setting them near the fire for several hours.*

Finally, use tongs to place the bone-dry tiles around the fire, inside

(continued next page)

MAKING THE TILES
(continued)

the firebox, until they are very hot and then use the long-handled tongs to bury them in the embers. Build a hot fire on top of the tiles. The tiles will begin to glow a dull red. Hold the tiles at a dull red for at least one hour.

Despite one's best efforts, a couple of tiles may partially explode during the initial firing so make 14 tiles to end up with 12 good ones.

 The Fire: *A roaring mature fire with a substantial bed of embers is needed to heat the tiles. If planning multiple batches, maintain a very hot fire until the last group of tiles has been heated.*

Once you begin heating the tiles, the process is demanding. It is essential that everything necessary for the baking be organized in advance—the tiles, the bricks or stand, the shovel, and the tongs—and that a space be cleared near the hearth for the dough that is brought from the kitchen. This is a fun bread to make, but it is not easy. It is best for two people to work together, one person forming the dough, while the other is heating the tiles.

To form the breads (20 to 30 minutes before baking): Regardless of the dough used, start by forming it into balls. Unleavened wheat and unleavened nonwheat breads should be comparatively thin. Form unleavened dough into balls that, when rolled or pressed flat, will be the size of the baking tile, 3 inches (7.5 cm) across and no more than ¼ inch (6 mm) thick. Wheat doughs that are leavened with yeast can be as thick as ½ inch (1 cm) when rolled flat. Prepare all the dough, either as disks for wheat breads or as balls of dough for nonwheat breads, place them on a floured board, dust them well with flour, and cover with a cloth. Bring the board to the hearth.

To rehydrate the leaves: If you plan on layering the dough between leaves, this is the time to prepare dried ones by rehydrating them in hot water for about 10 minutes. Plan on 2 chestnut leaves and 1 walnut leaf for each side of the tile.

To heat the tiles (30 minutes before baking): Heat the tiles to a dull red. Use the shovel or long-handled tongs to place them in the hottest part of the fire. Either bury them in the embers or lay them on top of a hot fire made with kindling. Use tongs to redistribute the tiles as needed to ensure they all glow an even dull red.

When the tiles are ready, use the tongs to remove them from the firebox and lay them side by side on the hearth to cool. Just before you think the tiles might be cool enough for baking, test them by slowly drawing a piece of dough across several tiles. As soon as this test no longer produces a black streak, use tongs to stack the tiles approximately 10 tiles high so they will be ready for the next step. If using nonwheat doughs, test the tiles by dusting them with flour. When the flour no longer immediately turns black, the tiles are ready. If measured directly using an infrared thermometer, the tiles should register about 600°F (315°C).

The first baking: Immediately take a tile from the top of the stack and place it on the hearth or, if using a stand, on the stand. Place a piece of dough on the tile and cover with a second tile, or, if using leaves, put 1 or 2 leaves, depending on type, between the dough and the tiles. Working quickly, continue sandwiching dough between tiles until you create a stack that is a maximum of 15 tiles (14 breads). If using bricks, support the stack on three sides. I find that a stack of 7 tiles (6 breads) is about the maximum stable stack when using bricks as supports. Some people, after a few minutes, reverse the stacks by placing the top tile on the hearth, or on the base of a stand, and rebuild the towers. When the breads are done, 10 to 15 minutes, remove them from between the tiles. If the breads are made with wheat flour, continue with the next step. Otherwise, put the breads in a basket lined with a cloth and serve.

The second baking: Use the shovel to spread embers beside the fire. Place the breads, a few at a time, on the embers. They should quickly begin to puff up into a ball. As a bread beings to puff, use the tongs to flip it over. When the bread is lightly browned, transfer it to a basket lined with a cloth, being careful of the steam that may be trapped inside, and serve.

MAKING THE BAKING STAND

If you find yourself making these breads often, construct a stand for them that will support a stack of 12 to 15 tiles. In Italy, stands are made of wood or iron. They are sometimes "double wide" for two stacks.

Place a tigelle in the center of a board 2 by 10 by 10 inches (5 by 25 by 25 cm). Draw a circle around the tile. Moving back 1 inch (2.5 cm) from the circle, make three marks to form the points of an equilateral triangle.

At each point, drill a hole 1 inch (2.5 cm) in diameter; drill entirely through the wood.

In each hole, glue a dowel 1 inch (2.5 cm) in diameter and 18 inches (45 cm) high.

When the glue is dry, cut out a piece of sheet metal, such as tin, the diameter of a tile and nail onto the wood. This prevents the wood from burning when stacked with tiles.

Simit

BASIC METHOD

Boiling and
   Ember Baking

EQUIPMENT

4-quart (4-l) saucepan
   with lid

Long-handled tongs

Tripod

Shovel

PRIMARY VENUES

Firebox and Hearth

ALTERNATE VENUE

Campfire

I N THE EARLY 1970S, A YOUNG COUPLE, Drew and Louise Langsner, made a journey through Greece, Turkey, and what was then Yugoslavia in search of the "hand made." Their book, *Handmade*, is a treasury of information about country life, about the houses, bread ovens, and many other handmade structures and tools that were an integral part of the lives they encountered. One particularly intriguing photograph, taken in the village of Rüzgarlar, in Bolu Province, Turkey, shows a boiled bagel-like bread—what Turks call *simit*—baking on the embers. In contrast to the recipe for Flat Bread (page 162), for which the embers cannot be too hot, *simit* requires an insulating layer of ash between the bread and the hot embers below. The bed of embers functions as a gentle to moderate griddle. As with all ember- and ash-baked breads, as long as the dough is dry when it comes in contact with ashes, the ashes won't stick. A close look at the photograph reveals small spots where the *simit* is browned and possibly lightly charred.

The Langsners didn't record the recipe. They are confident, however, that it was a simple leavened bread. The *simit* recipe I include here is made with either a yeast-activated sponge or a sponge made from dough held back from a previous baking. If you have a sour starter, use it in lieu of the yeast sponge and adjust the recipe accordingly.

The Fire: A long-burning fire with a substantial bed of embers, gentle to moderate flames while boiling the water, and gentle flames to no flames while baking the bread.

The day before, make the sponge: I provide a choice of two recipes. To make the yeast sponge, in a bowl, dissolve the yeast in the warm water. When the yeast is dissolved, add the flour, mix thoroughly, cover, and set aside overnight. To make the bread-dough sponge, in a bowl, combine the warm water, the bread dough, and the flour and stir to mix as best you can. Cover and set aside overnight.

The next day, make the bread dough: Uncover the sponge you made the previous day and stir it. The sponge should be a mass of bubbles. (If it is not, either proceed with the recipe and expect the rising to take longer, or dissolve ½ teaspoon dry yeast in a little warm water, and add that to the sponge before proceeding.) To make the dough, put the water in a large bowl and add the sponge, the flour, and the salt. Stir with a spoon or with your hands to form a homogeneous dough.

When the dough is thoroughly mixed, turn it out onto a floured work surface. Wet your hands, washing them clean of dough if necessary, and knead the dough until soft and elastic, about 3 minutes. Cover the dough with a damp cloth and let rise until it doubles in bulk. As a rule, the slower the rise, the better the flavor. This rise may take 4 to 8 hours. You can influence the speed by controlling the temperature of the dough. Expect a longer rising time in a cool place, a faster rising time in a warm place.

When ready to bake, punch down the dough, put it on a floured work surface, and divide it into 8 to 10 pieces, each weighing 2 to 3 ounces (50 to 75 g). Roll each piece into a cylinder approximately 9 inches (23 cm) long and 1/2 inch (1 cm) in diameter, dusting with flour as needed. Connect the ends to form a circle. Place the formed breads on a well-floured cloth, cover with a second cloth, and let rest for 20 minutes while you boil the water.

Fill the saucepan three-fourths full of water (at least 3 quarts/3 l) and cover it. If your fireplace is equipped with a crane, hang the pan from it and bring the water to a boil over the fire. Otherwise, put the covered saucepan on the tripod so the saucepan sits within 2 to 4 inches (5 to 10 cm) of the flames. Proceed with the instructions for boiling water on page 257. When the water boils, uncover the saucepan and drop the dough circles, 1 or 2 at a time, into the boiling water. As a bread rises to the surface, remove it with a slotted spoon and place on a rack to dry. Repeat until all of the dough is boiled. Throughout the process, keep the pan covered as much as possible and refresh the embers as needed to keep the water boiling. When all of the dough has been boiled, and the breads on the rack are dry to the touch, they are ready to bake. Shovel the embers back into the fireplace.

Use the shovel to push the fire in the fireplace to one side and create a deep, flat bed of embers far enough from any remaining burning wood that the side heat from the flames will not influence the baking of the breads. Let the embers cool for 2 minutes.

Place the breads, dry-side down, on the prepared bed of embers. After 5 to 10 minutes, using the long-handled tongs, flip each bread and bake for another 5 to 10 minutes. When done, the breads will have risen, be spotted with gold, and sound hollow. Remove from the bed of embers and brush off any ash. Serve the breads warm.

INGREDIENTS

(Makes 8 to 10 breads)

Yeast Sponge

1/2 teaspoon active dried yeast

1 cup (250ml) water, warmed to 110°F/43°C

1 cup (120 g) unbleached white flour

Bread-Dough Sponge

1 cup (250 ml) warm water

A scant 1/2 cup (75 g) bread dough from previous batch

1/2 cup (60 g) unbleached white flour

Bread Dough

Yeast Sponge or Bread-Dough Sponge (above)

1/2 cup (120 ml) water

2 1/2 cups (325 g) unbleached white flour

1 teaspoon salt

Brown Bread

BASIC METHOD
Steaming

EQUIPMENT

1-quart (1-l) steamed-
pudding mold, or
any 1-quart (1-l)
container with lid
(or lid improvised
with aluminum foil
and string)

Pot or saucepan with
lid large enough
to hold the mold

Tripod

Shovel

PRIMARY VENUE
Hearth

ALTERNATE VENUES
Campfire
Bread Oven

MOLASSES IS WHAT MAKES BROWN BREAD BROWN. In the late nineteenth century, American cookbooks often included a number of steamed brown breads leavened by baking soda and made with a mixture of flours—always cornmeal and whole wheat, but sometimes rye or barley. Molasses and whole grains meld into a firmly textured loaf of complex flavor—a little sweet, a little bitter—with the memory of the whole grains retained in the crumb. In New England, brown bread is often served with baked beans. Versions that predate the introduction of refined baking soda were leavened by saleratus (potassium bicarbonate), or yeast by way of a starter, which could have included beer barm.

We have grown accustomed to cookbook authors presenting us with a single authoritative recipe. But many nineteenth-century American cookbooks were anthologies very much in the spirit of moderated Internet recipe archives. An editor exerted some judgment, but ultimately it was up to the reader to decide which recipes had the most integrity.

For this brown bread, I have created a single recipe that more or less embraces the recipes of Mrs. Kent, Mrs. E. Wood, Mrs. L. Gilbert, Mrs. O. Wheelock, and others originally published in my great-aunt's favorite cookbook, the 1882 edition of *The Home Cook.*

Like the doughs for most steamed breads and puddings, this one should be a spoonable batter. Steamed breads are impossible to burn, but they can be undercooked. Allow up to three hours for steaming. The coarser the flour, and the more recently it was ground, the better the texture and the sweeter the flavor.

 The Fire: A mature fire with gentle flames to maintain the pot at a simmer for up to 3 hours.

Stir together the flours, salt, and baking soda in a bowl. Make a well in the center and add the sour milk, followed by the molasses. Stir with a whisk just enough to mix the ingredients into a thick batter. Butter the bottom and sides of the pudding mold and spoon the batter into the mold. (If using a 1-pound (450-g) coffee can, line the bottom with parchment paper and butter the paper.) If your mold does not have a lid, cover it with aluminum foil and tie in place with string. Place the covered mold in the pot. Add water to come halfway up the sides of the mold. Cover the saucepan and carry it to the fireplace.

Place the pot on the tripod positioned on the hearth within 4 to 6 inches (10 to 15 cm) of the fire. Use radiant heat from the fire and embers shoveled against the side of the pot nearest the fire to maintain the water at a simmer where it faces the flames. Replenish the water and adjust the fire and embers as necessary to maintain the simmer. If your fireplace has a crane, hang the pot near, but not over, the flames, so the water simmers but doesn't boil. The bread is done when it pulls away from the sides of the mold and a knife inserted into the center comes out clean, 2½ to 3 hours. Turn out onto a plate and serve warm.

Breakfast bread variation: Increase the molasses to 1 cup (300 g) and add ½ cup (75 g) raisins.

INGREDIENTS

(Serves 6 to 8)

1 cup (120 g) whole-wheat flour

1 cup (120 g) cornmeal

1 cup (120 g) rye, barley, or oat flour

1 teaspoon salt

1 scant teaspoon baking soda

2 cups (475 ml) sour milk or buttermilk

½ cup (165 g) dark molasses

English Toast

BASIC METHOD
Radiant Heat

EQUIPMENT
Long-handled fork

But I will do it for my father myself, said the youth. — Pray let me save you the trouble, young gentleman, said I, taking up a fork for the purpose, and offering him my chair to sit down upon by the fire, —whilst I did it. —I believe, Sir, said he, very modestly, I can please him best myself. — I am sure, said I, his honour will not like the toast the worse for being toasted by an old soldier. . . .

LAWRENCE STERNE, *The Life and Opinions of Tristram Shandy*

TOAST IS ENGLISH. Of course, other people grill bread, but the toast that Americans often eat for breakfast, or with tea, is a product of English tradition. Unfortunately, the American idea of toast is defined by the neutral flavor and predictable texture created in the electric toaster. It is not going too far to say that in England there was a time when toast was the personal food. The young man in the Sterne quote above is worried that this pushy stranger has taken over the project of grilling bread for his father. After all, only he, the son, knows precisely how his father likes his toast.

When you toast bread before an open fire you are in full control over the distance between the bread and the fire, and thus you control the nuances of toasting: how crisp, how deep the crispness, how much browning, and whether and how much flavor the toast picks up from the fire itself. A light searing very near the flame, or over embers, introduces a touch of smoke—and even a suggestion of bitterness—that makes toast with honey one of the incomparable foods.

English toast was never just about flavor. It was also about time and memory and a relationship with the hearth. Imagine yourself hunched before the fire on a damp morning in a stone farmhouse getting warm, making toast, letting the flames and the toasting clear one's mind for the day. It must have often been a meditation. Also, imagine in the late afternoon coming in from the life of the day to the hearth, and to another meditation with fire and bread. Finally, there was the sitting down to the table set for tea, to the hot cup and to that first bite into the perfectly crisped slice, a bite to bring calm into the day and settle one's troubled mind.

The long-handled toasting fork is the time-honored English method for grilling bread. It consistently produces the best results. However, it was never the only method. Another method was to stand bread on the hearth close to the fire. It was leaned against something—a brick would do, although the better-equipped hearth included an iron toasting rack. For a large tea party, I recommend toasting on a hearthside grill.

 The Fire: A new to moderately mature fire with moderate to high flames.

The basic method: Pierce a slice of bread with the long-handled fork so you can hold it near the flame, or over glowing embers, until the exposed face begins to turn golden brown. When the first side is toasted to your satisfaction, remove the slice from the fork and pierce it again, so the opposite side is toward the flames. When it is done, remove from the fire and, while still hot, lightly spread one side with butter. Continue until all the bread is toasted. Serve with honey, jams, jellies, and preserves. To toast many pieces of bread at once—for a tea party, for example—prepare on a hearthside grill (see Bruschetta, page 26). For tips on toasting refinements, read on.

Crispiness: Bread becomes crisp when it dries out. Control how deeply the crispiness penetrates by how quickly you toast the bread. The slower you toast it, the deeper the layer of crispiness. Bread can be crisped without being browned. To crisp, hold the bread at least 2 inches (7.5 cm) from the flames.

Browning: Bread browns when sugars in the crumb caramelize. Browning contributes flavor and requires high heat. Hold the bread near the flame or near hot embers. If you immediately begin browning it, the layer of crispiness will be very shallow. I advise developing at least some crispiness before bringing it close enough to the flames or embers to brown it.

Searing: Bring the toast within 1 inch (2.5 cm) of the fire for 1 to 5 seconds. Searing slightly burns the bread, introducing smokiness and sometimes a suggestion of bitterness. Save searing for the last step, after the toast has been both crisped and browned to your idea of perfection.

PRIMARY VENUE
Hearth

ALTERNATE VENUES
Barbecue
Campfire

INGREDIENTS
(Plan on 1 to 2 pieces of toast per person, but be prepared to make more)

Sliced bread, preferably hand sliced

Butter

Honey, jams, jellies, and preserves of choice

BEROWNE: *White-handed mistress, one sweet word with thee.*

PRINCESS OF FRANCE: *Honey, and milk, and sugar;*
there is three.

BEROWNE: *Nay, then, two treys, and if you grow so nice,*
Metheglin, wort, and malmsey; well run dice!

PRINCESS OF FRANCE: *There's half a dozen sweets.*

BEROWNE: *Seventh sweet, adieu!*

WILLIAM SHAKESPEARE, *Love's Labour's Lost*

DESSERTS

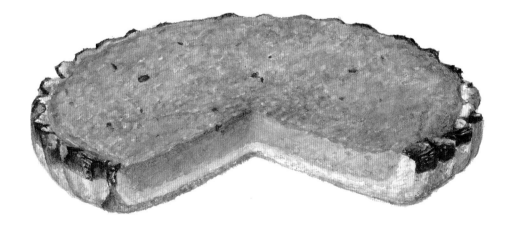

Tarte Tatin

BASIC METHOD
Hearthside Tripod

EQUIPMENT

10-inch (25-cm) frying
  pan with 3-inch
  (7.5-cm) sides and
  a lid that can be
  stacked with embers

Tripod

Shovel

Pot hook

PRIMARY VENUE
Hearth

ALTERNATE VENUES
Campfire
Wood Oven

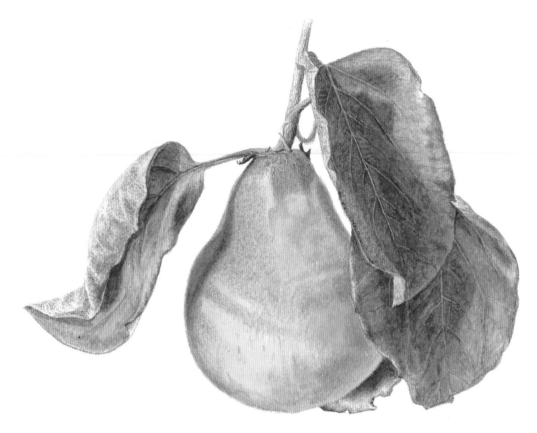

Quince

IT IS NOW MORE THAN A CENTURY SINCE PARISIANS were introduced to this tart by the Tatin sisters, owners of a restaurant in Lamotte-Beuvron, then a fashionable destination for the city's well-to-do residents during the hunting season. Time has augmented the dessert's reputation. It is now well entrenched as the tart of the Parisian café, and the Tatin sisters have managed one of the rarest feats—the achievement of immortality through a single dessert. This fact alone should be enough to convince you to try this recipe. What tart could lead to such fame? The *tarte Tatin* is a study in contrasts: the bitter taste of caramelized sugar against the sweet essence of apple; the crispness of the crust against fruit grown soft and translucent from long cooking.

This recipe returns Stéphanie Tatin's upside-down tart to what I believe were its hearthside origins. Slow cooking, and the addition of nuts to the crust, accentuate its textural contrasts. At my house, this tart reigns supreme as the monarch of the hearth-baked dessert. In order to maximize the dramatic effect, I always bake the crust during dinner, and flip the pie onto a serving plate at the table. Quince produces a more intense flavor than apples, and should be used in place of apples whenever the opportunity presents itself.

 The Fire: A mature fire with moderate flames to produce embers for use in cooking both the filling and the crust.

To make the caramel: Put the sugar into the frying pan. Place the pan on the hearthside tripod and shovel embers underneath to create high heat. When most of the sugar has melted, 3 to 5 minutes, begin to stir until all the sugar is melted and the color of medium-dark honey. Remove the pan from the hearth and set aside. Shovel the embers back into the fireplace.

To make the crust: Stir together the flour, sugar, and almonds in a bowl. Pour the mixture onto a work surface. Using a pastry blender, cut in the butter until it is uniformly the size of small peas. Gather the mixture into a mound, make a well in the center, break the egg into the well, and add the vanilla. Cut the liquid into the dough. When evenly distributed, complete the mixing by spreading the dough with the palm of your hand onto the work surface 2 to 4 times. Add a small amount of water if needed to create a uniform mass. Knead 2 to 3 times as you form the dough into a ball. Do not overwork. Cover with a cloth and set aside in a cool place, but not in the refrigerator, for at least 30 minutes.

To make the filling: Place a layer of sliced fruit over the cooled caramelized sugar in the pan. Sprinkle with sugar and dot with butter. Continue building layers of fruit topped by sugar and butter until all of the fruit is used up, finishing with a layer of sugar and butter.

To cook the fruit: Cover the frying pan and return it to the hearth. Place it on the hearthside tripod where the side heat will not significantly affect the cooking. Shovel an even bed of embers underneath to create high heat. Once you can see or hear the fruit bubbling, remove the lid. Let the heat fall to moderate. Keep the fruit bubbling until nearly all of the juices have evaporated. As the sugars begin to

INGREDIENTS
(Serves 8 to 12)

Caramel

1 cup (225 g) sugar

Crust

2 cups (250 g) flour

¼ cup (50 g) sugar

¼ cup (50 g) ground almonds

⅔ cup (150 g) unsalted butter, firm but not cold

1 egg

2 teaspoons vanilla extract

1 to 3 teaspoons water, if needed

Filling

4 pounds (1.75 kg) apples, peeled, cored, and thinly sliced, or 6 pounds (2.75 kg) quince, peeled, cored, and thinly sliced

1 to 3 teaspoons sugar for each layer of apple, depending on sweetness, or 2 tablespoons sugar for each layer of quince

1 tablespoon unsalted butter for each layer of fruit

Tarte Tatin
(continued)

Pot hooks

recaramelize, burning becomes a possibility. Be attentive to the heat under the pan, allowing it to fall if necessary. Remove the pan from the heat when the juices have thickened and the bubbles are relatively big and viscous. The fruit may be set aside for several hours.

To bake the crust: When you are ready to cook the crust, roll out the dough on a floured work surface into a round large enough to cover the fruit. The dough should be thin. Carefully transfer the pastry round to the pan, draping it over the filling and trimming away excess dough. Place the pan directly on the hearth, but back from the fire to minimize cooking from side heat. Pile the lid with embers. If the distance between the crust and lid is less than 1½ inches (4 cm), be cautious; otherwise, pile on embers as high as you can. After 8 minutes, use a pot hook to lift the lid. Check the progress, dump the old embers into the fireplace, and replace with fresh embers. Check again in 10 minutes, and continue checking and replacing the embers until the crust is light brown, usually in about 25 minutes. When it is ready, dump the embers from the lid back into the fireplace. Slide the frying pan onto the embers beside the fire for 10 to 20 seconds, just long enough to soften the sugars, then remove from the fireplace, slide a knife around the inside edge of the pan, and immediately, turn upside down onto a serving plate. A few apples may stick to the bottom. Use a spatula to dislodge them and replace them in the tart. Serve warm.

Pumpkin Pie

BASIC METHOD
Dutch Oven

EQUIPMENT
9-inch (23-cm) pie pan
Dutch oven with legs,
    large enough to
    accommodate pie
    pan
Shovel
Pot hook

PRIMARY VENUE
Hearth

ALTERNATE VENUES
Campfire
Bread Oven

WINTER SQUASHES were one of the few fresh foods eaten during the winter months by colonial and pioneer families in North America. They were boiled, baked in ashes, baked in ovens, and incorporated into soups, casseroles, and pies. Squashes can be eaten young and green in the summer, or they can be eaten mature, when the outer skin is thick and tough. Winter squashes are flexible foods. Baked squash puréed with milk and sugar makes a wonderful dessert, while baked squash puréed with water or a light stock makes a satisfying soup.

The squashes we call "pumpkins" are not part of a group recognized by botanists. "Pumpkin" is an ethnobotanical category that describes squashes drawn from all four of the main groups of squashes—*Curcubita maxima, C. mixta, C. moschata,* and *C. pepo*—on the basis of their color and shape. In selecting a squash for pumpkin pie, select one of any shape that has rich golden flesh. The sweeter the flesh, the more wonderful the pie.

A pie can be baked in a Dutch oven with the same ease that it is baked in a conventional oven. While I suggest you practice once before making *the pie* for Thanksgiving, my first effort was successful, and I think yours will be, too. A Dutch oven used for pie baking operates very simply. The metal of the oven is heated by embers and radiant heat from the fire. The hot metal

Pumpkin Pie
(continued)

INGREDIENTS
(Serves 4 to 6)

Crust for Tarte Tatin
(page 186)

1-pound (450-g) piece
pumpkin, seeded
and cut into wedges

2 cups (480 ml) water

2 eggs

1½ cups (350 ml) milk

½ cup (90 g) firmly
packed brown sugar

1 teaspoon ground
cinnamon

½ teaspoon ground
ginger

heats the air inside, and the hot air heats the food. As it happens, a thick pile of embers placed under a cold Dutch oven, and a thick layer of embers piled onto the lid, and a moderately hot fire from the fireplace striking the side of the oven, will heat the metal to around 350°F (180°C)—the temperature most of us are familiar with from baking in a conventional oven. Yes, part of the Dutch oven will get hotter than 350°F (180°C), and, yes, part will get cooler, but 350°F (180°C) is one of the Dutch oven's more natural temperatures. Because the bottom of the oven is liable to get hotter than the prescribed temperature when the embers are first put down, I line the bottom of the Dutch oven with a thin layer of ash to shield the bottom of the pie from the direct contact with the oven.

I prefer a crust for pumpkin pie that is more complementary to the filling than I find the standard American crust to be. Because of that, I recommend you use the crust with almonds called for in the recipe for *Tarte Tatin*.

 The Fire: A mature fire with gentle to moderate flames.

To prepare the crust: Prepare the dough for the *Tarte Tatin* crust. While the dough is resting, prepare the filling.

To make the filling: Put the pumpkin pieces and water in the Dutch oven. Cover and bring to the hearth. Place the Dutch oven near the fire. Begin by shoveling embers underneath the oven to create high heat. Replenish the embers as needed to maintain the water at a low boil. After 10 minutes, use a pot hook to lift the lid to check the pumpkin and adjust heat as required. The pumpkin is done when it is soft and can be easily mashed, 10 to 15 minutes. When done, return all the embers to the fireplace and transfer the pumpkin to a bowl. In the kitchen, use a spoon to scrape the pulp from the peel, then mash the pulp in a bowl with a fork, press it through a sieve, or run it through a food mill. You should have 1 cup (225 g).

Break the eggs into a bowl and whisk until blended, then whisk in the milk and brown sugar, mixing well. Add the pumpkin purée and the spices and mix until well combined.

Roll out the dough into a round 11 inches (28 cm) in diameter and ⅛ inch (3 mm) thick. Transfer the dough to the pie pan, pressing it into the bottom and sides. Trim the edge, leaving a ½-inch (1-cm) overhang, fold the overhang under, and crimp the rim. Reserve the trimmings to make cookies. Pour in the filling.

At the hearth, line the bottom of the Dutch oven with a layer of ash ½ inch (1 cm) deep. Center the pie pan on the layer of ash. Place the Dutch oven where it will receive moderate side heat from the fire, usually 4 to 6 inches (10 to 15 cm) back from the edge of the firebox. Again, shovel embers underneath the Dutch oven and on top of the lid to create high heat. Let the embers underneath the oven cool to a gentle heat, while maintaining moderate to high heat on the lid. Taking into account the side heat from the fire, maintain the Dutch oven at a moderate temperature (350°F/180°C) throughout the baking. After 45 minutes, use a pot hook to lift the lid and check the progress. Adjust the temperature according to what you see. The pie is done when a knife inserted in the center comes out clean, 50 to 60 minutes. Remove the embers to the firebox and remove the pie from the Dutch oven. Let the pie cool on a rack before serving.

Spider, circa 1850.
I improvise a Dutch oven with a lid
that I can pile with embers.

Golden Pudding: An Upside-Down Cake

THIS IS A RECIPE FOR one of the many desserts that the English call a steamed pudding, but that, in America, we think of as a cake. It is a cake with a beautiful outer coating produced by lining the baking pan with Golden Syrup, a trademarked English food developed in the 1880s. Golden Syrup is widely sold in much of the English-speaking world. If you can't find it in your local market, coat the pan with caramelized honey, caramelized sugar, or with marmalade, a practice that predates Golden Syrup.

Without the caramel coating, the recipe produces a basic white cake. I sometimes serve it as just that, but more often I use it as a base from which to develop other cakes—chocolate, lemon, almond—for afternoon tea and after-dinner dessert. My chocolate version has proved particularly popular among my friends, and so I include the recipe here.

Steamed puddings are the workhorses of the hearthside cake. Once you become familiar with the method, you will find that steamed puddings are actually easier to make than cakes baked in a conventional oven. As long as the cake mold is surrounded by water, the cake will not burn. Indeed, the only way to go wrong with steamed puddings is to undercook them. To be forewarned is to be prepared.

As with all mold-baked steamed puddings, this pudding is inverted onto the serving plate. Slices of fruit or a ring of toasted almonds placed on the bottom of the mold will be on top when the cake is presented at table.

Tripod, French, late eighteenth century, circa French Revolution

The *Fire:* *A mature fire with gentle to moderate flames to maintain the pot at a simmer for about 1¼ hours.*

INGREDIENTS
(Serves 6)

12 almonds

2 tablespoons (30 g) unsalted butter, at room temperature, plus butter for mold

2 eggs, separated

¼ cup (50 g) sugar

1 teaspoon vanilla extract

1 tablespoon grated lemon zest

¾ cup (175 ml) milk

1 teaspoon baking powder

1¼ cups (165 g) flour

4 to 5 tablespoons (75 to 95 g) Golden Syrup

Place the tripod on the hearth near the fire. Put the frying pan with the almonds over the tripod and shovel embers underneath. As the nuts begin to toast, shake the pan or stir the nuts with a wooden spoon to keep them from burning. When the nuts begin to brown, remove them from the heat and set aside. Melt the butter in the small saucepan pushed into the embers beside the fire and set aside.

Whisk the yolks with the sugar until they are pale yellow and form a ribbon when dropped from the end of the whisk back into the bowl, and set aside. Whisk the egg whites to form soft peaks, and set aside. Stir the vanilla, lemon zest, and milk into the egg-sugar mixture. Add the baking powder and then whisk in the flour. When just mixed, fold in the egg whites in three parts. Stop mixing as soon as the batter is smooth.

Butter the bottom and sides of the pudding mold, then coat the bottom and sides with the Golden Syrup. The syrup is unbelievably sticky, so use a rubber spatula to spread it. Place the reserved almonds on the bottom of the mold in an agreeable pattern. Spoon the batter into the mold. If the mold does not have a lid, cover it with aluminum foil and tie in place with string. Place the covered mold in the pot. Add water to come halfway up the sides of the mold. Cover the pot and bring to the fireplace.

Place the pot on the hearthside tripod positioned within 4 to 6 inches (10 to 15 cm) of the fire. Use radiant heat from the fire and embers shoveled against the side of the pot nearest the fire to maintain the water at a simmer where it faces the flames. Replenish water and adjust the fire and embers as necessary to maintain the simmer. If your fireplace has a crane, hang the pot near, but not over, the flames, so the water simmers but doesn't boil. The cake is done when it pulls away from the sides of the mold and a knife inserted into the center comes out clean, about 1¼ hours. When the cake is done, immediately remove it from the mold by inverting the mold onto a serving plate. Be careful not to splash yourself with the hot syrup coating the cake. Serve warm.

Chocolate variation: Omit the almonds and Golden Syrup. Place 1 ounce (25 g) unsweetened chocolate and a little milk in a small saucepan and push the pan near the fire to melt the chocolate. Increase the amount of sugar by 1 tablespoon for a barely sweet cake and substitute the grated orange zest for the grated lemon zest. After the cake is cool, dust with confectioners' sugar and serve.

Clafouti

BASIC METHOD

Dutch Oven or
 Hearthside Tripod

EQUIPMENT

5-quart (5-l) Dutch oven
 with legs, or 10-inch
 (25-cm) frying pan

Tripod if using
 frying pan

Shovel

Pot hook

INGREDIENTS

(Serves 4 to 6)

1 pound (450 g) fresh
 fruit such as sour
 cherries, figs, plums,
 or apples, or dried
 fruit such as pears,
 apricots, or prunes,
 soaked in warm
 water for several
 hours and drained

3 eggs

1¼ cups (350 ml) milk

2 to 6 tablespoons
 sugar, depending on
 sweetness of fruit

1 teaspoon vanilla
 extract

3 tablespoons brandy,
 rum, or eau-de-vie
 (optional)

¼ cup (30 g) flour

CLAFOUTI IS A DESSERT with its heart in the French farm. Frugal with ingredients—a small amount of flour, a couple of eggs, a little sugar, milk, fruit—it is quick to assemble and easy to bake. In France, the classic version is made with sour cherries. I suggest prune plums in the fall; pears or dried fruits in the winter. A clafouti can be placed in a mold and steamed, although I prefer to bake it on the hearth in an open frying pan or in a covered Dutch oven. Because it is delicious and so simple to make, a clafouti can easily play the role of a standby dessert, something to make at the last minute. Slow cooking keeps the custard tender, the fruit soft, and the bottom unburned.

 The Fire: A mature fire with gentle to moderate flames.

If using fresh fruit, pit and cut into small pieces with an eye to how the fruit will look when baked. Peeling is not usually necessary. If using rehydrated dried fruit, cut into small attractive pieces. Beat the eggs in a bowl until blended, then whisk in the milk, sugar, vanilla, and the alcohol, if using. Whisk in the flour, 1 tablespoon at a time. Butter the bottom and sides of the Dutch oven or frying pan. Line the bottom with parchment paper and butter the paper. Lay down the fruit on the paper and pour in the custard. The clafouti should be about 1½ inches (4 cm) thick. Cover the Dutch oven, but leave the frying pan uncovered.

Place the Dutch oven or the frying pan on the tripod on the hearth about 8 inches (20 cm) back from the edge of the firebox so the side heat from the fire will not significantly affect the baking. Begin by shoveling embers underneath the Dutch oven or frying pan to create moderate heat, and shovel embers onto the Dutch oven lid to create high heat. Let the embers underneath cool a little; refresh them as needed, a sprinkling at a time, to maintain gentle heat under the oven and frying pan while maintaining moderate to high heat on the Dutch oven lid. After 15 minutes, use the pot hook to lift the Dutch oven lid and check the progress. Adjust the Dutch oven temperature according to what you see. The clafouti is done when a knife inserted into the center comes out clean, about 20 minutes in the Dutch oven, and 40 minutes in the frying pan. When baked in the Dutch oven, the top is also browned. Return the embers to the fireplace. Serve warm from the Dutch oven or from the frying pan.

Grilled Grapes

IN THE FALL, WHEN DAYS BECOME SHORT and the nights chilly, grapevines turn yellow and the last of the grapes are harvested. If you have a choice, select bunches of grapes in which a few of the fruits are already a little shriveled. This is when the sugars are at their peak. Grilled grapes are excellent served as an accompaniment to strong-flavored meats—lamb, duck, and game—but my first recommendation is to grill them as a dessert. As the finish to a meal, grilled grapes have no peer. They are beautiful. They are sweet. They are unexpectedly different.

 The Fire: A mature fire with gentle to moderate flames.

Place the clean grill on the hearth close to the fire. Place the grapes on the grill and shovel a sprinkling of embers underneath. Add embers every few minutes until the grapes begin to cook. When the grapes are thoroughly hot, use your hands to take hold of the stem and turn the bunch. Continue cooking, increasing the heat as the grapes get hotter and cook more rapidly. When a few of the grapes have split open and have started oozing caramelized sugar, 15 to 20 minutes, transfer them to a plate, and return the embers to the fireplace. Use scissors to cut the bunches into several sections, then serve.

BASIC METHOD
Hearthside Grilling

EQUIPMENT
Grill
Shovel

PRIMARY VENUE
Hearth

ALTERNATE VENUES
Barbecue
Campfire
Bread Oven

INGREDIENTS
(Serves 4 to 6)

1 to 1½ pounds (450 to 750 g) late-season vine-ripened grapes (1 or 2 bunches)

Wafers, Pizelle, and Krumkake

BASIC METHOD
Hearthside Griddle

EQUIPMENT
Small saucepan
Stovetop wafer iron
   or antique open-
   hearth iron
Tripod
Shovel

PRIMARY VENUE
Hearth

ALTERNATE VENUES
Barbecue
Campfire

THE HOST—the small, round, stamped wafer of the Catholic service—is the prototypical wafer of European cuisine. The many elaborations of patterned wafers over the last several hundred years—wafers to sanctify special occasions, wafers to sell at festivals, cup-shaped wafers to hold ice cream—all exist in the shadow of the sacred wafer—the bread that becomes the body of Christ in the Catholic sacrament of Communion.

Wafers can range from the classic French *pain oublie*—a simple cracker of water and flour—to fragile cookies scented with orange flower water or rose water and flavored with saffron, reminders of wafers' medieval popularity. In modern times, wafers are often round. A dozen of them on a plate recalls a stack of harvest moons. Coffee or tea and golden moons by the fire is one of the more pleasant ways to sit out a winter afternoon.

Any wafer iron designed for the stovetop can be heated over a hearth-side tripod. *Pizelle* (Italian) and *krumkake* (Swedish) irons are fairly easy to find in kitchen-supply stores or through the Internet. Long-handled wafer and *pain oublie* irons from the nineteenth century and earlier are often incised with elaborate patterns. However, they can be heavy and awkward to maneuver. They require a stand on which to balance the handle while the wafers are baking and I find an assistant can also be helpful.

 The Fire: A mature fire with gentle to moderate flames.

To make the dough: Melt the butter in the small saucepan pushed into the embers of the fire and set aside. Break the eggs into a bowl and whisk until blended. Then whisk in the sugar and continue whisking until the eggs and sugar are pale yellow. Whisk in the melted butter. When thoroughly mixed, add the vanilla, orange flower water, cardamom, aniseeds, orange zest, and the flour. Stir just until the dough is smooth. Do not overmix. Let the dough rest for 20 minutes and turn out onto a floured work surface. The dough will be very sticky. Dust with flour and form into a long snake the diameter of a walnut. Cut into 18 pieces, each about 1½ inches (4 cm) long. Roll into balls and set aside.

Set the tripod on the hearth and shovel embers underneath to create high heat. Place the iron over the tripod and heat both sides until they are the temperature of a moderate griddle (350°F/180°C). A finger dipped in water and then touched to the griddle releases a drop of water that sizzles and breaks up into several sizzling drops before they evaporate. If the water seems to explode when touched to the griddle, it is too hot. Once the iron is hot, start baking by determining which of the iron's 2 plates is coolest and place that side on the tripod, open the iron, lightly oil both plates, and place a ball of dough in the center. Close the iron. Bake until the wafer begins to brown, 1 to 2 minutes. Remove the wafer from the iron and place on a rack to cool, or curl by letting the wafer cool over a rolling pin or another cylindrical form. The ideal rhythm is to cook each wafer in 1 to 2 minutes, and then to reverse the iron so the top plate—now the cooler plate—is on the tripod over the embers. After the first 2 wafers, oiling the wafer iron should not be necessary. Replenish the embers as necessary to maintain the heat and continue until all the wafers are baked. Serve the wafers when cool and crisp.

INGREDIENTS
(Makes eighteen
5-inch/13-cm wafers)

4 tablespoons (60 g)
    unsalted butter

2 eggs

½ cup (100 g) sugar

1 teaspoon vanilla
    extract

1 teaspoon orange
    flower water

½ teaspoon cardamom
    seeds

1 tablespoon aniseeds

Grated zest of
    2 oranges

2 cups (250 g)
    unbleached
    pastry flour

Vegetable oil, for
    oiling iron

Stewed Dried Fruit

BASIC METHOD
Hearthside Tripod

EQUIPMENT
Saucepan with lid
Tripod
Shovel

PRIMARY VENUE
Hearth

ALTERNATE VENUES
Campfire
Bread Oven

INGREDIENTS
(Serves 6 to 8)

4 cups (550 g) mixed
  dried fruits of choice
  such as prunes, figs,
  apples, apricots, and
  raisins, or a single
  fruit
4 cups (1 l) red wine
2 cups (475 ml) water
½ cup (50 g) sugar

IN THE ERA OF HEARTH COOKING, fresh fruit was rare and dear in wintertime. In the warmer months, the harvest of the orchard was preserved in the form of alcohol, syrups, jams, and dried fruits for eating when fresh fruits were absent. Long-storing apples and pears could be brought out of the cellar in the winter, but these were luxuries. A stewed mélange of dried fruits is the classic hearthside fruit dessert—a sweet parallel to meat stew. In February, when winter seems destined to last forever, this dessert of boiled dried fruits—thick, rich, wine deepened—will make you feel warm and bundled. Cooked on the hearth, it requires little attention aside from an occasional stirring. The flickering light of the open hearth colors the fruit, imparting a filigree of magic that distinguishes it from a compote cooked on the kitchen range. This is a dessert that never fails to give pleasure.

 The Fire: A mature fire with gentle to moderate flames.

Start in the evening for cooking in the morning, or in the morning for cooking in the early evening. Put the fruits in a bowl, cover with the wine and water, and let sit for 8 to 12 hours.

When you are ready to cook, put the fruits, the sugar, and liquid in the covered saucepan. Put the saucepan on the hearthside tripod so the pan is 6 to 8 inches (15 to 20 cm) from the fire. Shovel embers under and around the pan to create high heat. When the fruit begins to simmer on the side nearest the flames, 10 to 15 minutes, remove the lid and refresh the embers as necessary to keep the fruit simmering. Cook until the fruit is soft and the liquid is reduced to a light syrup. When done, remove from the heat, and add additional sugar if needed. Shovel the embers back into the fireplace and serve the stewed fruit. This dish can be prepared in advance and reheated.

Bread Pudding

I LOVED MY MOTHER'S BREAD PUDDING. I began helping her make it when I was very young. We cut the remnants of stale loaves into slices, buttered them on both sides, cut them into cubes, and put them into a soufflé mold, sometimes layered with raisins, sometimes not. We then flooded the bread with a basic custard of egg, milk, and sugar. My mother's bread pudding, like all of her cooking, was direct. I say direct, rather than simple, because she was very involved with flavor. She often tasted fruits and vegetables before buying them, and prepared everything so that the distinctive flavor of the primary ingredients came through, her bread pudding being no exception.

 The Fire: A mature fire with gentle to moderate flames.

Cut the bread into thick slices. Butter the bread on both sides and cut into 1-inch (2.5-cm) pieces. Set aside. Break the eggs into a bowl. Lightly beat them and whisk in the sugar, 4 cups (1 l) of the milk, and the vanilla.

To assemble the pudding: Butter the bottom and sides of the Dutch oven. Line the bottom with a piece of parchment paper. Cover the bottom with a layer of bread and sprinkle with raisins. Repeat the layers until you have used up the ingredients, finishing with a layer of bread. Pour in the milk mixture. Push the bread into the liquid with your hands until it is fully saturated, adding additional milk as needed so the liquid comes to just below the top of the bread. Cover the Dutch oven.

Place the Dutch oven on the hearth 6 to 8 inches (15 to 20 cm) back from the edge of the firebox so the oven receives gentle side heat. Begin by shoveling embers underneath the Dutch oven to create moderate heat and shovel embers onto the lid to create high heat. Let the embers underneath cool a little; refresh them as needed, a sprinkling at a time, to maintain gentle heat under the oven while maintaining moderate to high heat on the lid. After 30 minutes, use the pot hook to lift the lid and check the progress. Adjust the temperature according to what you see. The pudding is done when a knife inserted into the center comes out clean, 40 minutes to 1 hour. If the pudding is done but the top is not browned, remove all the embers from under the pudding, clean the embers off the lid, and pile the lid as high as possible with a fresh batch of embers. Bake for an additional 5 minutes. Return the embers to the fireplace and remove the pudding from the Dutch oven. Serve the pudding warm.

BASIC METHOD
Dutch Oven

EQUIPMENT
5-quart (5-l) Dutch oven with legs
Shovel
Pot hook

PRIMARY VENUE
Hearth

ALTERNATE VENUES
Campfire
Bread Oven

INGREDIENTS
(Serves 6)

1¼ pounds (550 g) stale bread, hand sliced and drawn from 2 or 3 different types
½ cup (100 g) unsalted butter, at room temperature
5 eggs
½ cup (100 g) sugar
5 to 7 cups (1.3 to 2 l) milk
2 teaspoons vanilla extract
¾ cup (100 g) raisins

Persimmon Pudding

BASIC METHOD
Steaming

EQUIPMENT
1-quart (1-l) steamed-
  pudding mold or
  any 1-quart (1-l)
  container with lid
  (or lid improvised
  with aluminum foil
  and string)
Small saucepan
Pot or saucepan with
  lid large enough to
  hold the pudding
  mold
Tripod
Shovel

PRIMARY VENUE
Hearth

ALTERNATE VENUES
Campfire
Bread Oven

*Kakikueba
Kanega narunari
Horyūji*

*Eating kaki
I hear the bell of
Horyūji*

Haiku by Masaoka Shiki

THE ENGLISH COLONISTS in America made steamed puddings with the small native persimmon of Virginia (*Diospyros virginiana*). The persimmons of contemporary commerce (*Diospyros kaki*) are from Japan, a country deeply enamored of the fruit, and the source of the best modern varieties, including Hachiya, the variety most commonly grown in European and American gardens. Hachiya persimmons are large, round, pointed fruits that, like the American native, are astringent when hard, and edible only when mushy soft.

Persimmon trees are one of the more distinctive temperate fruit trees. Although slow growing, they eventually become huge. In fall, their leaves turn a brilliant orange and the ripening fruits become all but invisible. When the leaves drop, hundreds to thousands of fruits are revealed to be hanging from the branches of a single tree — orange lanterns in the autumn night. It is a display of great beauty, but if it's your tree, it can also be a sight of despair. So many persimmons! What can be done?

If picked just before they are ripe, Hachiya persimmons can be dried. Ripe specimens can be made into wine, and into puddings — dense cakes of fruit and nuts that mark the passing of fall and the beginning of winter. My steamed pudding recipe results in a dense, sweet, deeply flavored dessert. I cannot recommend it too highly. Any fruits left on the tree will be eaten by birds, possums, and raccoons.

 The Fire: A mature fire with gentle to moderate flames to maintain the pot at a simmer for up to 2½ hours.

Butter the bottom and sides of the pudding mold. Line the bottom of the mold with parchment paper and butter the paper. Melt the butter in the small saucepan pushed into the embers beside the fire and set aside.

Break the eggs into a bowl and whisk until blended. Whisk in the persimmon purée, milk, melted butter, brown sugar, cinnamon, vanilla, walnuts, and raisins. Finally, whisk in the flour along with the baking soda. When thoroughly mixed, pour into the prepared mold. If your mold does not have a lid, cover it with aluminum foil and tie in place with string. Place the covered mold in a pot. Add water to come halfway up the sides of the mold. Cover the pot and bring to the fireplace.

Place the pot on the hearthside tripod positioned within 4 to 6 inches (10 to 15 cm) of the fire. Use radiant heat from the fire and embers shoveled against the side of the pot nearest the fire to maintain the water at a simmer where it faces the flames. Replenish the water and adjust the fire and embers as necessary to maintain the simmer. If your fireplace has a crane, hang the pot near, but not over, the flames, so the water simmers but doesn't boil. The pudding is done when a knife inserted into the center comes out clean, about 2½ hours. Invert onto a plate and serve warm or at room temperature.

INGREDIENTS
(Serves 6 to 8)

3 tablespoons (40 g) unsalted butter, plus butter for mold

2 eggs

1 cup (240 ml) puréed persimmon (1 to 2 large persimmons)

½ cup (120 ml) milk

½ cup (90 g) brown sugar

1 teaspoon ground cinnamon

1 teaspoon vanilla extract

½ cup (50 g) walnuts, chopped

1 cup (175 g) raisins

1 cup (120 g) unbleached all-purpose flour

½ teaspoon baking soda

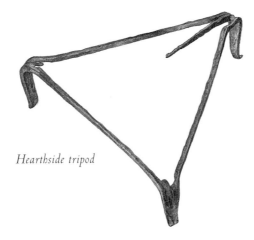

Hearthside tripod

Pain d'Épices

BASIC METHOD

Steaming

EQUIPMENT

Small saucepan

9-inch (23-cm) tube pan with improvised lid of aluminum foil and string

Pot or saucepan with lid large enough to hold the tube pan

Tripod

Shovel

PRIMARY VENUE

Hearth

ALTERNATE VENUES

Campfire

Bread Oven

Amidde the lond a castel he sighe,
Riche and real and wonder heighe.
Al the utmast wal
Was clere and schine as cristal;
An hundred tours ther were about,
Degiselich and bataild stout.
The butras com out of the diche
Of rede gold y-arched riche.

ANONYMOUS, *Sir Orfeo*

THIS IS THE GOLDEN CAKE—the cake of golden honey, of golden spices, of golden value when knights wore armor. It is a cake that carries with it the aroma of spring flowers and the enveloping heat of Arabia and the tropics. *Pain d'épices*—the English call it gingerbread—is the cake that best feeds the heart when winter is upon the land. Steamed on the hearth, eaten with cider to the poetry of minstrels and troubadours, it is a cake to make you smile deep inside.

While it is safe to assume that the recipes that have come down to us as *pain d'épices* are a comparative handful, there nonetheless remains a huge variety throughout Europe in terms of shape, texture, amount of spice, and method of cooking. In the spirit of medieval musicians who adjusted a melody's key and range to fit different instruments, a single recipe can often be changed by adjusting liquid, leavening, and the shape to fit different cooking methods. Soft doughs can be steamed while stiffer doughs can be baked in molds, on a griddle, or, if thoroughly dry, in the ashes.

This recipe is inspired by old French recipes in which a dough of rye flour, water, and honey was left to ferment for a period of months before being baked into cakes. In my recipe, the rye dough, given a boost with yeast, ferments for a few days, long enough to develop a distinct sour taste to contrast with the mellow sweetness of honey and spice. The cake can be eaten the day it is baked, but it is best eaten after two or three days. It is perfect for afternoon tea. Because it is made entirely of rye flour, this cake is dense. Serve thinly sliced, accompanied with butter.

 The Fire: A mature fire with gentle to moderate flames, to maintain the pot at a simmer for at least 2½ hours.

Days 1 to 3: In a small bowl, dissolve the yeast in the 1 cup (250 ml) of warm water. When the yeast is dissolved, add half the flour and the rest of the water. Mix, cover, and set aside at room temperature for 3 days. Once a day, for each of the 3 days, uncover the bowl, stir, and re-cover.

Day 4: Add the remaining flour. Mix, lightly knead, and if necessary, add flour or water to form a stiff dough. Form into a ball and cover lightly with a cloth. Set aside at room temperature for a minimum of 1 day or for up to 3 days.

Baking day: Start in the morning. In a spice grinder or clean coffee grinder, combine the peppercorns, cinnamon, ginger, allspice, cloves, and cardamom and grind finely. Set aside. Put the honey in a small saucepan next to the fire. Stir continuously until the honey is fluid and just warm. Remove the pan from the fire. Transfer the dough to a large bowl and mix in the honey. Use your hands to mix the dough until it is soft and whisk to eliminate all lumps. Add the aniseeds, nutmeg, orange zest, and the ground spices and whisk well. Butter the bottom and sides of a tube pan. Line the bottom with parchment paper and butter the paper. Spoon in the batter. Cover with a cloth and let rise in a warm place (78°F/25°C) for 2 hours. It will rise a little. Remove the cloth, cover the pan with aluminum foil, and tie down with string. Place the covered tube pan in a pot. Add water to come halfway up the sides of the tube pan. Cover the pot and bring to the fireplace.

Place the pot on the hearthside tripod positioned within 4 to 6 inches (10 to 15 cm) of the fire. Use radiant heat from the fire and embers shoveled against the side of the pot nearest the fire to maintain the water at a simmer where it faces the flames. Replenish the water and adjust the fire and embers as necessary to maintain the simmer. If your fireplace has a crane, hang the pot near, but not over, the fire, so the water simmers but doesn't boil. The cake is done when it pulls away from the sides of the pan and a knife inserted into the center comes out clean, 6 to 8 hours. Turn out onto a rack. Let cool completely, wrap in a cloth and store in a cool place for 2 or 3 days before serving. Serve thinly sliced.

INGREDIENTS
(Serves 24 to 36)

¼ teaspoon active dry yeast

1 cup (250 ml) water, warmed to 110°F/43°C, plus 2 cups (500 ml) cool water

6 cups (750 g) rye flour

24 peppercorns

3-inch (7.5-cm) piece cinnamon stick

1 nub dried ginger

12 allspice berries

24 whole cloves

Seeds from 9 cardamom pods

1½ cups (425 g) honey

3 tablespoons aniseeds

Scant ½ teaspoon freshly grated nutmeg

Grated zest of 3 oranges

Baked Apples

BASIC METHOD
Dutch Oven

EQUIPMENT
5-quart (5-l) Dutch oven
    with legs
Shovel
Pot hook

PRIMARY VENUE
Hearth

ALTERNATE VENUES
Campfire
Bread Oven

A BAKED APPLE IS ALWAYS a winter treat. Place a whole apple on the edge of the hearth near a hot fire, and turn the apple as it roasts. Fire concentrates flavors, intensifying whatever qualities the apple has. As always, the simpler the recipe, the more that is gained by the perfection of ingredients. The best apple for roasting is one that is firm, sweet, and perfumed, with a hint of astringency. When you take an apple of perfection and fill its core with honey, the flavors become even richer and warmer. The darker the honey, the better.

The recipe I include here, which uses a Dutch oven, is based on my own apple dream—that of coming in from a cold, muddy, gray November day to the sanctuary of a roaring fire and the warmth and delicacy of an apple spiced to suggest the Persian sun.

The Fire: A mature fire with gentle to moderate flames.

INGREDIENTS
(Serves 6)

6 apples

6 teaspoons currants
   or finely chopped
   raisins

6 almonds, halved

12 slivers candied
   ginger, plus
   2 tablespoons
   minced

6 pinches ground
   cinnamon

Rose water

About 1 cup (350 g)
   dark honey

1½ cups (350 ml) port

Slice off the top of each apple, reserving the caps, and core the apples, being careful not to cut through to the bottom. Put 1 teaspoon currants in each hollow core, pushing them down with your finger. Next, add 1 almond, 2 slivers candied ginger, a pinch of cinnamon, and a few drops of rose water. Finally, add 1 tablespoon honey and replace the cap on each apple. Place the apples in the Dutch oven, spooning a generous tablespoon of honey over each apple. Pour the port around the apples, add the minced candied ginger, and cover.

Place the Dutch oven on the hearth 4 to 6 inches (10 to 15 cm) back from the edge of the firebox so the oven receives moderate side heat. Begin by shoveling embers underneath the Dutch oven to create moderate heat and shovel embers onto the lid to create high heat. After 15 minutes, use the pot hook to lift the lid and check the progress. Adjust the temperature according to what you see. As the honey and juices thicken, they can burn, so watch the bottom heat. The apples are done when they are soft all the way through, 20 to 40 minutes. Transfer the apples to a serving plate and shovel the embers back into the fireplace. If the apples are done but the sauce has not thickened, remove the apples and continue cooking the sauce until it is reduced to a syrup. Serve the apples warm in individual bowls, spooning some of the sauce over each serving. The apples may be prepared in advance and kept warm on the hearth.

English bone apple corer, dated 1823

Roasted Chestnuts

BASIC METHOD

Ember Baking,
   Hearthside Tripod,
   or Dutch Oven

EQUIPMENT

Dutch oven with legs
   or frying pan and
   tripod

Pot hook, if using
   Dutch oven

Shovel

But let us leave them there, and return to our good Gargantua, who is at Paris very assiduous and earnest at the study of good letters and athletical exercitations, and to the good old man Grangousier his father, who after supper warmeth his ballocks by a good, clear, great fire, and, waiting upon the broiling of some chestnuts, is very serious in drawing scratches on the hearth, with a stick burnt at the one end, wherewith they did stir up the fire, telling to his wife and the rest of the family pleasant old stories and tales of former times.

FRANÇOIS RABELAIS, *Gargantua and Pantagruel*

CHESTNUTS ARE ONE OF the great foods. On Mount Amiata, a two-hour drive from Rome, chestnuts drop from the trees in October. In the season, cars line the shoulder where wild chestnut forests meet the road. Dozens of people can be seen stooped over, gathering nuts in the nearby forest. Children, teenagers, parents, grandparents, young couples—they all gather chestnuts, the glorious gift of the autumn forest, dream food of the open hearth, and free for the picking. At one time, chestnuts were a European famine food, something eaten in quantity when times were bad, but now they are a culinary luxury, and one of the few remaining seasonal foods in urban markets. You cannot buy a fresh chestnut in June.

Roman families return from the chestnut forests to their apartment kitchens to boil their harvest. But I think it likely that in each heart is the dream of chestnuts roasting in a pan over the fire, or of roasting them in the embers while sitting and talking before the hearth.

As one late fall afternoon turned to dusk, and the mist turned to rain, my friends and I roasted our chestnuts from the slopes of Mount Amiata by the fire on a stone hearth in a farmhouse with rooms that retained the spirit of the nearby countryside—rough, rugged, boulder strewn. The roasting was social. We talked, drank grappa, and ate cheese made from the milk of a flock of sheep whose bleating could occasionally be heard through a side window. Every now and then, one of us picked up a stick and poked at the roasting nuts. Finally, when there was agreement that the chestnuts were ready, we ate them—soft, hot, and sweet—as the room turned dark, but for the glow in the hearth.

 The Fire: A mature fire for the embers, and gentle to moderate flames if roasting in the Dutch oven.

PRIMARY VENUES
Firebox or Hearth

ALTERNATE VENUES
Barbecue
Campfire
Bread Oven

INGREDIENTS
(Serves 4)

16 to 24 large
  chestnuts in
  their shells

Preparing the chestnuts: Use a very sharp knife to make a deep cross on the rounded side of each chestnut. The shell can be slippery, so pay attention.

To roast in the embers: Use the shovel to create a bed of hot ash beside the fire by mixing 1 part embers into 1 part ash. If using an infrared thermometer, the ash should be around 375°F (190°C). Let the heat soak into the ashes for a few minutes and stir the prepared chestnuts into the ash. Stir every few minutes to promote even roasting. Check in 10 minutes. The nuts are done when the shells peel back at the cut and the meat is soft and tastes sweet, usually 10 to 20 minutes. Test a nut before removing them all from the ashes. When done, serve immediately.

To roast in a Dutch oven: Place the prepared chestnuts in the Dutch oven set on the hearth 4 to 6 inches (10 to 15 cm) back from the firebox so it receives moderate side heat. Shovel embers underneath the Dutch oven, and onto the lid, to create high heat. Let the heat under the Dutch oven fall to gentle while maintaining high heat on the lid. Use a pot hook to remove the lid after 8 to 10 minutes. Stir the nuts and check the cooking progress. Replace the lid and adjust the embers as necessary. Check again in 5 to 8 minutes. The nuts are done as described in the procedure, above, usually 15 to 20 minutes. Test a nut before removing them all from the oven. When done, shovel the embers back into the fireplace and serve immediately.

To roast in a frying pan: Place the prepared chestnuts flat-side down on the frying pan. Set the pan over a hearthside tripod and shovel embers underneath to create high heat. Let the heat fall to medium and shake the pan every few minutes to promote even roasting. Add embers as necessary, until the nuts are done, as described in the first procedure, above, usually 15 to 20 minutes.

Steamed Custard

BASIC METHOD

Steaming

EQUIPMENT

1-quart (1-l) mold

Pot or saucepan with
    lid large enough
    to hold the custard
    mold

Tripod

Shovel

PRIMARY VENUE

Hearth

ALTERNATE VENUES

Campfire

Bread Oven

INGREDIENTS

(Serves 4 to 6)

4 eggs

Scant ¾ cup (90 g)
    sugar

4 cups (1 l) milk

1½ teaspoons vanilla
    extract

Unsalted butter
    for mold

THIS STEAMED CUSTARD is a light dessert for dinner's end—a hint of sweet, a supple digestive. It is the ideal close to a full-flavored meal of grilled meat or a rich stew. It is also an appealing food on days when you feel a little under the weather.

To create crème caramel, caramelize ½ cup (100 g) sugar in the bottom of a saucepan over the hearthside tripod. Pour the caramelized sugar into the mold, let it cool, and add the other ingredients. If you caramelize sugar just to the point of burning, it turns bitter—which is just where I like it—a counterpoint to the sweetened custard.

 The Fire: A mature fire with gentle to moderate flames.

In a bowl, lightly beat the eggs until blended, then whisk in the sugar, milk, and vanilla. Butter the mold and pour the custard into it. Use aluminum foil to create a lid for the mold. Do not tie in place, however, as custard must be checked regularly. Place the covered mold in a pot. Add water to come halfway up the sides of the mold. Cover the pot and bring to the fireplace.

Place the covered pot on the hearthside tripod positioned within 4 to 6 inches (10 to 15 cm) of the fire. Use radiant heat from the fire and embers shoveled against the base of the pot nearest the fire to maintain the water just below the simmer where it faces the flames. Adjust the fire and embers as necessary to maintain the water temperature. If your fireplace has a crane, hang the pot near, but not over, the flames, so the water comes to just below the simmer. Custards set at between 180° and 190°F (82° and 88°C). If the custard gets too hot, the eggs will separate. Because it uses few eggs and little sugar, this recipe is not tolerant of error. Start checking the custard after 40 minutes. Cook it just to the point that a knife inserted in the center comes out clean, usually 1 hour, and immediately remove the mold from the fire. Set it in a bowl of cool water to stop the cooking. Serve the custard hot or at room temperature.

Shortbread

I ENJOY WATCHING MY FOOD COOK, and so I prefer baking shortbread slowly on a griddle over the course of two or even three hours rather than using the more traditional hearth method for cookies, which is baking them on an improvised cookie sheet set on a layer of ash within a Dutch oven. As a reward for your patience, you will find that slow baking creates a cookie that is unusually light. This same method can be applied to all cookies and is appropriate on a day when one is lazing around the fire. Getting the griddle too hot will burn the shortbread, while letting it get too cool only means more time, so, as long as you do not rush the baking, nothing can go wrong.

 The Fire: A mature fire with gentle flames to produce embers for the long baking.

To make the dough, stir together the flour(s) and sugar in a bowl. Pour the mixture onto a work surface. (If you omit the rice flour you do not need to compensate with additional flour.) Using a pastry blender, cut in the butter until it is uniformly the size of small peas. When evenly mixed, add the vanilla and complete the mixing by spreading the dough with the palm of your hand onto the work surface 2 to 4 times. Do not be discouraged by what may seem like a pile of sand. Add just enough of the water, 1 tablespoon at a time, to make it possible to form the dough into a uniform mass. Knead 2 or 3 times as you form the dough into a ball. Do not overwork. Cover with a cloth and set aside for 30 minutes. On a well-floured surface, flatten into a disk about a finger thick and mark off serving wedges with the tines of a fork.

Place the griddle on the hearthside tripod positioned so the fire's side heat will not affect the baking. Shovel a light sprinkling of embers underneath the griddle. Add more embers, a sprinkling at a time, over the space of a few minutes until the griddle is just gentle—no more than 225°F (110°C). A finger dipped in water and then touched to the griddle leaves a black mark in the shape of your finger before the water fully evaporates. When hot, slide the shortbread onto the griddle. Replenish the embers as needed to maintain very gentle heat until the shortbread is done. Once the dough is set, you may flip the shortbread, but it is traditionally baked on one side only. It takes 2 to 3 hours to bake. When done, the underside will be a light brown and it will smell delicious. Transfer to a rack to cool.

BASIC METHOD
Hearthside Griddle

EQUIPMENT
Griddle
Tripod
Shovel

PRIMARY VENUE
Hearth

ALTERNATE VENUES
Campfire
Bread Oven

INGREDIENTS
(Serves 6 to 8)

1⅔ cups (26 oz/ 725 g) unbleached pastry flour

¼ cup (25 g) rice flour (optional)

¼ cup (50 g) sugar

½ cup (4 oz/100 g) unsalted butter

2 teaspoons vanilla extract

Water

How do you do? How do you all do?——Quite well, I am much obliged to you. Never better.——Don't I hear another carriage?—— Who can this be?——very likely the worthy Coles.——Upon my word, this is charming to be standing about among such friends! And such a noble fire!——I am quite roasted. No coffee, I thank you, for me——never take coffee.——A little tea if you please, sir, by and bye,——no hurry——Oh! here it comes. Every thing so good!

JANE AUSTEN, *Pride and Prejudice*

BEVERAGES

The Bishop

Come, buy my fine Oranges, Sauce for your Veal,
And charming when squeez'd in a Pot of brown Ale.
Well roasted, with Sugar and Wine in a Cup,
They'll make a sweet Bishop when Gentlefolks sup.

JONATHAN SWIFT, *Oranges*

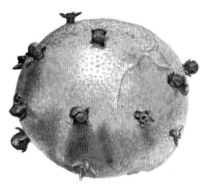

THE BISHOP is an English mulled beverage that dates back to at least the seventeenth century. It is usually made with red wine. This recipe, which calls for port, is particularly warm, rich, and deeply flavored. Taken near midnight when a meandering meal by the fire is ending— when the logs have burned down to embers, and the fire's shadow, after dancing all evening upon the walls, hugs the fireplace itself—the bishop, finished in alcohol's blue flame, is more magic potion than simple mulled beverage. I love this drink. To me it is an elixir, a drink to bring friends together, to make hearts one.

There are three steps to making the bishop: a clove-studded orange is roasted by the fire; a mixture of water and spices is boiled and reduced by half; and finally the port is heated with the orange and the spices, lit to burn off some of the alcohol, and served.

The ingredients list—port, orange, lemon, sugar, clove, cinnamon, mace, allspice, and ginger—is a reading of exotica. There is no place in the world where all these ingredients are grown together. One or another must travel a long way. The cloves are likely to have come from Zanzibar, where they were picked by a child who climbed into the clove tree to gather clusters of red berries. On the ground, the clusters were made into piles around which half a dozen people sat separating the berries from the leaves and stems. The berries were then laid out in vast aromatic carpets under the tropical sun and left to dry into the cloves we know.

Most of the steps necessary to make the bishop can be taken in advance, with the final heating of the port reserved for just before serving.

 The Fire: A mature fire with gentle flames to prepare the drink, then anything from the residual embers of a long-burning fire to a roaring blaze for ambience.

To prepare the orange: Roast the clove-studded orange on the edge of the hearth in front of the fire, turning it from time to time, until the orange begins to brown, about 20 minutes. Set aside.

While the orange is roasting, put the water and spices (except the nutmeg garnish) in the small covered saucepan on the tripod positioned on the hearth a few inches (7.5 cm) from the edge of the firebox. Shovel a thick layer of embers underneath. The water will boil in about 5 minutes. Remove the cover and continue boiling, adding fresh embers as needed, until the water is reduced by half. Remove the pan from the tripod and set aside. Shovel the embers back into the fireplace.

Squeeze the juice from the lemon quarters into a serving bowl. Add the spent lemon wedges and the sugar cubes and set aside.

When you are ready to serve, place the orange and the port in the medium-sized saucepan and add the spice liquid through a strainer. Place the pan on the hearth 4 inches (10 cm) from the fire. At your discretion, push embers against the base of the pan nearest the flames. Stir the wine to distribute the heat. When it is hot enough to drink, remove the orange and place it in the serving bowl. With the room illuminated only by candles and the light of the fire, strike a match and light the port. Let it burn for a dramatic moment, then pour the flaming drink into the serving bowl. When the flames have died down, sprinkle with nutmeg and serve in individual glasses.

INGREDIENTS
(Serves 6)

1 small orange, studded with 12 to 18 whole cloves

1 cup (250 ml) water

1/3 teaspoon ground cinnamon

1/4 teaspoon ground mace

1/4 teaspoon ground allspice

1 small nub dried ginger, crushed

1 lemon, rubbed with sugar cubes and quartered

4 to 6 sugar cubes

1 bottle (750 ml) port

Freshly grated nutmeg, for serving

Herbal Infusions

I am sorry to say that Peter was not very well during the evening. His mother put him to bed, and made some camomile tea; and she gave of a dose of it to Peter! "One table-spoonful to be taken at bed-time."

BEATRIX POTTER, *Peter Rabbit*

Dried strawberries

WILD-STRAWBERRY TEA IS one of the most lovely drinks of northern Europe. A bouquet of dried forest strawberries steeped in a cup of hot water brings the sweetness of early summer to the darkness of deepest winter. As medicine for the soul, there are few drugs as efficacious as a cup of herbal tea taken before the fire. My own approach to these beverages is largely sensual and associative. I enjoy infusions that remind me of a summer walk, an afternoon in an orchard, an hour spent in a spice market in a foreign country.

I have not explored the aspect of the open hearth that linked foods with medicine. For those of you interested in brewing potions, I cannot recommend too highly the encyclopedic, yet highly readable, *A Modern Herbal* by Mrs. Maude Grieve. This two-volume book was first published in 1931, and is in print. As of this writing, it is also online. Mrs. Grieve provides the folk history, cultivation requirements, culinary uses, and medicinal qualities, including instructions for preparing infusions, of a large number of plants. In the time of the open hearth, most households maintained both a kitchen garden and a medicinal garden, with a few plants, such as thyme, having a place in both.

The Fire: A mature fire with gentle to moderate flames.

To simmer water: Some teas are infused by steeping in hot water, and others by being simmered. Start either method by simmering water in a covered saucepan or in a teakettle set 2 to 4 inches (5 to 10 cm) from the fire, either on the hearth or next to the fire in the firebox. It takes 10 to 12 minutes to bring 2 to 4 cups (500 ml to 1 l) of water to a simmer. For detailed instructions, please see Boiling, page 256. Once the water is simmering, either add the ingredients to the saucepan or kettle and continue simmering or remove from the heat and pour the hot water into a teapot along with the selected herb. Set the teapot by the fire to stay warm while the tea steeps. See individual recipes for specific directions.

Canela: Cinnamon *(Cinnamomum zeylanicum)* is the bark of a tropical tree. In Mexico, where canela is often a daily drink, it is credited with the qualities of a general tonic. For 4 servings, put 12 inches (30 cm) cinnamon stick in 5 cups (1.25 l) water. Simmer for 45 to 60 minutes until a rich, red tea is created. While simmering, add water as needed to maintain the original level. Canela is always served with milk and sugar. Per cup: 3-inch (7.5-cm) piece cinnamon stick.

Chamomile: Into the early twentieth century, chamomile tea was taken only as a medicine. My paternal grandmother was so traumatized by a childhood of being served chamomile tea to cure ills, that many years ago when I asked for a cup at her house after having just discovered the drink at college, she recoiled in horror, as if I had asked for a cup of motor oil. My grandmother's dread notwithstanding, chamomile tea has a reputation for settling an unsettled stomach and tastes so good that it is a pleasure to drink even when all is well. Steep 1 teaspoon per cup for 10 minutes in a teapot of hot water set beside the fire. Serve with honey.

Dried fruits: Infusions made with dried fruits release the warm scent-laden air of ripening orchards into the soft light of the autumn and winter fire. Per cup: 1 bouquet dried wild strawberries, 4 dried apple rings, 6 dried cherries. Gently simmer for 5 minutes before serving through a strainer.

Thyme: In regions of southern Europe where a particularly pungent strain of *Thymus vulgaris* grows wild in the mountains, many people use it in their everyday cooking and also as a daily tonic. Thyme tea goes particularly well with honey. Plant two dozen thyme plants in your garden to develop your own supply of dried sprigs for the winter. Steep 1 teaspoon dried or 2 or 3 fresh or dried sprigs per cup, for 10 minutes in a teapot of hot water set beside the fire. Serve with honey.

INGREDIENTS

General Guidelines

1 to 3 teaspoons herbs
  or spices per cup

3 or 4 pieces dried
  fruit per cup

Milk or sugar (optional)

Sage

Thyme

Spiced Coffees of Africa and Arabia

BASIC METHOD
Pot Buried in Ash

EQUIPMENT

Cezve, jebena
   or any small metal
   coffeepot

Small metal or ceramic
   bowl or plate tongs
   for burning incense
   (optional)

Thin-gauge aluminum
   frying pan or
   saucepan with long
   handle and wicker
   mat for roasting
   beans (optional)

Shovel

PRIMARY VENUE
Firebox

ALTERNATE VENUES
Barbecue

Campfire

FROM ARABIA, NORTH Africa, and Ethiopia, the mythic home of coffee, comes a legion of coffee-transforming flavors that remains largely regional in practice. Dried ginger, pepper, cardamom, cinnamon, clove, coriander, rose water—these are ingredients that augment coffee's qualities, and that evoke the romance of the exotic, returning us to one of coffee's first attractions. European coffee culture adopted sugar as a coffee additive, but of the spices, only cardamom was embraced, and that largely by the Swedes. Mexico developed a taste for cinnamon, but for the most part, the world of spiced coffee remains unexplored outside of Africa and Arabia.

Spiced coffees are wonderful. They are wonderful if you live in the desert where heat flattens out flavor, and they are wonderful where the snow reaches to the horizon. A shot of sweet pepper coffee served with gingerbread in front of the fire on a snowy or rain-swept afternoon wakes you, and warms you, as no other dessert can.

The Arabic coffeepot has a distinctive flared base. The shape was developed in the fifteenth century for brewing coffee in hot sand or hot ash, and the now-classic pot, known as a *cezve*, is still used throughout North Africa, Arabia, Turkey, Greece, and up through central Europe into Russia. Well into the late 1980s, many cafés in Moscow brewed coffee to order in a single-cup *cezve* heated in a thermostatically controlled box of hot sand.

At its best, a *cezve* slowly heated in sand or ash brews a cup of coffee that reveals the nuance of bean and roast. To this day, many coffee lovers in Arabia and Africa roast their beans just before brewing. In the Horn of Africa, the roasting of the beans, the pounding, the brewing, the burning of frankincense, and, finally, the serving is a daily ritual that brings together family and friends.

In traditional coffee-making ceremonies, details are everything. The shape of the pot; the bean; the roast; the degree to which the beans are pounded or ground; the spicing; the sugar, salt, or butter that might be added; the details of the boiling; the incense, if any; the cup that is used; the way in which the coffee is poured into the cup; the order and way the cups are presented; the way each cup is held and the coffee drunk; the number of cups that are taken at one sitting—each of these elements, and more, are woven into the meaning of coffee. What I describe here is the basic recipe, and some of the ritual, for coffee as it is usually made in Ethiopia and Eritrea. Although I call for a *cezve* for brewing the coffee, the traditional pot used in Ethiopia and Eritrea is called a *jebena*. It is made of terra-cotta, and has a bulbous base and a narrow neck.

The contemporary fashion in Arabia is to serve coffee in small glasses, but I recommend the more ancient custom of serving it in small, ceramic cups—Chinese teacups are used in the Horn of Africa—as these better suggest the sacredness of the godlike gift of clear thinking promised by an infusion of the roasted ground bean of the African coffee tree.

Cezve

 The Fire: A mature fire with gentle flames for roasting beans, and hot ash for brewing the coffee.

Pound roasted coffee beans (see roasting instructions on the next page if you wish to roast your own beans) in a mortar until you have a mix of coarse and fine grind, or use a grinder for a medium-coarse grind. If using whole spices, pound or grind the selected spice along with the coffee.

Put the water, ground coffee, and ground spice—if it is not already ground with the coffee—into the *cezve*. It should be two-thirds full.

Bring the *cezve* to the hearth and bury the bottom third of the *cezve* in hot ash. Allow 5 minutes for the water to reach a simmer. If the coffee is not heating, remove

INGREDIENTS
(Serves 4)

1 ounce (25 g) roasted Ethiopian or other coffee beans, or 4 heaping demitasse spoons medium-roast, medium-grind coffee, or 1 ounce (25 g) Ethiopian green coffee beans or other green beans

½ cup (120 ml) water

One of the Following Spices:

Seeds from 1 or 2 cardamom pods

6 to 10 peppercorns

5 whole cloves

1 nub dried ginger

½-inch (1-cm) cinnamon stick

About 1 teaspoon sugar for each cup

Frankincense (optional)

the pot from the ash, stir in fresh embers, and rebury the pot. As soon as the coffee begins to simmer, remove the *cezve* from the ash and stir the contents. Following tradition, after this brief cooling, return the *cezve* to the hot ash and repeat the pattern 2 more times. After the third time, let the grounds settle for a few minutes. When the grounds have settled the coffee is ready to be served.

Put sugar to taste in each cup, light the optional incense as described below, pour the coffee through a fine sieve, and serve along with a small spoon. If continuing with the coffee ceremony in the tradition of the Horn of Africa, make coffee 2 more times. Each time, add ½ cup (120 ml) water to the used grounds and brew as described above. The incense, however, is burned only for the first cup.

To roast the beans (optional): Put the green coffee beans in the aluminum pan. You may need to extend the handle by attaching a long stick or dowel. Roast the beans over hot embers or over the flames. Shake the pan as you would for popcorn to roast the beans as evenly as possible and to prevent burning. After a few minutes, the beans will begin to turn from green to yellow to brown. Finally, you will hear them pop as they expand and they will begin to smoke. The beans are done when they have plumped out and have reached the color you like, from light brown to black.

Pull the smoking pan away from the fire and, still shaking the pan, bring the beans near to each guest so they may breathe in the smoke. Pour the beans onto the wicker mat to cool before grinding.

To light the incense (optional): Using the tongs, remove a few embers from the fireplace and place them in the bowl. Drop a few pieces of incense on the embers. The incense should only burn for a few minutes.

Variations: An old Ethiopian and Eritrean tradition calls for adding salt to taste in place of sugar, while a modern practice calls for adding a pinch or two of salt along with the sugar. In North Africa, rather than adding spices to coffee, it is often served with a few drops of rose water in each cup.

Coffee with Chicory

. . . and one of the blessings of peace has been the disappearance of the various brews which we had to drink out of politeness, but which were no more chocolate than an infusion of chicory is Mocha coffee.

JEAN-ANTHELME BRILLAT-SAVARIN, *The Philosopher in the Kitchen*

T O PURISTS, IT IS ANATHEMA. Toasted chicory root, like toasted acorns, dandelion root, or carrot, are coffee adulterants. In time of war, each of these extenders, or substitutes, hints at one or another of coffee's qualities, and brings something of coffee's memory to a cup of hot water. In time of peace and prosperity, even a discreet inquiry about chicory in fine restaurants, or among coffee roasters, is met with horror. Chicory is a facet of culinary culture in which the experts and the people diverge. Toasted ground chicory is sold in grocery stores in many parts of France, and in New Orleans the regional affection for chicory coffee is a remnant of eighteenth-century French influence.

My first taste of coffee was of chicory coffee served by a lockkeeper in northern France. I was eleven years old. It was 1963. We sat around a small kitchen table, and the lockkeeper served all of us coffee, even me. I looked over at my mother. She smiled. I was an adult!

When you feel the need to drink coffee all day—which can happen on the same kinds of days when you start the fire early in the morning—chicory coffee is a good choice. Chicory "extends" coffee by providing flavor, and an even greater blackness, to what would otherwise be a watery cup. But be warned: if the pot is left to sit, too much chicory produces an overpowering bitterness. When you find the right mix of coffee and chicory, you will have created a rich, slightly sweet, lightly caffeinated beverage that you can drink for hours on end.

BASIC METHOD
Pot Beside the Fire

EQUIPMENT
Teakettle
Shovel

PRIMARY VENUES
Firebox
 or Hearth

ALTERNATE VENUES
Barbecue
Campfire

Chicory root

Coffee with Chicory
(continued)

INGREDIENTS

(Serves 2 to 4)

4 cups (1 l) water

2 tablespoons coarsely
  ground French roast
  coffee

1 tablespoon chicory

Milk and sugar
  (optional)

 The Fire: A mature fire with gentle to moderate flames.

If your fireplace is equipped with a crane, hang the teakettle over the fire from the crane. Otherwise, place the kettle 2 to 4 inches (5 to 10 cm) from the fire, either on the hearth or set beside the fire within the firebox. At your discretion, push embers against the base of the kettle where it is nearest the flames. A kettle with 4 to 6 cups (1 to 1.5 l) of water will come to a simmer on the side nearest the flames in 12 to 15 minutes. As soon as the water comes to a simmer, prepare the coffee. Mix the coffee and chicory and make the coffee the way you usually do, such as through a filter or in a French press pot. Alternatively, put the coffee, chicory, and hot water into a teapot warmed on the hearth, stir it, let the coffee settle, and pour through a fine sieve into cups. Offer milk and sugar.

Hot Rum or Brandy

Hot water poured into a shot of rum or brandy, along with a curl of lemon peel and an optional spoonful of honey, is a welcome palliative for the minor aches and pains of colds, and a reliable cure for blue funks, winter's chill, and sleeplessness. It is also virtually mandatory for occasions when one wants to settle in for a long fireside talk. Hearthside drinking is a pleasure all its own, a melding of warmths—the warmth of the fire on your face, the soft warmth of the glass in your hand, and the firewater itself.

 The Fire: A mature fire with gentle to moderate flames to heat the water, and a blazing fire for ambience.

Place the kettle 2 to 4 inches (5 to 10 cm) from the fire, either on the hearth or set beside the fire within the firebox. At your discretion, push embers against the base of the kettle where it is nearest the flames. A kettle with 2 to 4 cups (475 ml to 1 l) of water will come to a simmer on the side nearest the flames in 10 to 12 minutes.

Put the lemon peel into a cup or glass. Add the hot water and rum, stir, and serve. If using honey, mix it with a little water in the bottom of the glass first before proceeding with the recipe. If you have a sore throat, add the lemon juice.

BASIC METHOD
Pot Beside the Fire

EQUIPMENT
Teakettle
Shovel

PRIMARY VENUES
Firebox
    or Hearth

ALTERNATE VENUES
Barbecue
Campfire

INGREDIENTS
(Per person)

⅔ cup (150 ml)
    hot water

1 curl lemon peel,
    yellow part only

2 tablespoons rum
    or brandy

1 teaspoon honey
    (optional)

Squeeze of lemon juice
    (optional)

Indian Chai

BASIC METHOD
Hearthside Tripod

EQUIPMENT
Saucepan with lid
Tripod
Shovel

PRIMARY VENUE
Hearth

ALTERNATE VENUES
Barbecue
Campfire

Sharod

INDIAN MILK TEA, OR *chai,* is a sweet smooth drink, often lightly spiced with ginger or cardamom. It is appropriate to the heat of the Indian tropics and to the cold of the Indian Himalayas, and a pot of it is often my hearthside companion. In India, *chai* is at the center of hospitality customs. More than once when I have been invited to tea, a child has been sent out to milk the cow. *Chai* provides the kind of energy—both quick and sustained—that helps rebuild spirits made tired by a day working in the fields. *Chai* is the Indian drink of life.

When I first made this tea for an English friend, he did his best to remain relaxed, but he couldn't help mentioning that his mother had impressed upon him the overriding importance of never stewing tea. He need not have said a thing. As the tea merrily boiled, his face, and the stiff way he was sitting, told the story. As delicious as it is, Indian milk tea, a mélange of tea, milk, water, sugar, and spices, is always boiled, thus viewed from the English teapot, it is always ruined tea.

But exactly how long should the tea be boiled? There is no programmatic answer. Indian tea is not Arabic coffee with its prescribed rules. Boil the tea until you feel it is ready. For some, this means a superficial boiling. For others, it is boiled even to the point of being reduced. Which path to follow? Here is the advice of Sharod, a Rajasthani who, for thirty years, has sat crosslegged from morning until night in front of a small burner making tea at his tea stall: "Tea and ladies are brothers, equal. Boil boil boil boil boil! Loving loving loving loving loving! Ladies cold, no loving! Ladies hot, I kiss! Cold water, cold milk, tea, sugar—no interest. 'Lady, come here my bed.' 'Oh, oh, stop!' Boil boil boil boil boil!" So, how long to boil the tea? How ready, how boiling, do you want your lover?

 The Fire: A mature fire with gentle to moderate flames.

Put all the ingredients in the covered saucepan. Put the pan on the hearthside tripod so the pan sits within 4 to 6 inches (10 to 15 cm) of the fire. Push embers against the base of the pan where it is nearest the flames. In about 5 minutes, the tea nearest the heat will simmer. Lift the pan and shovel a thick layer of embers under and around the tripod. Replace the pan. In 2 to 3 minutes, the *chai* will boil. Remove the lid and maintain the pan at a simmer or low boil for 3 to 10 minutes, depending on your mood. If the *chai* begins to foam over, remove from the tripod, give it a swirl, and set back on the tripod to continue boiling. Remove from the heat and pour through a strainer into small cups to serve.

INGREDIENTS
(Serves 4)

¾ cup (175 ml) water

½ cup (120 ml) milk

1 scant teaspoon Darjeeling tea

1 tablespoon sugar

3 nubs fresh ginger, each the size of a thumb's first joint, crushed, or 1 cardamom pod, crushed

Mulled Wine

When Gawain had gazed on that gay lady,
With leave of her lord, he politely approached;
To the elder in homage he humbly bows;
The lovelier he salutes with a light embrace.
He claims a comely kiss, and courteously he speaks;
They welcome him warmly, and straightway he asks
To be received as their servant, if they so desire.
They take him between them; with talking they bring him
Beside a bright fire; bade then that spice
Be freely fetched forth, to refresh them the better,
And the good wine therewith, to warm their hearts.

ANONYMOUS, *Sir Gawain and the Green Knight*

FIRE, SPICES, WINE, AND WARM HEARTS are the four corners of the world of mulled beverages. While tropical spices are no longer the exotic ingredients they were when *Sir Gawain and the Green Knight* was written, the scene described in the fourteenth-century poem is one of timeless temptation: a beautiful woman, a bright fire, a plate of aromatic spices, and a bottle of wine.

Mulled wine traces an unbroken lineage from Rome through medieval Europe to the cafés of Paris, where *vin chaud* is a standard of the café menu. Long considered a medicinal beverage to counter the effects of a cold, you may with clear conscience rest on folk wisdom to support the belief that drinking mulled wine is a winter duty.

There can never be a definitive mulling recipe. To mull is to improvise. The whole panoply of spices is open to you, along with the full range of brewed and fermented beverages—cider, pale ale, brown ale, white wine, red wine, mead, port, champagne. I recommend sweetening with honey because honey, particularly the darker varieties, contributes to melding the flavors of beverage and spice to create a warmer, more nuanced drink. Alcohol evaporates at a lower temperature than water, so the hotter you heat the beverage, and the longer you mull it, the less alcohol there will be when you start drinking. Keeping this in mind, neither simmer nor boil. When it is hot, drink! I include three mulling methods: mulling in a saucepan beside the fire, mulling with a hot poker, and mulling with a spice concentrate.

Serve in individual glasses, but, when appropriate, remember that, between both lovers and comrades, the ancient tradition of passing the cup from hand to hand and lip to lip, is still observed.

 The Fire: A mature fire for embers and a roaring fire for ambience.

Basic mulling: Put all of the ingredients except the rose water in the medium-sized covered saucepan. Place the pan 4 to 6 inches (10 to 15 cm) from the fire, either on the hearth or set beside the fire within the firebox. Push embers against the base of the pan where it is nearest the flames. Stir the wine to distribute the heat. When hot enough to drink, remove from the hearth, add the optional rose water, strain into cups, and serve.

Mulling with an iron poker: Put all of the ingredients except the rose water into the narrow pitcher. Place a poker in the hottest part of the fire until it glows red. Remove from the fire and use it to stir the beverage. If the poker is covered with ashes, knock them off before stirring. Repeat until the beverage is hot enough to drink, add the optional rose water, strain into cups, and serve. The more massive the poker, the more heat it stores, and the faster the mulling. Expect to heat the poker between 4 and 6 times.

Two-step mulling: Employ this method if you want to develop fully the flavor and aroma of the spices. Put 1 cup (250 ml) water and the spices in the small covered saucepan on the hearthside tripod. Shovel a thick layer of embers underneath. The water will boil in about 5 minutes. Remove the cover and continue boiling, adding fresh embers as needed, until the water is reduced by half. Remove the pan from the tripod and shovel the embers back into the fireplace. Use this spice concentrate in place of the spices in Basic mulling or in Mulling with an iron poker, above.

INGREDIENTS
(Serves 4)

1 bottle (750 ml) red wine

2 to 3 tablespoons honey

1 teaspoon ground cinnamon

1 teaspoon whole cloves

2 tablespoons diced candied ginger

2 pinches of coarsely ground pepper

2 teaspoons dried orange peel

1 teaspoon rose water (optional)

Bob carried in his left hand one of those iron models of sugar-loaf hats, before mentioned, into which he emptied the jug, and the pointed end of which he thrust deep down into the fire, so leaving it for a few moments while he disappeared and reappeared with three bright drinking-glasses. Placing these on the table and bending over the fire, meritoriously sensible of the trying nature of his duty, he watched the wreaths of steam, until at the special instant of projection he caught up the iron vessel and gave it one delicate twirl, causing it to send forth one gentle hiss. Then he restored the contents to the jug; held over the steam of the jug each of three bright glasses in succession; finally filled them all and with a clear conscience awaited the applause of his fellow creatures.

CHARLES DICKENS, *Our Mutual Friend*

Lamb's Wool

OB, OF DICKENS'S SIX JOLLY PORTERS, uses a specialized
English tool for mulling his beverage: an iron cone that he thrusts
into hot embers and then into the drink to heat it. For Bob, the
mulling cone is both a practical tool and a theatrical prop to bring an additional quotient of ostentatious display to his presentation of the mulled
beverage—a move that will, presumably, increase his tips. However, despite
the comedy of the scene, Dickens gets at something that I think is true:
mulled beverages lend themselves to presentations that emphasize the mys-
tical in alcohol and the magic of a ritual activity.

Mulling cones are extremely wonderful tools, not least because, as
Dickens noticed, they are the source of a gentle and very satisfying hiss
when the first drink is poured. They are useful for mulling, and also for boiling water, which was their primary purpose on the medieval hearth. A copper mulling cone is an easy commission from a metal shop. The cone
illustrated here dates from the reign of King George III. It is five inches
(13 cm) in diameter at the top, and nine inches (23 cm) long. The handle is
made of iron. If you commission a mulling cone, before using it, have the
interior tinned, as for copper saucepans.

I present here a particularly smooth and warm mulled ale called lamb's
wool. It is a sweetened spiced ale that includes either the pulp of roasted
apples or, more traditionally, roasted crab apples floating in the drink, as in
Shakespeare's song from *Love's Labour's Lost.*

> *And sometime lurk I in a gossip's bowl,*
> *In very likeness of a roasted crab,*
> *And when she drinks, against her lips I bob*
> *And on her wither'd dewlap pour the ale.*

Lamb's wool is the drink that by tradition goes into the wassail bowl
on Twelfth Night, but it is also a drink to be enjoyed by the autumn and
winter fire with friends. Brown ale makes the most deeply flavored lamb's
wool, but any beer with body will do.

BASIC METHOD
Pot Beside the Fire

EQUIPMENT
Aluminum foil
Saucepan with lid

PRIMARY VENUES
Firebox or Hearth

ALTERNATE VENUES
Barbecue
Campfire

Lamb's Wool
(continued)

INGREDIENTS

(Serves 4)

6 crab apples, each
studded with 1 whole
clove, or 3 small
apples, cored and
each studded with
1 whole clove

1 quart (1 l) brown ale

5 tablespoons (100 g)
honey

½ teaspoon ground
cinnamon

½ teaspoon ground
allspice

Freshly grated nutmeg,
for garnish

The Fire: A mature fire with gentle flames to roast the apples and mull the ale, and a blazing fire to drink it by.

Place the apples on aluminum foil (to catch the drippings) on the edge of the hearth. Turn the apples as they begin to cook, moving them back from the fire if they begin to burn. The apples are done when they are soft all the way through, with pulp leaking out of at least one crack in the skin. This should take 15 to 20 minutes.

Leave crab apples whole, but quarter small apples. Put the apples, ale, honey, cinnamon, and allspice in the saucepan and cover. Place the covered saucepan in the firebox with one side 2 to 4 inches (5 to 10 cm) from the fire. The mixture is ready when it just begins to simmer on the side nearest the flames, 10 to 15 minutes. Pour into a bowl warmed on the hearth. To serve, ladle into glasses and include a piece of apple, or a whole crab apple, in each glass. Garnish each serving with a pinch of nutmeg.

Coffee and Bread

B READ BROKEN INTO A BOWL of sugared café au lait is the breakfast of millions in Europe and South America. It is an economical meal, a quick way to make cereal, and a good use for stale bread. It is the perfect breakfast to eat standing up before rushing to work.

But it also can be a breakfast suited to quite a different morning—to a lazy, cozy morning before the fire. In a robe, sitting by the hearth reading the newspaper, a new fire dancing in the fireplace, the warmth of orange light on face and arms, a bowl of café au lait with a dozen torn pieces of bread, the coffee sipped, the bread eaten with a spoon—a winter dawn becomes a welcome morning.

The best water temperature for making coffee is water that is just below the simmer. This is the temperature of the water called for in this recipe. It brews a cup with the fullest, richest taste.

 The Fire: A moderately mature fire with moderate flames.

Prepare the water for the coffee and the milk at the same time. Put the water in a covered saucepan and put the pan 2 to 4 inches (5 to 10 cm) from the fire, either on the hearth or set beside the fire in the firebox. Push embers against the base of the saucepan where it is nearest the flames. In about 10 minutes, the water nearest the heat will simmer, at which point it is ready to be used. Put the milk in the other covered saucepan and push the pan to within 4 to 6 inches (10 to 15 cm) of the fire. As soon as the milk begins to simmer on the side closest to the flames, stir the milk to distribute the heat. When the milk is hot, but not fully simmering, pull the saucepan back a little from the fire to keep it warm.

Once the milk and water are both hot, make the coffee the way you usually do, such as through a filter or in a French press pot. Alternatively, with the saucepan off the heat, you may stir the ground coffee into the water and let it sit for 2 minutes before proceeding to the next step. Shovel the embers back into the fireplace.

When the coffee and milk are both ready, pour half the coffee and half the milk into each of 2 small bowls. If the coffee was made in a saucepan, pour it through a fine sieve. Add sugar to taste and serve with the bread. The bread is broken into the bowl, allowed to become soggy, and then eaten with a spoon.

BASIC METHOD
Pot Beside the Fire

EQUIPMENT
2 small saucepans
  with lids
Shovel
Coffee-making
  equipment such as
  filter, French press
  pot, or fine sieve

PRIMARY VENUES
Firebox or Hearth

ALTERNATE VENUES
Barbecue
Campfire

INGREDIENTS
(Serves 2)

6 tablespoons freshly
  ground French roast
  coffee
2 cups (500 ml) water
2 cups (500 ml) milk
Sugar (optional)
2 to 4 thick slices *pain
  de campagne* or
  other coarse country
  bread

Tea

BASIC METHOD
Pot Beside the Fire

EQUIPMENT
2 teakettles
Pot holder

THE TEA SERVICE
2 teapots
Teacups with saucers
Tea spoons
Milk pitcher
Sugar bowl with spoon
  or tongs
Butter and butter knife
Jam pot with spoons
Serving plate for toast
  or toast rack
Plates
Napkins

And a tray was soon brought. How pretty, to my eyes, did the china and the teapot look, placed on the little round table by the fire! How fragrant was the steam of the beverage, and the scent of the toast!

CHARLOTTE BRONTË, *Jane Eyre*

TEA AND TOAST! The English flirted with coffee in the seventeenth century, but by the end of the eighteenth century, tea had won the field as England's stimulant of choice. As the English adopted tea, they also transformed it, married it to toast, brought it into the pattern of the day, and created a beverage, and a private daily domestic ritual, that has survived three hundred years of radical social change. It is only in the past few years that tea and its rituals have come under challenge—by coffee, which is once again finding a welcome home on the English side of the channel.

English tea is tea with milk, a combination that has been adopted in one form or another by England's former colonies—India, Kenya, Australia, New Zealand, America—but that stands outside the bounds of the two great tea-drinking cultures of China and Japan, in which the flavor of tea is rarely merged with other ingredients. By contrast, English afternoon tea is less about subtleties of taste than about the comfort and power of the routines surrounding its consumption. There is an essential truth about rituals, including domestic ones: they stop and then control time. English teatime stands outside of clock time. Each family has its own talismanic implements that are part of the essential office of tea: the sugar tongs, toasting fork, teapot, toast rack, tea spoons, teacups.

Every household tea ritual has its own nuances. I grew up seven thousand miles from England, in the shadow of the English tea tradition. Every weekday afternoon at four o'clock I had tea with my mother; it was her way of keeping in touch with her teenage son. The setting itself was informal, the breakfast room, but the tea was always set up before we began, and the pastry fresh. English tea-serving custom can be very precise. For example, among several of my English and Indian friends, the milk must be poured into the cup first, the tea second, and sugar, if any, is added last. For them, any departure from this sequence results in a palpable sense of discomfort. The arbitrariness of social custom is something that is easy to laugh at, but in the end, what, besides these apparently arbitrary social customs, links us to our lives?

In nineteenth-century English literature, hearthside tea stands for normality—safety, home, family, friends—which is why one of the most poignant literary teas is that of Dr. Jekyll on the night of his death. Along with the odor of sweet almonds that could be detected near his still-warm body, Dr. Jekyll's pursuers found all the components of the domestic happiness he had forsaken through his malignant quest—the hearth fire, the singing teakettle, and the implements set out for tea. Woe unto us who turn from life's simple pleasures.

PRIMARY VENUES
Firebox or Hearth

ALTERNATE VENUES
Barbecue
Campfire

INGREDIENTS
(Serves 6)

6 cups (1.5 l) water

7 teaspoons leaf tea such as Assam, Darjeeling, English breakfast, or black currant

Milk or lemon (optional)

Sugar (optional)

 The Fire: A mature fire with gentle to moderate flames to heat the water, a cheerful fire while drinking the tea.

If your fireplace is equipped with a crane, hang 1 teakettle over the fire from the crane, and place one beside the fire. Otherwise, place both kettles 2 to 4 inches (5 to 10 cm) from the fire, either on the hearth or set beside the fire within the firebox. At your discretion, push embers against the base of the kettles where they are nearest the flames. A kettle with 4 to 6 cups (1 to 1.5 l) of water will come to a simmer on the side nearest the flames in 12 to 15 minutes.

While the water is heating, set a table for tea in front of the hearth and prepare the toast (see English Toast, page 182).

When the water is hot, fill both teapots with water. Add tea to one of the teapots and set it on the hearth near the fire to stay warm while it brews. Place the other teapot by the fire to stay warm. The water in this second teapot will be used to dilute cups of tea that might be too strong and to add water to the first teapot to make a second round. After the tea has steeped for 10 minutes, remove the teapot to the table and serve the tea through a strainer.

Caudles and Possets

BASIC METHOD

Pot Beside the Fire
   or Boiling

EQUIPMENT

Saucepan (with lid for
   caudle)

Tripod for caudle

Shovel

I do wish he would try a hot posset of a night,
just before going to bed.

ANTHONY TROLLOPE, *Charming Fellow*

THE DAMP COLD OF ENGLAND, Wales, and Scotland produced a huge repertoire of mulled beverages, including some, like
egg-thickened ales, sweetened spiced alcoholic gruels, and sweetened, spiced alcoholic whey, that could substitute for meals. Over
the centuries, fashion and changing habits have brought one or
another mulled beverage to the fore, but in general, all mulled
beverages have fallen into disuse, and none more so than beverages
that can double as meals-in-a-cup.

Caudles, or sweetened gruels, and possets, or sweetened whey, have a
seven-hundred-year history in English literature. I do not pretend that these
recipes, no matter how declarative the presentation, are singularly definitive.
There is no single recipe for either drink. Over the course of centuries, each
has undergone substantive changes in character, and even existed side by side
in very different forms. What I can say is that the recipes presented here are
very good, have an authentic English tradition on their side, and are an
excellent basis on which to begin your own experiments.

In Shakespeare's plays, the caudle was out of favor as a social drink—
it was banished to the sickroom as a medicine—but possets were enjoyed by
many of his characters as an evening drink. A posset spiked with Lady
Macbeth's poison was nearly the nightcap-of-undoing for Duncan's guards.
I can personally attest that when sleep is hard to find, a posset—minus the
poison—makes a lovely late-night drink. The first step in making a posset
is to heat milk, and then to curdle it with alcohol. Hamlet's father, in
describing how he was killed by the henbane that was poured into his ear,
says that it "posseted his blood." When my wife wakes to noises in the
kitchen, it is often me making a posset.

Caudles range from a drink slightly thickened by water strained of boiled grains to the recipe included here, which is a sweetened, spiced alcoholic porridge that is a meal in itself. Drink the caudle in front of a roaring fire when the cold has sapped your strength, then take a nap. All will be well.

 The Fire: A mature fire with gentle to moderate flames.

To make posset: Put the milk, honey, and spices in the saucepan. Put the pan near the fire and bring slowly to a simmer on the side closest to the flames. Stir to distribute the heat evenly. When the milk is at a simmer, pull the pan away from the fire, add the alcohol, and stir once. Taste for sweetness. Pour the now-curdled milk through a strainer into 2 serving glasses. When making a quantity of posset, reserve the curds for a pastry filling.

To make caudle: Put the water in the covered saucepan. Put the pan on the tripod set on the hearth so it sits within 4 to 6 inches (10 to 15 cm) of the fire. Push embers against the base of the saucepan where it is nearest the flames. In about 10 minutes, the water nearest the heat will simmer. Lift the saucepan and shovel a thick layer of embers under and around the tripod. Replace the saucepan. In 2 to 3 minutes, the water will boil. Add the oats in a thin stream. Stir occasionally to keep the oats from sticking. As long as the oats simmer on the side closest to the heat, it is not necessary to refresh the embers under the pan. When the oats are tender, 30 to 40 minutes, add the spices, honey to taste, and the brandy. Shovel the embers back into the fireplace and serve the caudle in 2 large cups.

INGREDIENTS
(Each recipe serves 2)

Posset

2 cups (475 ml) milk

2 rounded teaspoons honey

8 whole cloves, ground

½-inch (1-cm) cinnamon stick, ground

1 cup (250 ml) wine

Caudle

2 cups (475 ml) water

6 tablespoons (25 g) cracked or rolled oats

4 whole cloves, ground

1 nub fresh ginger the size of a thumb's first joint, finely grated, or ¼ teaspoon powdered ginger

Honey

¼ cup (60 ml) brandy

Chocolate

BASIC METHOD

Pot Beside the Fire

EQUIPMENT

1 medium-sized
    saucepan with lid

1 small saucepan
    with lid if making
    Mayan chile
    chocolate, and
    without lid if
    making French
    chocolate

Molinillo
    (a carved
    wooden tool
    for whipping
    chocolate)
    or whisk (optional)

Tripod

Shovel

*When sugar, cinnamon and cacao are joined with the delicious aroma of
vanilla, one reaches the highest point of perfection to which this drink can
be brought.*

JEAN-ANTHELME BRILLAT-SAVARIN, *The Philosopher in the Kitchen*

OURS IS NOT THE FIRST AGE OF scientific achievement, innovation, and culinary experimentation. There have been others, including the Baroque period, a golden age for European culture, an age of exploration flush with new scientific ideas, new art, and new foods. This was a period when the entire cuisine of Europe was turned upside down. It wasn't a matter of just a few foods moving into the fringes of cuisine—a shiitake mushroom here, a packet of tofu there—but rather a period of culinary transformation on a scale that is hard to imagine even on a time frame of two hundred years.

Among the Maya, and in the court of Motecuhzoma, the Spanish found chocolate in the form of a sophisticated drink that was prepared in many different ways with many different flavorings. It could be a cold drink, or a hot one. It could be sweet, or savory. One of the flavorings that was often added to Mayan and Aztec chocolate was dried chile, of which the Maya and Aztecs had many varieties. When the Spaniards were offered chocolate with chile they drank and felt as if they were floating. Their eyes sparkled. This was amazing! And it still is. The first of the three recipes included here is one for unsweetened chocolate and chile. Take a risk. Try it.

While the sweet, hot, and richly flavored chocolate drinks the Spanish introduced to Europe constituted a more limited approach to making chocolate-based beverages than the ones they encountered in their voyages of conquest, the chocolate drinks of the European aristocracy circa 1650 were significantly more dynamic than the ones we know today.

The Spanish introduced hot chocolate into Europe in the form of a concept that could be, and was, incorporated into a culinary culture of astonishing courage and vitality. Flavoring chocolate was often a competitive game between cooks. In addition to pepper in the form of long pepper (*Piper longum*), cooks drew upon a wide range of herbs, spices, fruits, and flowers to flavor chocolate including anise, ambergris, jasmine, nutmeg, rose petals, vanilla, annote, and citrus. Hot chocolate was a richly flavored and scented drink up until the spread of French court cuisine in the late eighteenth century. The practice of making complex chocolate remained current in America, even into the early nineteenth century through the long-popular *The Art of Cookery Made Plain and Easy*, by Hannah Glasse. The second chocolate recipe is based on one from the Spanish court of the seventeenth century. Take it as a place to start freeing your mind and palate of a lifetime of thinking about hot chocolate as a drink for children.

As an institution, the French court set itself the task of moving civilized life forward a notch, which, when it came to food, meant a war on spices and strong flavors. In their defense, as someone who seldom enjoys foods that are buried in a muddle of flavors, I admire the spirit of their quest to simplify hot chocolate, to strip away the Baroque flavorings so that the chocolate could speak for itself, even as I am amazed that this eighteenth-century reform solidified so thoroughly into convention that it is only now, two centuries later, that we are beginning to see experiments with putting back in some of those flavorings. The French developed a simple chocolate recipe, the one that is still used by all premium chocolate makers: cacao, sugar, and a very mild flavoring, vanilla.

When it came to hot chocolate, the *ancien régime* was partial to one additional flavoring, cinnamon, an affection that carried into the early part of the nineteenth century and is reflected in Brillat-Savarin's effusive praise

Chocolate
(continued)

INGREDIENTS

Mayan Chile Chocolate
(Serves 2)

1½ ounces (45 g) unsweetened chocolate

2 cups (500 ml) water

1-inch (2.5-cm) piece dried cayenne chile or other dried hot chile

Spanish Baroque Chocolate
(Serves 4)

3 ounces (90 g) unsweetened chocolate

1 quart (1 l) water or milk

1 vanilla bean, split lengthwise

6-inch (15-cm) cinnamon stick

24 whole cloves

1 teaspoon aniseeds

1 teaspoon dried orange peel

1 teaspoon annatto seeds (optional)

4 tablespoons sugar

quoted at the beginning of these recipes. For the third recipe, I merge the customs of the eighteenth and the twenty-first centuries. Parisian cafés sell a fabulous hot chocolate—sinfully rich would not be out of place as a qualifier—under the name *chocolat ancien.* A waiter brings to the table a pitcher of melted chocolate along with a pitcher of hot milk, and you mix them to suit your taste. My recipe blends this modern service—industrially refined chocolate and milk, rather than hand-processed chocolate and water—with the *ancien régime's* flavorings of vanilla and cinnamon. The result is a cup of hot chocolate that achieves the highest standards a cup of hot chocolate can achieve, or in Brillat-Savarin's actual words, *"Le ne plus ultrà de la perfection à laquelle cette préparation peut être portée."*

 The Fire: A mature fire with gentle to moderate flames.

Mayan Chile Chocolate: Place the chocolate, water, and piece of chile in the small covered saucepan. Put the pan on the hearth 4 to 6 inches (10 to 15 cm) from the fire. Push embers against the base of the pan where it is nearest the flames. As the chocolate melts, stir to mix. Maintain the chocolate at a simmer on the side nearest the fire for 15 minutes. When done, pour through a sieve into a pitcher and let the chocolate cool. Optionally, just before serving, use a *molinillo* or a whisk to whip up a head of foam. Serve in cups.

Note: *There are many different kinds of chiles, each with their own taste and level of hotness. The spiciness and flavor of this drink is significantly affected by which kind you use.*

Spanish Baroque Chocolate: Put all of the ingredients in the covered saucepan. In the seventeenth century, this chocolate drink was made with water, but you may want to substitute milk. Cook as directed for Mayan chile chocolate, above.

Strain the liquid through a sieve into a pitcher warmed on the hearth. Scrape the seeds from the vanilla bean into the hot chocolate and discard the pods. Taste for sugar. Optionally, just before serving, use a *molinillo* or a whisk to whip up a head of foam. The more cocoa butter in the chocolate, the more easily it creates a head of foam. Serve hot.

French Chocolat Ancien: Place the chocolate and cream in the small saucepan near the fire. As the chocolate begins to melt, stir until it forms a sauce that is both smooth and easily poured. If necessary, add additional cream, 1 tablespoon at a time. Remove from the heat, stir in the sugar, and pour into a small pitcher. Place on the hearth to keep warm, but place it well back from the fire so it doesn't continue to cook.

Place the vanilla, cinnamon, and milk in the larger saucepan and cover. To develop the flavor of the spices, heat the milk slowly by placing the covered saucepan on the tripod positioned 4 to 6 inches (10 to 15 cm) from the fire. Push embers against the base of the saucepan where it is nearest the flames. Stir as the milk begins to heat. In about 12 minutes, the milk nearest the heat will begin to simmer. Just as the milk begins to simmer, remove from the heat. Remove the vanilla bean from the milk, use the tip of a knife to scrape the seeds into the milk, and discard the pods. Remove and discard the cinnamon stick. Pour the chocolate into a pitcher warmed by the hearth. Serve the hot milk along with the melted chocolate in a small pitcher.

French Chocolat
Ancien
(Serves 4)

3 ounces (90 g)
  unsweetened
  chocolate

¼ cup (60 ml) heavy
  cream, plus more
  if needed

4 tablespoons sugar

1 vanilla bean,
  split lengthwise

3-inch (7.5-cm)
  cinnamon stick

1 quart (1 l) milk

*Tripod, French, late eighteenth century,
circa French Revolution*

But Joe had got the idea of a present in his head and must harp upon it. "Or even," said he, "if you was helped to knocking her up a new chain for the front door . . . or some light fancy article, such as a toasting-fork when she took her muffins——or a gridiron when she took a sprat or such like——"

CHARLES DICKENS, *Great Expectations*

REFERENCE

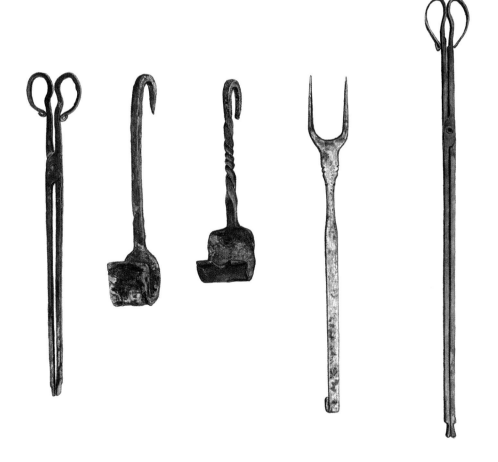

All About the Fireplace

THIS SECTION IS ABOUT THE FIREPLACE, its history, its different parts, how to operate it safely, what kind of preparation is helpful when using a hearth for cooking, what kind of wood to burn, how to light a fire, and something about the three major components of the fireplace fire: flame, embers, and ash.

ANDIRONS AND THE FIRE GRATE

Most fireplaces are equipped with andirons—two iron stands placed parallel to each other and perpendicular to the hearth—or with an iron grate on legs called a fire grate. The purpose of both is to raise the logs up above the fireplace floor so they can be easily lit. Once they are burning, the supports are no longer needed. In fact, logs burn longer, and more steadily, when they are sitting directly on ash. Hearth cooking regularly requires easy access to embers and ash beside and beneath the fire, and also the ability to move food and pots near to the flames. Both andirons and a fire grate, though to different degrees, impede the work of the hearth cook. Because of this, I recommend that you remove them from your fireplace. But, then, how do you light the fire? I suggest using two logs in the manner of andirons. See Lighting the Fire for details.

ASH

Ash has many uses in hearth cooking, and a number of recipes in this book cannot be made without a substantial quantity of ashes. A well-regulated working fireplace has a layer of ash 4 to 6 inches (10 to 15 cm) deep across its floor. The first role of ash is passive. Logs sitting on ash burn more slowly than logs sitting above the ash on andirons or a fire grate, and a slower, more steady burn is desirable for hearth cooking. Ash has other, more direct roles to play. With the aid of a shovel, ash is sprinkled on embers to cool them, distributed to insulate food from intense heat, and mixed with embers to function as a heat sink that can be used like an oven for baking all kinds of foods. Finally, in the traditional practice of hearth cooking, ashes are used each evening to bank the embers of the nighttime fire.

BANKING THE FIRE

Throughout the age of hearth cooking, fires were banked down at night with a layer of ash and rekindled in the morning. In this way, the hearth fire was kept burning for months, and even years, at a time. Wait to bank the fire until the logs have burned down in the late evening and are mostly embers, and then cover them with a few inches of ash (about 7.5 cm). In the morning, dig into the mound of ashes to uncover the glowing embers. Add kindling, and blow the fire to life. A blow stick—a metal rod 4 feet (1.2 m) long and ⅜ inch (9 cm) in diameter—is ideal for this purpose. In my fireplace, twenty-four hours after covering the embers of a hardwood fire with a mound of ash, the ashes will range from 160° to 400°F (70° to 200°C) and will include live embers. The hot ashes can be used for cooking (see Pot Buried in Hot Ash, page 263, and Ash Baking, page 255).

EMBERS

Embers are the workhorse of hearth cooking. They are an explicit component of most of the cooking methods used in this book, and are an important source of the radiant heat that projects onto the hearth—sometimes an even greater source than the flames. Embers are also a portable heat source. They can be moved around within the fireplace or shoveled onto the hearth. They provide a heat source that is scalable. You can heat with one ember or a shovelful, which means that embers provide the hearth cook with a tool for finely regulating the amount of heat applied to a dish.

The most common direct use for embers is on the hearth. As a rule, the first load of embers shoveled under the cooking pot, griddle, or grill brings the cooking utensil up to temperature. The addition of subsequent embers, usually a sprinkling at a time, maintains the cooking utensil at the temperature that cooks the food at precisely the rate you want to cook it. With embers, you are always in control of the process. One reason you have this control is that embers are never hotter than the moment they are shoveled onto the hearth. If you are inattentive when cooking with embers, the only harm done is that they cool and the food takes a little longer to finish. With embers, you work with a pattern of rising and falling temperature. I visualize this as the rise and fall of hilly terrain. When you add embers, think of yourself as pushing the temperature up an imaginary slope to the point you want it. You will find that it is easy to keep the peak temperature from exceeding the top temperature at which you want to cook.

Use common sense when handling embers on the hearth. It is generally safe to shovel embers out of the fireplace onto the third of the hearth closest to the flames, toward the center of the fireplace opening. The recipes in this book call for comparatively small amounts of embers. They are never used on the scale of charcoal in a barbecue, and live flame is never a component of cooking with embers on the hearth.

Glowing embers generate fumes. In a well-maintained, properly designed fireplace, the fumes produced by embers on the hearth are pulled up the chimney by the fire burning in the fireplace. Never burn embers on the hearth unless you have a fire going, and always shovel embers back into the fireplace as soon as you have finished using them for cooking. And, of course, if you feel that it is unsafe to shovel embers onto the hearth, then don't. There are many options for cooking on your hearth that do not require embers being moved from the fireplace. Never do anything in or around your fireplace that you do not know to be safe.

FIRE AND FLAME

Metaphorically speaking, fire is life. More prosaically, in the context of the open hearth, the flame is the first visible product of combustion, the rapid oxidation of wood. In the modern kitchen, cooks with gas ranges do most of their cooking over flame, and when many people think of hearth cooking, they think of a pot hanging over the fire. In practice, unless one is boiling water in a cauldron for a large group of people, no hearth recipe requires placing a cooking vessel over flame. In fact, you almost invariably have more control over the cooking process when you cook over embers and beside the flame than when you cook directly over flame.

I have written this book for people with ordinary fireplaces and standard kitchen equipment who are preparing modest quantities of food for small families or a few guests. Only one recipe, that for a single egg fried in a spoon, calls for cooking over flame. This does not mean that flames are not important in hearth cooking, however. The heat that radiates sideways from the fire to heat the side of a pot is a steady, reliable heat source. This radiant heat (page 264) is one of the principal heat sources used in hearth cooking. Huge meals can be cooked with nothing more than the heat falling on the side of a stockpot (see Pot-au-Feu, page 114). The faster the flames consume the wood, the sooner the wood is turned into embers. As embers are essential for many of the cooking techniques described in this book, flames are often managed to create embers.

FIREBOX

The area enclosed by three walls under the chimney where the fire burns. Many recipes in this book are cooked within the firebox beside the fire, buried in hot ash, or directly on embers.

FIREPLACE AND HEARTH

I arrived in a Tibetan village in Yunnan, China, midmorning. It was a beautiful day—the mountain sky a crisp blue, the air fresh with the hint of approaching winter. It was a classic Tibetan village of elaborately carved and painted wooden houses. Near the peak of each thatched roof smoke rose lazily into the autumn air. It was the smoke coming through the thatch, more than anything else, that gave the day a romantic gloss. In historical terms, it is only recently that the smoke in Europe's thatched-roof cottages began to rise through brick chimneys, rather than lazily through the thatch.

The open hearth of this book is the open hearth of the European fireplace as it was developed in Italy during the Renaissance. It is the basic design, even now, of the fireplaces built in contemporary homes. In Europe, over a period of a few hundred years that began in the eleventh century, the hearth that had been built on the floor of the main room with smoke rising to the ceiling moved toward a wall. Eventually, the hearth was built into the wall itself, under a chimney. By the sixteenth century, the hearth-in-the-wall had become the architectural focus of the room through the influence of Italian Renaissance architects. Functionally, there is no reason why fireplaces are not built flush with the wall. It is to Renaissance architects that we owe the nonfunctional, but aesthetically pleasing, mantle and attendant architectural features.

To be strictly correct, the hearth extends from the back of the firebox, which is the back wall of the chimney, forward, out of the firebox into the room. Masons refer to the portion of the hearth that is inside the firebox as the "inner hearth," and the portion that extends into the room as the "hearth extension." However, in common usage, the hearth extension is called "the hearth" and, for the most part, I employ that usage. In the majority of American houses with fireplaces, the hearth extension is clearly differentiated from the floor in the rest of the room. In Europe, however, many houses have tile floors that come right up to the inner hearth, eliminating any demarcation between where the inner hearth ends and the floor begins.

There are also fireplace parts we cannot see, such as the throat and the smoke chamber. The chimney itself is more than a straight flue to the outside. In fact, it is the extent to which all the interior parts of a fireplace—firebox, throat, smoke chamber, and flue—are working together that determines how much heat is radiated into the room versus how much goes up the chimney.

The most efficient fireplaces are those built on the principles of the brilliant eighteenth-century fireplace designer, Count Rumford. Rumford fireplaces are tall and shallow to reflect more heat, and they have streamlined throats to eliminate turbulence and carry away the smoke with little loss of heated room air. Properly designed, Rumford fireplaces radiate substantial quantities of heat into the room and approach the efficiencies of modern wood stoves.

Any masonry fireplace, regardless of design and size, can be used for cooking. In my opinion, however, the ideal working fireplace is one in which the back wall reflects at least some heat forward into the room, and which has a hearth that projects in front of the firebox 30 to 36 inches (75 to 90 cm) into the room, with a further 6- to 8-inch (15- to 20-cm) separation between the hearth and the start of any carpet. As for width, the wider the fireplace, the more recipes you can prepare at the same time. My own fireplace is 26 inches wide (65 cm). A width of 6 feet (2 m) would be better.

FIREPLACE INSERTS

Many fireplaces have been "modernized" by the addition of a metal box— a wood stove with glass doors. There are many different designs, and to what extent you can use a fireplace with an insert for cooking depends on its design. If you can operate the insert with the doors open, it should be possible to cook with radiant heat by placing a pot in front of the fire on an improvised platform. Roasting on a spit, from a string, or on a stand should also be possible, as should some baking and roasting in the ashes and embers. I am by no means familiar with all fireplace inserts, but I can't think of one I've seen where it would be safe to shovel embers out of the insert onto the hearth.

FIREPLACE PREPARATION

Any masonry fireplace that is in safe working condition—the chimney has been recently swept, the bricks surrounding the firebox are well pointed, the flue damper, if any, is operational—can be used for hearth cooking. Many of the recipes in this book assume that the fireplace floor is covered with at least 4 inches (10 cm) of ash. If you have been in the habit of sweeping out the ashes so the floor is bare, stop! Leave the ashes that are there, and let others accumulate. If you have been using your fireplace as if it were an incinerator—which you never should—then sweep out the contaminated ashes, and start fresh. The hearth-cooking techniques described in this book assume that the fire is built on two logs that function as andirons and that the mature fire is burning directly on the bed of ashes (see Lighting the Fire). Therefore, for the best results in cooking most of the recipes in this book, I suggest removing the andirons or fire grate (see Andirons and the Fire Grate).

FIREPLACE SAFETY

Follow commonsense safety practices. Every fireplace is different, and only you know the particulars of your situation. Do not follow any instruction in this book that you do not regard as a safe practice in your own fireplace. Safety always comes first.

▶ *If you have not had the fireplace and chimney inspected recently—and the chimney swept—do it now, then adopt a regular schedule for sweeping it. If chimney sweeps are not listed in your phone directory, call your local fire department.*

▶ *Burn dry, well-seasoned, untreated wood. Small quantities of newspaper may be used to light the fire.*

▶ *Follow all standard fireplace safety practices, such as keeping combustibles clear of the hearth, never leaving a fire unattended, and so on.*

▶ *Hearth cooking sometimes requires you to work around very hot fires. Consumer-grade oven mitts are not designed for live fire and beds of hot embers. They can—and will—catch fire when used around the hearth. Purchase Kevlar gloves (page 250) for proper protection.*

▶ *See Embers for a discussion of how to use embers safely on the hearth.*

▶ *Deep-frying is a cooking method I would approach on the open hearth cautiously, if at all. On my own fireplace, I have made the judgment never to deep-fry.*

FIRES THAT FAIL TO THRIVE

Assuming that the wood you are burning is dry and well seasoned, and that the flue damper, if any, is open, a fire that smokes or fails to thrive is probably the result of insufficient oxygen in the room to feed the flames. While this might sound improbable, it isn't. Robust fires require substantial quantities of oxygen, and weather-stripped houses may not be able to provide it. The solution to a fire deprived of oxygen is to open a window to provide more air for combustion.

A traditional fireplace in an old house pulls the air for combustion from inside the house. This works well in a drafty house with cracks around doors and windows, but if your old house is well sealed, there may not be enough air-flow to feed the fire. If your fireplace was built in compliance with building codes that consider energy efficiency, it is likely that the air for combustion comes from outdoors. Look for the external air intake where the inner hearth meets the hearth extension, or within the firebox at the base of a sidewall. If the fire isn't thriving, it may be either because the air intake is not big enough for a roaring fire or because it is blocked with ash. The quantity of ash I recommend be retained on the inner hearth floor will block most air intakes.

If lack of oxygen is your fire's problem, opening a window will quickly solve the problem. If it doesn't, call a chimney sweep to inspect your chimney.

FIREWOOD

For the fireplace cook, there is only one important question to ask about firewood: is it hardwood or softwood? Hardwoods burn hotter and longer than softwoods. They also produce embers that are hotter and longer lasting than softwood embers. Hardwoods are always preferred for hearth cooking, and the recipes in this book were all tested with hardwood fires. Green fireplace logs should be aged six to twelve months before burning. Cut and split wood in early summer to burn in the fall and winter. Keep the woodpile in a spot protected from both rain and snow. In English-speaking countries, wood is sold by the cord. A cord is a tightly stacked pile of cut and split firewood measuring 4 by 4 by 8 feet (1.2 by 1.2 by 2.4 m). Wood comes in varying lengths. In my region, firewood is either 16 or 24 inches (40 or 60 cm) long. When you are cooking, you need working room beside the fireplace fire, making 16-inch (40-cm) logs most practical for small fireplaces.

It is helpful to have on hand small-diameter firewood for when you want to create more heat with flame or generate fresh embers quickly. Hardwood, whether logs split into narrow pieces or lengths of small branches, quickly produces excellent embers. Wood must always be dry, well seasoned, and sound. Rotten wood does not produce embers and has no place in a cooking fire.

FLUE DAMPER

Many fireplaces, particularly those built in cold climates, have a damper built into the flue that enables you to regulate the flow of air in the chimney to and from the outside. If your chimney has a damper, be sure you open it before lighting the fire, and be sure you close it again when the fire burns out. During the winter in cold climates, the closed flue damper keeps freezing air from coming into the house when there is no fire in the fireplace.

LIGHTING THE FIRE

If your fireplace has a flue damper (see Flue Damper), be sure it is set to the open position. If you live in a particularly cold climate, after opening the flue, you may need to warm the air in the chimney by burning a few newspapers on top of the wood before you begin to light the wood from underneath. Fires burn more steadily when the mature fire rests directly on the ashes. In order to light the fire, however, the logs must be raised a few inches above the hearth. Using five dry, well-seasoned logs, create the fire as follows: Remove the andirons or fire grate from the fireplace. In their stead, place two logs in the firebox pointing toward the back wall and parallel to each other in the manner of andirons. On top of these log-andirons, place three more logs in the standard triangular formation—two parallel to each other with 1 or 2 inches (2.5 cm or 5 cm) between them and the third log on top. Loosely crumple a piece of uncoated newspaper, push it under the logs, and light it. As the first piece of burning paper reaches its hottest point, slowly add a second loosely crumpled piece to the fire with the goal of maintaining this high heat. Continue until the logs are lit. You know the logs have caught when they continue to flame even after the newspaper fire has died down. Dry, well-seasoned hardwood logs will usually light with one or two pieces of paper. Logs that are still a little green, or wet, or both, will take more pieces, even up to twenty. The illustration on page 13 shows a fire built as I have just described.

If you are not familiar with lighting log fires, the best way to learn is to have a friend teach you. I have also posted step-by-step instructions on my Web site, ***williamrubel.com.***

MANAGING THE FIRE   **For advice on how to approach managing a fire for cooking,** and for the definitions of the terms I use to describe fires, see The Fire (page 16).

Equipment

*Flame, embers,
and ash — these
are the tools of the
historical cuisines.
With these, imagina-
tion, and little else,
you can cook meals
of distinction from
the foods of prehistory
to the present on
your living room
fireplace or on an
outdoor campfire.*

T HE SPIRITUAL CORE OF HEARTH COOKING IS found in the past among the subsistence farmers of Europe, Canada, and America who created fabulous meals with virtually no special-ized equipment, and among the many millions of subsistence farmers in other parts of the world who still cook on wood fires. The basic equip-ment required for this book is minimal. You will find an illustrated list on pages 12 and 13.

The annotated list that follows describes every tool or piece of equipment referred to in this book, even when it is not essential to own it. All of these tools can be purchased (see the supplier information on page 278), plus I provide dimensions for the iron and copper tools referenced most frequently so that you may more easily commission them from a met-alsmith. I have also included an entry on Commissioning Tools, which I hope everyone will read. If you are involved with re-creating period meals—Roman, medieval, Renaissance, colonial American, or some other cuisine—you will inevitably have heard of a tool that is not here. The only tool for which there is no substitute is live fire. Flame, embers, and ash— these are the tools of the historical cuisines. With these, imagination, and little else, you can cook meals of distinction from the foods of prehistory to the present on your living room fireplace or on an outdoor campfire.

The primary method or methods in which each tool or piece of equipment is used follows its name. In Methods (page 254), you will find information on each method, as well as a list of recipes that rely on it.

Aluminum Foil	Grill, Hearthside	Spider
Bricks	Kevlar Gloves	String-Roasting Equipment
Cezve	Mechanical Spit	Terra-cotta Cookware
Commissioning Tools	Mortar and Pestle	Thermometer, Infrared
Cookware	Mulling Cone	Tiles
Crane	Oiled Paper	Tongs, Long-Handled
Dutch Oven with Legs	Pot Chain	Tripod, Hearthside
Fork, Long-Handled	Pot Hook	Tripod, Long-Legged
Griddle, Hearthside	Shovel	

ALUMINUM FOIL

Method in which used:

Steaming, 266

Historically, foods were often wrapped so they could be baked either under a mound of hot ash or on the ashes beside the fire. French cuisine has preserved this hearth technique in the form of baking *en papillote*. Less formally, the method is used every time a potato is wrapped in foil and buried in the coals of the barbecue or campfire. Wrapping foods to bake them beside the fire, or buried in ash, is a practical technique that can be applied to many preparations that we now reserve for the oven. Traditional wrappings include leaves, clay, salt, and edible and inedible flour crusts. Cooks in colonial America used oiled paper to roast pike in the ashes.

Of many possible wrappings, aluminum foil is the one wrapping that I do not specify in this book. The primary reason for this is that aluminum foil, unlike any of the other wrappings, including oiled paper, completely seals foods, so they steam more thoroughly, and thus taste different. One of the purposes of this book is to help readers uncover flavors that are created by forgotten techniques of hearth cooking, and to inspire experiments that will create a dynamic new cuisine of the open hearth. When foil is the only practical choice, use it, but whenever possible, if you must substitute one wrapping for another, select one from among the traditional choices.

Foil makes excellent impromptu lids. The steaming recipes call for the use of foil to fashion covers for molds. I also use foil to cover pots for which I do not own a lid.

BRICKS

Methods in which used:

Hearthside Griddle, 260
Hearthside Grilling, 261
Hearthside Tripod, 262
Pot Beside the Fire, 263

You may use common red bricks set on their broad face to improvise a stand that can be used in place of an iron hearthside tripod as a stand for hearthside cookware. The short height of the brick is roughly the same height as the legs of equipment designed for use on the hearth. Thus, with between two and four bricks, you can improvise a stand for a pot, a griddle, a grill, or a Dutch oven. This may not be the most aesthetic long-term solution to hearth cooking, but with bricks and standard kitchen cookware you can cook virtually any recipe in this book.

Historically, and even today in many parts of the world, three rocks are used as the pot stand. I suggest bricks only because they are easier for most of us to find than river rocks, but I can certainly imagine that some readers will find rocks that would both be functional and look beautiful on the hearth.

CEZVE

Method in which used:

Pot Buried in Hot Ash, 263

The Turkish coffeepot with a flared base is designed for heating coffee in hot sand or ash. The shape is common to a large part of the world, including most of central Europe. Any metal coffeepot that does not have plastic or wooden parts can be used as a substitute. Enamel coffeepots are widely available at camping supply stores.

COMMISSIONING TOOLS

The prime years of open-hearth cookery were also those when every village had a forge. People were accustomed to commissioning the tools they needed, and a fine tool was intended to last a lifetime. Then, as now, fine tools were comparatively expensive, and were given as gifts at the time of marriage and for other special occasions. For wealthier clients, tools were made with great care to be both distinctive and beautiful. Where regions specialized in a particular food—for example, baked apples in Normandy, crêpes in Brittany, mulled beer in

England—specialized tools were developed to facilitate the cooking. In addition to commissioning tools from blacksmiths, more affluent households also commissioned cookware from coppersmiths.

I encourage you to develop your own imaginative commissions. Bringing back the tradition of open hearth cookery also means reinvigorating the tradition of creating tools for your own use. Start with something simple, like a short-legged tripod. Begin with the simplest design. As you and your blacksmith develop confidence in each other, increase the complexity of the commissions. A word of advice: Always work out the details of a commission with the blacksmith or coppersmith before getting your heart set on a particular design to be sure that what you have in mind is practical, and that you can afford it. When working with craftspeople, the personal relationship is everything. Be patient. Few smiths run production shops. It is customary to pay 50 percent down upon placing an order, with the balance due on delivery. In my experience, smiths are always unusually inventive. They can work from a photograph, a book illustration, or a rough sketch.

COOKWARE

Methods in which used:
All methods that call for pots, griddles, or frying pans

You may use the saucepans, griddles, and frying pans from your kitchen in conjunction with a short-legged tripod or bricks. If shopping specially for the hearth, then cookware made of terra-cotta is always my first choice (see Terra-cotta Cookware). My second choice is cast-iron cookware, the heavier the iron, the better. However, I would like to emphasize that there is no need to wait to buy special cookware to begin cooking on your hearth. Aside from a Dutch oven with legs, I use the same assortment of terra-cotta, iron, copper, steel, and aluminum cookware around my hearth that I use in my kitchen.

CRANE

Method in which used:
There is an entry for Crane on page 258 in the methods section although no recipe requires its use.

An iron bracket on a pivot attached to one side of the fireplace, the crane was common in England, which meant it was common in colonial America. A fireplace with a crane to one side is the iconic American image of the open hearth. The height of the cooking pot from the fire is determined by using the crane in conjunction with pot hooks or adjustable trammels. Cooking temperature is then regulated by swinging the crane so the cooking vessel is closer to, directly over, or farther away from the fire. Temperature is also regulated by controlling the heat of the fire itself. Many European fireplaces were equipped with a pot chain, a stationary chain that hung within the chimney over the fire, rather than with a crane.

DUTCH OVEN WITH LEGS

Method in which used:
Dutch Oven, 258

Around 1670, the famous Dutch artist Pieter de Hooch created a beautiful painting of a young woman cooking while sitting on a chair by her hearth. She is depicted using a three-legged terra-cotta pot placed on the hearth near the fire. Her cooking pot is oval. Embers taken from the fireplace are both under the pot and on its lid, which has a lip to hold them. In fact, the young woman is shown with a pair of long-handled tongs in her hand with which she is adjusting embers on the lid. The cooking pot depicted is functionally identical to what we, in America, call a Dutch oven. The only substantive difference between the seventeenth-century version and the modern American one is that the latter, made of cast iron, usually has a handle so it can be hung over the fire.

Modern American Dutch ovens come in many sizes, both round and oval, and can be large enough to roast a turkey. Dutch ovens intended for the hearth, and for campfires, have three short legs, typically 2½ inches (5 cm) high, sides 4 inches (10 cm) high, and a lid with a lip to hold embers. The 5- to 7-quart (5- to 7-l) sizes, whether round or oval, are most appropriate for the hearth. A Dutch oven can be improvised from any saucepan or frying pan with the help of a tripod or bricks and a metal lid that will support embers. I bake the *Tarte Tatin* (page 168) in a standard aluminum kitchen frying pan with an aluminum lid. To raise the frying pan up off the hearth so embers can be shoveled underneath, I use a short-legged tripod, but one could use two bricks.

FORK, LONG HANDLED

Methods in which used:
Ash Baking, 255
Ember Baking, 260
Toasting bread and roasting sausages

A two pronged, long-handled fork, sometimes called a toasting fork, is even more useful around the hearth than it is around a barbecue. The hearth fire can get so hot that it is difficult to get near it. Thus, the longer the handle, the better. The fork is used to remove foods baking under the ash and on embers, for toasting bread, and for roasting foods such as sausages before the flames. Any fork designed for use around the barbecue will work, with the fork having the longest handle being the best choice. A long-handled fork can be improvised by tying a stick or dowel to the handle of a meat fork. Many blacksmiths make toasting forks.

GRIDDLE, HEARTHSIDE

Method in which used:
Hearthside Griddle, 260

Any griddle, whether made of terra-cotta or metal, can be used on the hearth with embers shoveled underneath if it is supported by a short-legged tripod or two common red bricks set on their broad face. The griddle should be held about 2½ inches (6 cm) above the hearth. The thicker the griddle, the easier it is to maintain it at a stable temperature. Griddles also come with handles that permit them to be hung from a crane or pot chain above the fire, although the recipes in this book do not call for such a griddle.

GRILL, HEARTHSIDE

Methods in which used:
Hearthside Grilling, 261
Roasting on a Stand, 266

Eighteenth- and early-nineteenth-century grills designed for use on the hearth over embers were about 11 inches (28 cm) on a side, with legs 2½ inches (6 cm) high, and a long handle. A hearthside grill can be improvised out of two bricks set on their broad face and a small barbecue grill.

KEVLAR GLOVES

Oven mitts designed for use around the kitchen are not intended for use around live fire. The temperatures reached on the open hearth can be much higher than those encountered in the kitchen, and it is sometimes necessary to shield your hands from the heat. Buy a pair of heat- and fire-resistant gloves—these are usually made of Kevlar—from a supplier of industrial safety equipment.

MECHANICAL SPIT

Method in which used:
Spit Roasting, 266

For most of culinary history, when meat was spit roasted, the spit was turned by hand. Children turned spits, so did slaves and serfs. The mechanical spit was one of the first laborsaving devices introduced into the kitchen. By the eighteenth century, there were mechanical spits of various types turned by many different means, including the updraft of the air in the chimney. Clockwork spit motors were manufactured in a variety of sizes. They ranged from powerful motors capable of turning a substantial weight of meat in a large fireplace, to motors for small, portable spits built for cooking one or two chickens or comparably sized roasts on a parlor fire.

All spit roasting takes place on the hearth, in front of the fire. Neither embers nor flames are ever placed under meat roasting on a spit. However, it is not necessary to own a mechanical spit to roast meat on the hearth. Meat can easily be roasted on the end of a looped string or on a stand (see String Roasting, page 267 or Roasting on a Stand, page 266). For more information on spit roasting, see page 266.

MORTAR AND PESTLE

Old ways can be best. Crushing herbs is the best way to develop their flavor. For making my various herb and garlic sauces and my herb stuffings, a mortar and pestle provides the winning combination of quality output and convenience of use. If you don't have a mortar and pestle, use a small food processor, or finely mince the garlic and herbs and add them to the oil or butter in a bowl.

MULLING CONE

Method in which used:
Pot Buried in Hot Ash, 263

In the Middle Ages, water was sometimes boiled in copper cones thrust deep into a bed of hot ash. In the late eighteenth and early nineteenth century, tin-lined copper cones were used in England to mull wine and beer. The cone pictured on page 226 is 5 inches (13 cm) in diameter at the top, 9 inches (23 cm) long, and has an 8-inch (20-cm) iron handle.

OILED PAPER

Methods in which used:
Ash Baking, 255
Ember Baking, 260

Heavy, brown wrapping paper and the paper of brown-paper grocery bags are both ideal. Cut paper into pieces the size you need for the recipe and rub with vegetable oil until saturated. The oil raises the temperature at which the paper burns and also protects the paper from liquids the food may give off when baking. I usually specify wrapping foods in a double layer of oiled paper. For more formal presentations, make the inner wrapping parchment paper and the outer wrapping the more rustic oiled paper.

POT CHAIN

A chain that is hung over the fire from which one can hang a pot or a griddle. Pot chains are popular among campers who suspend pots over the fire from a tripod with 3 foot (1 m) legs. Pot chains were more commonly installed in fireplaces on the European continent than in England or in America, where the crane was popular, although one should assume that a pot chain, or a rope thrown over a rafter, was used in poorer households everywhere.

POT HOOK

Methods in which used:
Dutch Oven, page 258, and any method that can be adapted for use with a crane

Iron pot hooks of different lengths, or adjustable hooks called adjustable trammels, are used in conjunction with cranes or pot chains to control the distance cooking vessels or griddles hang above the fire. I also use a pot hook to lift the lid of the Dutch oven when it is laden with embers. A pot hook for lifting the lid of the Dutch oven can be improvised out of a wire hanger.

SHOVEL

Methods in which used:
All methods, 255–268

SPIDER

Method in which used:
Hearthside Tripod, 262

STRING-ROASTING EQUIPMENT

Method in which used:
String Roasting, 267

TERRA-COTTA COOKWARE

Methods in which used:
Hearthside Tripod, 262
Pot Beside the Fire, 263
Pot Buried in Hot Ash, 263

The small shovel that comes with most fireplace sets is an absolute requirement for hearth cooking. The shovel is used in nearly every recipe in this book to move embers or ash within the firebox, or to move embers onto the hearth for use in cooking and then back into the firebox when the recipe is complete.

The spider is a three-legged iron frying pan used on the hearth with embers underneath. You may improvise a spider by setting an iron frying pan on a tripod or on bricks. The ideal distance from pan to hearth is about 2½ inches (6 cm).

A hook, string, and two skewers about 8 inches (20 cm) long make it possible to roast any meat to perfection. The string itself and an occasional push provide the power to turn the meat. With the addition of a pole the width of your fireplace opening, you can use the string method to roast more than one roast or several birds at the same time hanging side by side in front of the fire.

In Italian, *terra-cotta* means "burnt earth." Terra-cotta cookware is made from clay that is fired at a comparatively low temperature—even as low as that of the fireplace itself. The clay often includes impurities in the form of sand and small stones. Terra-cotta cookware was one of the first great technological achievements and it remains unsurpassed as the cookware of choice for hearth cooking.

The heat of the fireplace is dynamic. It is always getting either hotter or cooler. It never stays the same. The reason terra-cotta is the best material for hearth cookware is the combination of clay's poor heat-conducting qualities with its excellent heat-retaining qualities helps to smooth out the natural cycles of the fire.

As a rule, look for terra-cotta pots that are unglazed on the exterior. Find invisible cracks by striking the bottom of the pot with a coin. If it rings sharp and bright, the pot is fine; but if it has a dull or hollow sound, it is cracked. Terra-cotta cookware can be used the same way you use metal cookware. You can expose it to direct flame, set it in front of a hot fire, or even nestle it in a bed of embers. One difference, however, is crucial: hot ceramic will immediately crack when exposed to water, so always let the pot cool before washing.

The first time you use a new terra-cotta pot, soak it in water by both partially filling it and by immersing its base in water. You will hear the sound of thousands of tiny bubbles as the clay absorbs the water. Let the ceramic soak until the absorption stops, usually in three to ten minutes. If you don't use a pot for a long time, soak it again before using it.

In the past, all terra-cotta pots were intended for use with live fire. Unfortunately, comparatively high-fire, fine-grained ceramic cookware is now being sold as terra-cotta. To ensure against cracking, soak all fine-grained terra-cotta in water for a few minutes before each use.

THERMOMETER, INFRARED

Methods in which used:

Infrared thermometers are used to read surface temperatures. For the hearth cook, using an infrared thermometer means knowing some things that were previously unknowable except by intuition. How hot is the ash? How fast is the food cooking inside the Dutch oven? How hot is the griddle? The infrared thermometer takes guesswork out of the very part of hearth cooking that is otherwise the most difficult to master. As of this writing, the cost of infrared thermometers is beginning to fall, with models now appearing in stores for the price of this book. This is a tool that can help you become an expert hearth cook because it delivers immediate feedback. For example, since you can directly and instantly measure the exterior temperature of a Dutch oven, you can see if the side nearest the flames is too hot or too cool, so you can confidently adjust its position as the situation requires. Infrared thermometers are sold with a preset temperature range. A temperature range of up to 450°F (230°C) is acceptable, while a range of up to 750°F (400°C) is ideal.

TILES

Method in which used:

Low fire tiles a few inches (7.5 cm) in diameter can be used for baking bread. The tiles are heated in the fireplace, pulled onto the hearth to cool a little, and then stacked sandwiched with dough. The heat in the tiles bakes the breads. Instructions for how to make tiles for bread baking is found in the recipe for Tile-Baked Breads, page 174.

TONGS, LONG-HANDLED

Methods in which used:

Most fireplace sets come with tongs, but these are designed for handling large pieces of wood, and can be heavy and cumbersome to use when manipulating food cooking on the embers. Buy the longest tongs designed for use on the barbecue, or commission a pair of thin tongs from a blacksmith. Iron tongs 24 to 30 inches (60 to 75 cm) long made of 1/4-inch (6-mm) square iron stock are ideal.

TRIPOD, HEARTHSIDE

also called **Short-legged Tripod**

Methods in which used:

Tripods are, in effect, portable legs for pots, grills, griddles, and saucepans. They sit on the hearth, usually near the fire. The griddle or cooking vessel sits on top of the tripod, and embers from the fireplace are shoveled underneath. Tripods designed for the hearth have three legs typically 2 1/2 inches (6 cm) high. Some tripods come in the shape of a ring 8 inches (20 cm) in diameter, or in the shape of an equilateral triangle about 8 inches (20 cm) on a side. It is often useful to have two tripods. A tripod, also sometimes referred to as a trivet, is an easy first commission from a blacksmith. If you lack a tripod, improvise one with two common red bricks set on their broad side.

TRIPOD, LONG-LEGGED

Method in which used:

Tripods intended for use with flaming wood, rather than with embers, typically have legs 5 inches (13 cm) long, with the legs attached to a ring on which the pot or griddle sits. The long-legged tripod is used in the firebox beside the fire with kindling as the source of flames. The wider one's fireplace, the more likely one can use a long-legged tripod. Standard-sized modern fireplaces are usually not wide enough to accommodate a fire, a deep bed of ash, and a long-legged tripod. A long-legged tripod can always be used in conjunction with a campfire.

Methods

This section is a reference that you can use when planning meals based on technique. At the start of each method are the recipes that call for it.

HEARTH COOKING IS AN ART OF INCOMPARABLE DEPTH and flexibility. It utilizes all three aspects of the fireplace fire—flame, embers, and ash—and it takes advantage of the spatial qualities of live fire, with cooking taking place under, beside, in front of, and, more rarely, over the flames. Between the many combinations one can make with the different elements of the fire and cooking locations, the opportunities for extemporaneous solutions to the timeless challenge of how to cook food so it tastes wonderful and looks enticing are almost limitless.

This section is a reference that you can use when planning meals based on technique. At the start of each method are the recipes that call for it. Planning a meal by method can be helpful if you have a limited set of tools, or your hearth is small and you have to plan what to cook with an eye to what space is available on the hearth and in the firebox. This section can also be useful when adapting modern and period recipes to the hearth. The method descriptions will help guide you to a technique appropriate to the recipe you want to cook. Lastly, this section is for people who like to read the manual before they start a project, as well as for those who start first, and only read the manual when they run into trouble. I do suggest, however, that everyone read the entry on radiant heat before they begin, as it details concepts that can be applied to most of the other techniques.

Ash Baking	Long-legged Tripod
Boiling	Pot Beside the Fire
Cooking over Flame	Pot Buried in Hot Ash
Crane	Radiant Heat
Dutch Oven	Roasting
Ember Baking and Ember Roasting	Roasting on a Stand
Hearthside Griddle	Spit Roasting
Hearthside Grilling	Steaming
Hearthside Tripod	String Roasting
	Tile Baking

ASH BAKING

The most ancient oven is a mound of hot ashes. The ash oven can be gentle enough to roast an egg, or so fiercely hot that a 6-pound (2.7-kg) brisket bakes to perfection in 45 minutes. In this method, foods are baked directly in hot ash. They may be wrapped or unwrapped. Wrappings might include clay, oiled paper (page 251), or large leaves. Since foods must be baked in ashes without the addition of water, ash-baked foods often have a remarkably intense flavor. This is a method whereby foods emerge "most themselves." They may also, depending on chance or your purposeful technique, acquire a light taste of smoke, in which case the flavor is one that cannot be replicated in a conventional oven.

From the perspective of written culinary history, ash baking is a nearly invisible, though often central, cooking method. There are occasional references to ash baking in early food literature. Athenaeus, for example, writing in Rome early in the second century, refers to a recipe in a now-lost cookbook: "Smother the bulbs in the ashes, moisten with sauce, and eat as many as you will. . . ." References to ash baking continue in the food literature of the late Middle Ages, the Renaissance, and colonial America. In my own field research in Europe, and in Africa and Asia where cooking still takes place on open fires, I have encountered ash baking. Whether a hearth cook would have prepared a winter squash for a pie, pudding, or soup by first baking it in ashes, or by first boiling or steaming it, would have depended on the circumstances and the preferences of the cook. If the cook only had one pot, or if the cook fetched water from a long distance, I think it is fair to assume that ash baking would always have been favored over boiling. For historical re-creationists, ash baking provides a window to the cuisine of the poor, and brings authenticity to the preparation of many recipes.

The ash oven is one of the more useful hearth techniques to master because it requires no tools other than the standard fireplace shovel and a fireplace with a few inches (7.5 cm) of ashes on its floor. It is a method well suited to hearth cooking at a friend's house, in a hotel fireplace, or in a country cabin. I include recipes that utilize the ash oven to cook foods in three different ways: unwrapped (Ash Cakes, Brisket Baked in Ash), wrapped (Chicken in Clay, Chicken or Fish Baked in Wrappings), and, in a closely related method, in covered pots in the method Pot Buried in Hot Ash (Baked Beans).

In practice, how easy or difficult is it to bake in ashes? On the face of it, it's easy. Bury a potato in hot ashes and it will cook. However, a practical cuisine is one in which the cook can predict when dinner will be ready, which is possible only if you know the temperature of the ash oven. Knowing the temperature of the ashes is an old problem. Platinus, a fifteenth-century Italian author, alludes to the difficulty in his book, *On Right Pleasure and Good Health,* in the context of the admittedly tricky challenge of roasting eggs in ash. I have developed two solutions to the problem of knowing the temperature of ash. Both solutions make ash baking predictable.

The first solution is to replicate the same conditions each time you prepare a particular recipe. Once you fix the cooking temperature, you can then cook based on time alone. The three-minute egg is the classic example of this concept. We know the egg cooks in three minutes because we know its size and we know the temperature of boiling water. Think of this first ash-baking method as the layer method. It works like this: starting on ash—embers, ash, food, ash, embers. The first layer of embers, optional in some recipes, provides bottom heat. The food is kept from direct contact with those embers by a thin layer of ashes. The food is covered with a layer of insulating ash and then is piled with the hottest bed of embers you can muster. This method depends on the concept that "hottest" is the easiest temperature to replicate. The skill is in getting the thickness of the insulating ash correct. Too thin and the food burns, too thick and it doesn't cook. Use ½ to 1 inch (1 to 2.5 cm) for the best results.

The second solution uses twenty-first century technology. I directly measure the temperature of the ash with an infrared thermometer (page 253). To create a bed of ash of a specific temperature, mix embers into ash, give the ash time to soak up the heat, and then dig into the ash with a shovel. Use an infrared thermometer to measure the ash where you have hollowed it out, and also measure the temperature of the ash as it falls off the shovel. Continue adding embers (or cold ash) until you arrive at the temperature you desire.

In a conventional oven, hot air circulates around the food. Thus, if the air is 350°F (180°C), the air touching the food will always be 350°F. In the ash oven, however, air does not freely circulate around the food. The ash touching the food quickly cools. Furthermore, unless there is a heat source pumping fresh heat into the ashes, the ash is also always cooling. Taking both of these factors into account, you may need to begin baking in an ash oven at a temperature that is higher than you would choose in a conventional oven to achieve the same overall cooking time. For example, you might start baking a potato at 550°F (290°C) in an ash oven rather than at the 375°F (190°C) you would choose in a conventional oven.

Ash baking is a technique that can command all of the space within the firebox. When cooking several dishes for a single meal on a standard-sized fireplace, you may need to take this into account when planning the order in which you cook the meal. The ash-baking recipes that tend to be the most disruptive to the rhythm of hearth cooking are those that call for baking something large, like a chicken wrapped in clay.

BOILING

Recipes using this method:

The simmer and the boil are the primary touchstone temperatures of European cuisine. In a fifteenth-century English manuscript we read, "And when hit begynneth to boyle, skem it clene..." an instruction that could just as well have been written today. When recipes in this book call for water to be brought to a boil, it is only for small quantities, from 1 cup (250 ml) to 12 cups (3 l). The method I describe for boiling water works well for these small quantities. To boil larger quantities, use a crane (page 249), a pot chain (page 251), or a long-legged tripod (page 253).

When adapting period or modern recipes to the hearth, you will often find that a simmer on the side of the pot nearest the fire is adequate. A slightly lower cooking temperature usually means nothing more than longer cooking times. "Boyled" meats are actually better when prepared at a simmer. A simmer is easy to achieve on the hearth. See Pot Beside the Fire, Radiant Heat, and my recipe for Pot-au-Feu.

To boil water, place a hearthside tripod on the edge of the hearth as close as possible to the fire. Place a saucepan (or teakettle) with water on the tripod so the saucepan sits within 4 to 6 inches (10 to 15 cm) of the fire. Push embers against the base of the saucepan where it is nearest the flames. In some minutes, the water nearest the heat will simmer. At that point, lift the saucepan and shovel a thick layer of embers under and around the tripod. Replace the saucepan on the tripod. In a short time, the water will boil. Maintain the heat with embers pushed against the side of the saucepan nearest the flames and by refreshing embers underneath the saucepan.

The following are boiling times that I reliably achieve on my hearth using this two-step process.

1 cup (250 ml) water in a covered saucepan,
5 minutes to simmer, and 1 minute to boil

2 cups (475 ml) water in a covered saucepan,
10 minutes to simmer, and 2 minutes to boil

4 cups (1 l) water in a covered saucepan,
12 minutes to simmer, and 3 minutes to boil

6 cups (1.5 l) water in a covered saucepan,
15 minutes to simmer, and 3 minutes to boil

3 quarts (3 l) water in covered saucepan,
40 minutes to simmer, and 8 minutes to boil

If your fireplace is equipped with a crane, you can boil water in a pot hanging from it over the hottest part of the fire. If you live in a house with a fireplace that is wide enough, you may be able to boil water over a fire made of kindling by placing the pot or kettle on a long-legged tripod set on the floor of the inner hearth, beside the fire.

COOKING OVER FLAME

Recipe using this method
Fried Eggs, 78

Cooking over flame is familiar to everyone who uses a modern kitchen. There are two ways to cook over flame in a fireplace. One is to hang a pot from a crane (page 249) or pot chain (page 251), and the other is to set a pot over a long-legged tripod (page 253) set beside the fire within the firebox. The temperature of the air above a fireplace fire can be very hot—the flames of a roaring log fire can put out substantially more heat than even a commercial gas burner. Only one recipe in this book, an egg fried in the bowl of a spoon, calls for cooking over flame. For all the other recipes, including a large simmered meal for fifteen to twenty, the techniques I describe that rely on embers and radiant heat work perfectly. Historically, these methods, rather than cooking directly over flame, are the ones that were employed for most of the dishes prepared in complex multicourse meals. The types of recipes that most benefit from cooking over flame are those that can benefit from a sustained rolling boil.

Griddles can be hung over fire from a crane or pot chain. They can also be placed over a long-legged tripod beside the fire, but in my judgment one has more control over the griddle's temperature when employing a griddle on the hearth as described in Hearthside Griddle. As I explain in the section on embers (page 241), the fact that embers are never hotter than when you first start using them is an advantage when you need to regulate temperature carefully, as you always do with a griddle.

CRANE

Recipes using this method:

No recipe in this book requires a crane. If you have a crane, use it for recipes that call for boiling or simmering. Most of the soups, many of the beverages, and all of the steaming recipes, for example, are appropriate for use with a crane.

If your fireplace is equipped with a crane, this is how to use it. Swing the crane out from the fireplace so that it is pointing into the room. Bring your pot or griddle to the hearth. Decide how low you want the bottom of the pot or griddle to hang inside the firebox, and either hang the utensil directly from the crane or adjust the height by hanging it from a hook or adjustable trammel. Now, swing the crane toward the fire. Whether you swing the pot or griddle over the flames, or keep it to the side, depends on the amount of heat required.

When using a crane, you can cook directly over flame, but you don't have to. You can also cook to the side of the flames in the fire's radiant heat. If your fireplace is large enough, it is possible to have two fires, one managed for the pot that hangs from the crane, and the other managed for other cooking purposes. If your hearth is small, then the single fire will be the fire over which the pot is swung. A log fire can produce a huge amount of heat. For many recipes in this book, in all but one of the steaming recipes, that for mussels, the pot would not be swung over the flames of a hot fire, but rather would hang so its leading edge is 6 to 8 inches (15 to 20 cm) from the flames. The water in the pot nearest the flames will thus simmer rather than boil. If you are hanging a Dutch oven from a crane, you can still pile embers onto its lid.

DUTCH OVEN

Recipes using this method:

When a Dutch oven with legs is utilized on the hearth, it becomes the most exquisite cooking tool imaginable. I cannot overemphasize its flexibility, nor the subtlety of technique it offers the cook. A Dutch oven is far more versatile than a conventional kitchen oven, and for the small-scale cooking of the modern home, it beats all alternatives. Virtually every savory and many of the sweet dishes cooked in the modern kitchen oven—stews, beans, casseroles, roasts, pies, cakes, breads— were originally baked in a hearthside Dutch oven or an equivalent piece of cookware. The Romans relied on a version of the Dutch oven called a *testo* for hearth baking, and for pies and baked goods the French used a vessel called a *tourtière*, which can be thought of as a larger version of a Dutch oven, or *daubiére*, as it is called in French. If you are interpreting early recipes—for example, those from the Middle Ages, the Renaissance, and up to the early part of the nineteenth century—you should usually take "oven" to mean either a bread oven or a piece of hearth cookware being used in the manner of an oven.

The Dutch oven is placed on the hearth anywhere from the very edge of the hearth where it meets the firebox, to as much as 10 or 12 inches (20 to 25 cm) away from the firebox. As a rule, the distance you set the Dutch oven back from the firebox is determined by the extent to which you want side heat to contribute to the cooking—whether the heat falling on the side of the Dutch oven nearest the fire is gentle, moderate, or high as described below. As the amount of heat radiating out of the firebox onto the hearth varies, it isn't possible to give a fixed distance. I usually cook with the Dutch oven placed about 6 to 8 inches (15 to 20 cm) back from the firebox.

A Dutch oven placed on the hearth can be heated from three different sources: embers shoveled underneath, embers placed on the lid, and side heat, the heat from the fire that radiates onto the side of the oven closest to the flames (see Radiant Heat). Each of these sources can be applied and adjusted separately from one another. At different points in the cooking process, one of them may become more, or less, important. In practical terms, this means that the cook has a wide range of options for how to apply heat to the food, and considerable control over the speed of the cooking and the texture and look of the finished dish. When making long-cooking stews, a paste of water and flour can be used to seal the lid of the Dutch oven, and if the lid has a lip, water can be kept on the lid to help conserve moisture further.

The great mystery of Dutch oven cookery is knowing how hot it is inside the pot. Experienced hearth cooks can intuit the temperature. With the aid of an infrared thermometer (page 253), you can measure the external temperature directly and thus know the internal temperature. With or without an infrared thermometer, by lifting the lid to see how the food is cooking—use an iron pot hook (page 251) if the lid is laden with embers—you quickly develop a feel for Dutch oven cookery. Conceptually, the first load of embers both under the oven and on the lid goes to heat up the metal. Subsequent loads establish the working temperature.

The heat that falls on the side of the oven facing the flames can play a significant role in the cooking of the dish. Sometimes a recipe is baked in a Dutch oven exclusively by this radiant heat. Iron is isothermic, meaning that heat spreads out evenly within the metal. Heat applied to one side moves through the metal to the opposite side, so heating a Dutch oven on the side facing the flames also heats it on the side facing toward the room. In my recipes, I refer to three temperatures for side heat: gentle, moderate, and high.

Gentle side heat (slow oven): The heat striking the side of the pot or Dutch oven heats that side to between 160°F (70°C) and 250°F (120°C). Liquids touching the side are at a low to active simmer.

Moderate side heat (medium oven): The heat striking the side of the pot or Dutch oven heats that side to between 250°F (120°C) and 350°F (180°C). Liquids touching the side are at an active simmer to a fast boil.

High side heat (hot oven): The heat striking the side of the pot or Dutch oven heats that side to between 350°F (180°C) and 475°F (240°C). Liquids touching the side are boiling rapidly, and there may be some burning.

EMBER BAKING
AND EMBER ROASTING

Recipes using this method:

Like ash baking, this is a cooking method that was once common, but about which little has been written. I have seen references to ember baking in late-Medieval sources. Cooks of otherwise more refined dishes purposefully resorted to this rustic method for the subtle flavor it imparted to the food. I think it is fair to assume that ember baking, though rarely mentioned in texts, was common throughout Europe and America up to at least the early decades of the nineteenth century. In India today, hundreds of millions of women regularly bake bread directly on the embers. I have also seen the method employed in China, Mexico, and several countries in Africa. In cooking terms, a bed of embers is analogous to a hot griddle. Ember baking is the hearth-cooking method that consistently produces the most unique flavors, ones that cannot be replicated in the kitchen oven.

In ember baking, food is laid directly on the embers and heated by bottom heat. This book includes two ember-baked breads, Flat Bread and Simit, and many ember-baked vegetables. Embers from hardwoods are always preferred to those of soft-woods because they burn hotter and longer. The temperature of an iron griddle is regulated by controlling the intensity of the heat source underneath the griddle. In the case of embers, the intensity is controlled by manipulating their surface. The griddle is cooled either by letting the embers develop a layer of ash or by sprinkling the embers with ash. The griddle is made hotter by knocking off accumulated ash, by fanning the embers, and/or by adding fresh embers. Counterintuitively, the biggest problem you will encounter cooking on embers is not that ash sticks to the food—if food is dry to begin with, ash will not stick—but that the food snuffs out the embers.

A pair of long-handled tongs (page 253) is often required for handling food on embers. Some foods, such as Roasted Red Peppers and Roasted Artichokes (See Ember-Roasted Vegetables), are cooked so hot that one cannot easily work around the embers without wearing gloves (see Kevlar Gloves, page 250).

EMBER ROASTING

See **Ember Baking and Ember Roasting.**

HEARTHSIDE GRIDDLE

Recipes using this method:

Place a metal or terra-cotta griddle over a hearthside tripod (page 253) or straddling bricks (page 248). The ideal distance of the griddle above the hearth is approximately 2½ inches (6 cm). Shovel embers evenly underneath the griddle. Unless you know that you are baking on the griddle at the hottest temperature you can possibly achieve, it is usually best to work up to the temperature you want by adding embers underneath the griddle, a sprinkling at a time, over the course of a few minutes, waiting between each additional load for the heat to sink into the metal.

There are two advantages to using a griddle on the hearth over embers, rather than over a burner on the kitchen stove. The first is that the heat is always evenly spread underneath the griddle, no matter how large it is. The second is in the nature of embers as a heat source. Embers are never hotter than when you shovel them underneath the griddle, and so overheating a hearthside griddle is seldom a problem. Once the griddle is brought up to temperature, it is comparatively easy to keep the griddle heated within a narrow temperature range by adding embers, a sprinkling at a time, as one senses the food is cooking slower. The thicker the griddle, the more stable the heat.

In my recipes, I refer to four griddle temperatures: gentle, moderate, hot, and smoking.

Gentle, 225° to 250°F (110° to 120°C): A finger dipped in water and then touched to the griddle leaves a black mark in the shape of your finger before the water fully evaporates.

Moderate, 325° to 350°F (165° to 180°C): A finger dipped in water and then touched to the griddle releases a drop of water that sizzles and breaks up into several sizzling drops before they evaporate. The hotter a griddle gets, the more parts the drop breaks into, and the faster it evaporates. It is difficult to express in words the timing, but I would say that the water does not evaporate instantly. It evaporates in the space of a pause.

Hot, 400° to 425°F (200° to 220°C): A finger dipped in water and then touched to the griddle releases a drop of water that sizzles and breaks up into several sizzling drops that almost immediately evaporate. If the drop of water seems to explode when it touches the griddle, however, the griddle is too hot.

Smoking: Oil brushed onto the griddle smokes.

HEARTHSIDE GRILLING

The hearthside grill (page 250) sits on the hearth, in front of the fire. The best location is toward the center of the fireplace and close to the fire itself. Embers from the fireplace are shoveled underneath the grill, and the fire in the fireplace pulls any smoke generated by grilling up the chimney. Hearthside grilling is an additive process—you shovel embers under the grill only as you need them. Because the legs of a hearthside tripod are so short, typically 2½ inches (6 cm), the food being grilled is very close to the embers. Small changes in temperature are immediately registered in the speed of the cooking, making this method one in which the cook has nuanced control over the process. Grilled Strips of Meat (page 120) is a good recipe with which to begin.

It is the use of embers from the fireplace, and the ease with which you can scale the heat up and down that makes hearth grilling a process over which you have total control. The recipe for Grilled Saffron Milk Caps is the most challenging of the grilling recipes. It is a recipe for grilling a kind of wild mushroom. The mushroom is grilled for an hour, but it is never browned. While you should always start with an even layer of embers under the grill, one of the ways you have a fine level of control over the cooking process is that as the cooking progresses you can apply extra heat to one portion of the grill, or take heat away from another portion, as the cooking demands. In practice, I often increase the temperature of the embers under meat and poultry just before taking them off the grill in order to give the meat the exact color I would like.

HEARTHSIDE TRIPOD

A tripod (page 253) is the single most useful piece of culinary fireplace equipment. It is a set of portable legs that makes possible the hearthside use of any pot, frying pan, or griddle. Tripods intended for the hearth have very short legs, 2½ inches (6 cm) is typical. They are only used with embers, and never with flaming wood. A pair of common red bricks set on their broad face makes an excellent substitute.

The basic instructions for using a tripod are simple: place the tripod on the hearth, put the cooking utensil on top, and shovel embers underneath as needed.

For safety reasons, tripods should be placed toward the center of the hearth and within the third of the hearth closest to the firebox. There must always be a fire in the fireplace to pull fumes generated by the embers up the chimney. Within this general area of the hearth, and taking safety concerns particular to your fireplace into account, the precise location is determined by the extent to which, if any, you want the fire's side heat to influence the cooking. In some of my recipes, I suggest that the radiant heat be a part of the cooking process, and in other recipes I suggest it not be.

The methods Boiling and Pot Beside the Fire also use the hearthside tripod. What differentiates this method from those is that in this method bottom heat from the embers is the primary cooking heat. Radiant heat falling on the side of the cookware is incidental to the cooking process. As with the method Hearthside Grilling, you will find that embers provide you with significant control over the cooking process, however, in this case, the type of cookware you use will have a significant influence over how you experience the cooking process. For example, compared with metal cookware, you will find that using terra-cotta on a tripod requires less attention, but the cookware will also seem "sluggish." It responds slower to fresh embers than does metal cookware.

LONG-LEGGED TRIPOD

No recipe in this book requires a long-legged tripod. If you have one, use it for recipes that call for boiling or simmering.

If your fireplace is wide enough, you may be able to place a long-legged tripod (page 253) on the floor of the inner hearth, a couple of feet (60 cm) away from the fire. If this is possible, you can put cooking pots or a griddle on the tripod and cook over a fire made of burning kindling. I do not specifically call for this method because this book is written for people with a standard-sized living-room fireplace. However, this method is well suited to cooking around a campfire or fire pit, in addition to cooking in a very large fireplace.

Once the tripod is in place, shovel embers underneath and lay down kindling wood. Blow the kindling into flame. Place the cooking vessel or griddle on the tripod and heat over a flame that is appropriate for the recipe. In my opinion, cooking over flame is best suited to recipes that do best over high heat. My recipes for Sautéed Greens (page 141) or Fava Beans (page 152) would do well on a long-legged tripod. The tripod is also well suited to boiling water and to the first stages of cooking foods, like beans, that can benefit from sustained boiling during an initial cooking period. Whenever a recipe benefits from slow cooking, or when there is a risk of easily burning the food, the methods that rely on embers or radiant heat such as Hearthside Tripod or Pot Beside the Fire are a better choice.

POT BESIDE THE FIRE

POT BURIED IN HOT ASH

Place a covered pot 4 to 6 inches (10 to 15 cm) from the fire, either set on the edge of the hearth or set beside the fire within the firebox. Use a shovel to push embers against the base of the pot where it is nearest the flames. That is all there is to it. From working on the kitchen stove, we are used to the idea of heat being applied under a pot, but heat falling on the side of a pot is just as effective for most cooking purposes. The food will come to a simmer or low boil on the side of the pot nearest the flames. The overall temperature will be lower than if the food were cooking at a full simmer or boil, and thus will take a little longer to cook than you might be used to.

I specify this method for some recipes in which sitting before the hearth is part of the recipe. *Aïgo Bouido* (page 44) is a good example. I also recommend it for quickly preparing small quantities of ingredients, like melting butter, and for small amounts of liquid that you don't want to boil, like milk and mulled beverages, as well as for cooking large quantities of ingredients, as slowly as possible, such as the Pot-au-Feu (page 114).

The country cuisines of Europe often include foods that are the result of slow cooking. Stews, long-simmering meats, soup stocks, potted meats, steamed puddings and cakes, and the many sauces that are cooked at a bare simmer for a long time are all appropriately cooked entirely by side heat using the method a pot set beside the fire, or as you find in my Dutch oven recipes for stews, beginning with bottom heat, and then by side heat for the remaining part of the cooking period.

This is a variant on ash baking. Historically, when hearth fires were routinely banked down at night to be rekindled in the morning, there was always a deep reservoir of hot ash at a stable temperature in which a pot could be buried. In my fireplace, there remain areas of ash that are 400°F (200°C) twenty-four hours after the fire has been banked. In the traditional practice of hearth cooking, beans and stews were often cooked in the banked embers of the nighttime fire. In many ways, this was an ingenious use of waste heat, a means of taking advantage of heat that would otherwise simply dissipate. The hot ash was often used to start a cooking process at night that would continue into the next day, such as cooking a meat stew made from an old, tough farm animal. In the past, hearth cooks were opportunistic about cooking venues. If the bread oven was being heated for bread, then they might use the oven to bake the stew. But if the oven wasn't being fired up, and it rarely was, one option was to bury a pot in the ashes of the nighttime fire. If you read old recipes, you can, as a rule, assume that if something was supposed to bake for a very long time at a very low temperature, burying the pot in hot ash was one way this was achieved.

Burying a pot up to its neck in hot ash and then going to bed is a cooking method that takes practice to make reliable. I have developed a method for baking in ash that achieves the same effect—slow, long cooking—but that is more easily controlled. In my method, the pot is buried in ash in the morning and heated by a fire that is built next to the ash-mounded pot. See the recipe for Baked Beans (page 40) for full details.

If you want to experiment with a more historically authentic method of cooking in ash, I advise you to develop a very thick bed of ash—one at least 6 inches (15 cm) deep—and to keep a fire burning for at least two days before baking in a buried pot. Shoveling embers into the ash during the day will help create deep areas of ash that are evenly hot. The two factors that influence the success of this cooking method are the temperature of the ash in which the pot is buried and the proximity of a reservoir of hot embers that could pump heat toward the pot for at least the initial few hours it is in the ash. A goal for most dishes you will want to prepare this way is for the pot to come up to a boil and then to cool slowly, so that in the morning it is still cooking in the range of 160°F (70°C). The skill required by the traditional technique is that of judging the temperature of the ash and the rate at which it will cool. The temperature of ash can now be directly measured with an infrared thermometer. See both Ash Baking and infrared thermometer (page 253) for more details.

RADIANT HEAT

Recipes using this method:

The gentle warmth of the fire that feels so nice against your face is radiant heat. That same heat, though falling much closer to the side of a roast, falling on an egg lying on the hearth, or striking the side of a Dutch oven, contributes to the cooking, or may even be the only heat source used to make a recipe. I call this heat "side heat." The side heat that projects out from the fireplace onto the hearth is usually a combination of heat from flame and embers. At different times in the cycle of the fire, the heat may be more flame than embers, or more embers than flame.

In working with side heat, it is helpful to keep in mind that radiant energy is strongest when you are very near its source, but that its strength rapidly falls off as you move away from the source. If you hold your finger $1/16$ inch (2 mm) from the surface of a glowing ember, it will be very hot, but at 2 inches (5 cm) away, you may not even be able to feel any warmth. The heat radiated by flames and embers obeys Newton's Inverse Square Law. In the hearth cooking techniques described in this book, most cooking takes place to the side of the flames, and not over the flames, so understanding how radiant heat works will help you make the recipes work.

As described by Sir Isaac Newton's Inverse Square Law, radiant energy drops off with the square of the distance, so a very minor shift in the position of a pot from the fire can have a tremendous effect on the amount of heat striking its side. For example, a pot sitting 4 inches (10 cm) from the fire receives four times the heat of a pot sitting 8 inches (20 cm) from the fire. Thus, if the leading edge of the first pot is 400°F (200°C), the leading edge of the second pot will be 100°F (38°C).

Using side heat, rather than bottom heat, as a primary heat source is something those of us raised with the modern kitchen stove are unfamiliar with, but it is an important source of heat on the hearth. In many ways, a slow simmer on the side of the pot nearest the fire is the natural temperature of the open hearth. As long as a fire is burning in the fireplace, there is a place on the hearth and a place within the firebox next to the fire where the ingredients on the side of the pot closest to the heat will simmer. I think of this as the "sweet spot." Many European recipes for stocks, stews, beans, and "boiled" meats take advantage of this sweet spot to produce rich-tasting, succulent foods with minimal work on the part of the cook.

When using side heat, temperature is controlled by moving whatever is being cooked—whether it is an egg, an apple, heads of garlic, or something in a pot—toward or away from the fire. By taking advantage of the fact that small changes in distance have a significant effect on the speed of cooking, you gain full control over the cooking temperature. When cooking in pots, you can also control the heat through the quantity of embers, if any, pushed up against the side of the pot closest to the flames. Taking advantage of the fire's radiant heat to cook your dinner requires no special tools. It is one of the hearth methods that can be used anywhere there is an open fire.

ROASTING

To cook meat, chicken, ducks, and other birds with dry heat is to roast. There are three methods of roasting before the fire: string roasting, spit roasting, and roasting on a stand. For all three, the item being roasted is turned in the hot air at the edge of the hearth near the fire. In spit roasting and string roasting, the turning is automatic. In roasting on a stand, you must turn the meat by hand.

Conceptually, think of the air in which the meat is turning as the air of an oven. The hotter the air, the faster the meat cooks. Neither embers nor flames are ever placed under hearth-roasted meat. What goes under the meat is a pan to catch the drippings. Because embers may be pushed up against the drip pan, I always suggest there be at least some water in the pan to keep the drippings from burning. A variant that is not included in the book's recipes, but that I recommend, is to catch the drippings of small birds, such as quail, on pieces of toast placed under the turning birds in lieu of a drip pan.

To best achieve the classic golden crust of hearth roasting, the fireplace fire—the combination of flame and embers—should be extremely hot, and in most of my roasting recipes I call for a mature hot fire. Put in terms of oven roasting, to match my fastest roasting times, the fire must be hot enough to heat the air where the meat is closest to the fire to between 375° and 450°F (190° and 220°C).

As I have said elsewhere in this book, hearth cooking is tolerant of different approaches. There are many options for approaching most recipes, and the consequences for not following my guidelines precisely is rarely severe. In the case of the hotness of a roasting fire, Hannah Glasse, in her 1747 cookbook, *The Art of Cookery Made Plain and Easy,* put it best: " . . . according to the goodness of your fire, your meat will be done sooner or later."

While embers and flame work together to provide the radiant heat for roasting, embers often play the dominant role because they are often closer to the meat than the flames.

To ensure even roasting, all meat should be well trussed and formed into as symmetrical a shape as possible. Managing the fire so that it is just right when you start to roast is one of the hearth roaster's most critical skills. If you misjudge the cycle of the fire and it is not hot enough, burn kindling to create a rapid rise in temperature. Kindling or fresh logs can, of course, be added to the fire at any time during the roasting process.

On small fireplaces, roasting can dominate the hearth, making it difficult or impossible to cook anything else at the same time. If, in addition to the roast, you are planning several hearth-cooked dishes for dinner, you may have to cook some of them before or after the roast is finished.

ROASTING ON A STAND

Recipes using this method

This is the roasting method you can do anywhere. Meat is placed on a stand in front of the fire on the hearth or set beside the fire in the firebox. The meat is then turned with a fork as needed, more frequently—perhaps a quarter-turn even every three minutes—if the meat is placed near intense heat; less often—even once every thirty minutes—if the heat is less intense or the distance from the fire is greater. A stand can be a grill set up on the hearth between two bricks, or it can be aluminum foil laid down on the ashes beside the fire. This method always works well for roasts, but it can be more difficult to apply to large birds, such as chickens or turkeys, unless you can devise a stand to hold the bird upright to facilitate turning. See Roasting on a Stand (page 124) for a full description of the method.

SPIT ROASTING

Recipes using this method

Spit roasting is the roasting method with which most people are familiar. Meat is attached to a metal spit that is placed in front of the fire parallel to the ground, and turned in the fire's radiant heat. Mechanical spits have existed for hundreds of years. On the hearth, the spit motor, whether it is a clockwork or an electric motor, is placed to the side of the hearth where it is shielded from heat. The spit runs from the motor to a stand, which sits on the edge of the hearth extension, as close to the fire in the firebox as possible. Neither fire nor embers are ever placed directly under the roasting meat, however. Only a drip pan sits beneath the meat. See Spit Roasting (page 127) for a full description of the method.

STEAMING

Recipes using this method

Steaming, or perhaps more accurately put, baking in a *bain-marie* (water bath), is an almost effortless way to cook. Nineteenth-century American cookbooks, which reflected the practice of the many cooks of the day who didn't have ovens, recommend steaming for a wide range of cakes, quick breads, and puddings. In this Anglo-American system, simmering water replaces the hot air of the oven as the means of transferring heat to the batter, dough, or custard that sits within a covered mold. Since you are baking at the temperature of simmering water— 210°F (100°C)—rather than the oven's 350°F (180°C), steaming takes more time than oven baking, but achieves the same results.

To steam on the hearth, simply put the covered pot, with the water and the covered mold inside, on a hearthside tripod set close to the fire, usually within 4 to 6 inches (10 to 15 cm) of the flames. Push embers against the pot where it sits nearest the flames to bring the water to a simmer on the side closest to the heat. Manage the fire to maintain the water at a simmer until whatever you are steaming is done. This method is very similar to Pot Beside the Fire.

I have not included recipes in this book for English potted meats or French terrines, but both foods can be baked in a water bath following my instructions for steamed cakes and puddings. Chinese cuisine has a rich steaming tradition. In the

Chinese method, dough and other foods are directly exposed to steam, usually by placing them in bamboo baskets that sit over boiling water.

STRING ROASTING

① Loop
② Handle
③ Skewer

This is a flexible method for roasting on the hearth. It is applicable to large meat roasts and to large birds, such as turkeys. When string roasting, the birds and meat hang from a string that is tied to a hook usually placed either in the ceiling or under the mantle. The string—either a loop of string or, for very small birds, a single strand—turns the meat with only an occasional push from the cook. For the recipes in this book, string roasting is accomplished as follows: the meat is pierced with a skewer through its short direction, a string handle is attached to one end of the skewer, passed through the bottom of the loop that hangs from the hook, and then attached to the other end of the skewer. With the meat in place, it turns in front of the fire hanging from the loop, first turning in one direction, then in the other. The string-roasting method is fully explained on page 62. What follows is technical information on how to position the hook and prepare the two required sets of strings, the one being the loop that hangs from the hook, and the other, the handle that attaches the meet to the loop.

Hook placement: Mount a small hook in the ceiling or mantle so that it is centered over the fireplace and so that when the meat hangs in front of the fire from a string attached to the hook, the leading edge of the meat, the side that is closest to the flames, hangs exactly over the imaginary line that divides the inner hearth from the hearth extension. Because Rumford fireplaces are shallower and reflect more heat into the room than more conventional fireplaces, owners of Rumfords may need to position the hook so the meat will hang a little farther away from the fire.

The longer the string, the longer the meat will turn without being given a push by the cook. Therefore, the ceiling is the ideal location for the hook. However, the position of the mantle may preclude a ceiling hook because the string must clear the mantle by 1 inch (2.5 cm). Some mantles will push the meat too far from the fire; if this is the case, place the hook on the underside of the mantle.

The string: Use only natural-fiber string. In addition to length, the thinness of the string influences the length of time the meat will turn before needing a little push. A 12-pound (5.5-kg) turkey hanging from a loop of thin rope 5 feet (1.5 m) long turns for a little more than 1 minute, while the same bird hanging from kitchen string of the same length turns for 10 minutes. Therefore, use the thinnest string that will handle the weight.

The loop: Make two loops, one out of household string for a turkey and heavy roasts, and one out of kite string or No. 10 crochet yarn for chickens and smaller roasts.When stretched taut, the looped string should hang 2 to 6 inches (5 to 15 cm) below the top of the fireplace opening. The loop can be reused.

The handle: Think of the handle in terms of the handle of a shoulder bag. In this case, the handle is made of string and has a loop on each end. I would start by making a set of four string handles, one 12, 18, 20, and 22 inches (30, 45, 50, and 55 cm) in length when stretched out—including the knotted loop on each end. The loop on each end should be big enough to easily slip over the end of the skewer, about 1 inch (2.5 cm). The bottom of the meat should hang about 8 inches

(20 cm) above the hearth. Through experimentation, you will determine the length of string-handle appropriate to your fireplace and to what you are cooking. A turkey, for example, will require a much shorter string-handle than a Cornish game hen. The handles can be reused.

Note: String roasting is usually the most practical method for roasting more than one of something, two roasts, three chickens, five ducks, twenty-five quail. This is accomplished by hanging a stick from the hook, and then hanging the roasts, chickens, etc., from strings tied to the stick.

TILE BAKING

Recipe using this method
Tile-Baked Breads, 174

This is a bread-baking method that is poorly documented. The concept is simple: place terra-cotta tiles in the fireplace until they glow dull red, then remove them to the hearth, and when they have sufficiently cooled, stack them sandwiched with dough, and bake until the breads are cooked. This method makes it possible to bake large quantities of bread without an oven in what amounts to waste heat, the heat of the fireplace fire that would otherwise be lost up the chimney. There is an archeological record of bread baking on tiles that goes back at least to a Babylonian excavation of 1750 B.C. I have seen a documentary showing people of the Omo tribe in Ethiopia baking breads by surrounding hot rocks with dough, a method that would not leave an archeological record. Besides baking in ash (see Ash Cakes, page 158) and on griddles or in pots (see *Les Galettes de Sarasin*, page 172, and Irish Soda Bread, page 170), how did people in isolated European farmhouses without bread ovens bake bread when snowed in during the winter? Was the technique of baking bread between hot tiles, a method still practiced on special occasions in a small region in northern Italy, practiced elsewhere in Europe?

williamrubel.com

A WEB SITE IS NOT A BOOK. A book is fixed in time while a Web site is always a work in progress. The breadth of material that I include on the Web site will depend to some extent on the participation of my readers. I invite you to visit my Web site and then to write to me with information that you would like to share with other enthusiasts of the open hearth. I wrote this book with the Internet and the Web site in mind. Following is some of what you can expect to find at *williamrubel.com:*

Suppliers: There is an up-to-date list of suppliers, including small suppliers, and craftspeople. There are drawings of tools to make commissioning tools easier, and there is information on fireplaces that you can use when talking with masons about building the most ideal fireplace for hearth cooking.

Methods: There is always more to say about how to cook on the open hearth. This book is a first word, not the last word on the subject. Methods not explored in the book that I come across, and that my readers tell me about, are presented on the Web site.

Community: Even while I have been writing this book I have, through the Internet, been contacted by people from all over the world—from many parts of the United States, Europe, the Middle East, Africa, Asia, and South America. While it will take some time, I am hopeful that through this Web site I will be able to bring together enthusiasts of the open hearth, wherever you are, so that all of us working together can breathe new life into this ancient craft.

Errata and Lacunæ: If you write to me pointing out an error, or something important that was left out, I will post the correction on an Errata and Lacunæ page for the benefit of other readers.

Bread ovens, vegetable gardening, wild mushrooms, homemade alcohol, traditional cooking, and more: As I believe is clear from the text of this book, I have many interests. You will find interests other than hearth cooking explored at my Web site, and to the extent that these other interests are also your interests, I welcome your questions and comments.

Key to Cooking Venues

Besides the single option I define for each recipe, you will find information that indicates my judgment as to whether, and how easily, the recipe can be prepared in other locations around the hearth, or in the barbecue, campfire, or wood-fired bread oven.

WHAT IF YOU DON'T HAVE A FIREPLACE or you want to cook on a friend's fireplace or on a fireplace in a rented cabin that might not be equipped like your fireplace at home? What are your options besides the single option that I define in each recipe? If your friend doesn't want you to cook on the hearth, can the recipe be cooked in the firebox, beside the fire? Can you use a barbecue or a campfire? What if you have a wood-fired bread oven? Can you use the oven for any of the recipes?

Fortunately, hearth cooking is an inherently flexible enterprise. There is always more than one way to approach any dish. All of the recipes in this book are written for one or the other fireplace location — in the firebox or on the hearth. In each recipe, you will find that I have identified which of these two locations is the primary cooking venue. You can use this key as a way of planning what you will cook. On a small fireplace, you may only be able to cook one recipe in the firebox at one time, so this key will help you plan.

If you don't have a fireplace, or if it is the summer and thus too hot to cook on an open fire indoors, use your barbecue or cook in a backyard campfire or fire pit. If you are lucky enough to have a bread oven, you can also use that for many of the recipes. Suggestions for adapting recipes in this book from firebox to hearth, and hearth to firebox, and from the fireplace to a barbecue, campfire, or bread oven, are made in the following pages.

PRIMARY VENUES
Firebox
Hearth

ALTERNATE VENUES
Barbecue
Campfire
Bread Oven

FIREBOX

There exist fireplaces that are so large you can actually walk inside the firebox, even while a fire is burning. If you are lucky enough to have such a fireplace, then everything I specify for cooking on the hearth can also be cooked inside the firebox because it is large enough for you to maintain an area free of ashes that can be used in the way I suggest using the hearth—as a place for shoveling embers underneath pots, grills, and griddles set above the hearth on short legs.

You will find that all of the methods that employ the firebox, such as Ash Baking (page 255), Ember Baking (page 260), and Pot Beside the Fire (page 263), are methods that work well under improvised circumstances. If at a friend's house, for example, you want to use your friend's fireplace to cook a meal, but you want to keep your friend's hearth ash-free, look for the recipes that use the firebox.

As I say many times in this book, open-hearth cooking is an inherently flexible adventure. "Impossible" is not in the vocabulary of open-hearth cooks. When you cook on a small fireplace you will find that hearth real estate can become valuable. There are times on my own fireplace when I cannot fit all the pots on the hearth that need to be there. I then make compromises. For example, I might slip a frying pan with a frittata onto the embers beside the fire so I can use the space on the hearth for a Dutch oven. It is not the ideal cooking method for the frittata—I specify Hearthside Tripod as the method—but it works. If you take an improvisational "but it works" attitude, you will find that quite a few of the recipes I specify for cooking on the hearth can, in a pinch, be moved into the firebox.

HEARTH

The most nuanced cooking takes place on the hearth. This is where you have the most control over temperature. It is the primary venue for many of the methods of this book including Dutch Oven (page 258), Hearthside Grilling (page 261), Hearthside Tripod (page 262), and all the roasting methods (pages 265–267). While I can imagine more situations in which you will be likely to transfer a recipe from the hearth to the firebox, than from the firebox to the hearth, the hearth's flexibility certainly works both ways. Even for recipes like Baked Beans (page 40), where the bean pot is buried in ash, or Chicken in Clay (page 75), where the chicken is wrapped in clay and buried in ash, you could cook the dishes, with equal results, by placing the pot or the clay-wrapped chicken on the hearth in front of a hot fire.

BARBECUE

Can you cook it in the barbecue? A typical American barbecue is a box with a fixed grill that sits over a bed of embers, usually charcoal. This type of barbecue is not as flexible a cooking tool as a campfire or fire pit, both of which are suitable for cooking every recipe in this book. The recipes I identify as suitable for the barbecue are the most obvious—those that use grilling or that call for cooking under the ash or on the embers.

What of the other recipes? Just because I don't suggest the barbecue as an alternate cooking venue doesn't mean it cannot be used. But it does mean that using the barbecue will depend on the size and configuration of your barbecue, and in some cases your imagination and determination to succeed. The other methods that use bottom heat, Hearthside Tripod (page 262) and Hearthside Griddle (page 261), can be adapted to a barbecue, but you will probably not be able to just follow the instructions and proceed. If you remove the grill so pots can be set on the barbecue floor beside burning coals, most of the recipes in this book that use the method Pot Beside the Fire (page 263) or Steaming (page 266) could be brought to your barbecue. The primary limitation will be whether the pot is too big. When a pot is filled with liquid, as it is for beans or for the recipe Chicken in a Pot (page 60), the challenge on a barbecue is how to first bring the liquid up to the simmer. Once the liquid is simmering, embers pushed beside the pot should be enough to hold it at that temperature. To bring a pot up to temperature, I suggest burning kindling wood on top of the charcoal until the pot is simmering on the side nearest the fire. Stir to distribute the heat and then maintain embers at the pot's base for the balance of the cooking time with an occasional boost from a kindling fire if needed.

CAMPFIRE

Every recipe in this book can be cooked equally well on a campfire. One way to think of the modern fireplace is to think in terms of a campfire brought indoors and built into a wall under a chimney. Historically, this is pretty much what happened. The campfire's first migration into the house took place a long time ago. In Greek literature, the hearth that Odysseus comes back to after his long travels is a ring of rocks on the living room floor. The smoke rose to the ceiling and, over time, covered everything with soot. It was sooty armaments that, at the very end of the story, his son, Telemechus, takes out of the great hall and hides in the storeroom out of reach of his father's enemies. In Europe, the fireplace as we know it only became a common feature of ordinary houses a few hundred years ago. Even into the twentieth century, there were still remote settlements in which the hearth remained as it had been in the time of Homer, and as, in fact, it remains in large parts of the world—a campfire built directly on the floor of the main room with no provision for a chimney.

The recipe instructions can be applied to campfire cooking without modification. In terms of a campfire or fire pit consider the firebox as the area where the fire is burning, and the hearth as the immediate area in front of the fire. If you are used to cooking in campfires that are closely ringed with rocks, you may need to modify your campfire design a little. Keep the perimeter of rocks, but extend the perimeter a little on one side to create a hearth extension where you can work with the Dutch oven, the grill, the griddle, and pots set on tripods, bricks, or stones. If you build a campfire in your backyard, situate it so that it is sheltered. Wind makes fire management difficult.

The campfire is the perfect venue for those of you who are intent on cooking large meals in cauldrons. Large pots can be suspended over the fire from a chain (see Pot Chain, page 251). The campfire is also the ideal venue for the long-legged tripod (page 253).

BREAD OVEN

Until the nineteenth century, the oven used by most Europeans and Americans was invariably of brick, adobe, or stone and fired with wood—either logs or, in much of Europe, faggots, large bundles of thin branches. Traditional bread ovens function as follows: wood is burned inside the oven to make the oven walls hot. When the walls are white and the wood is largely reduced to ashes, the oven is swept out and baking is accomplished on the heat stored in the oven's floor and walls.

Historically, the principal function of the wood oven was to bake bread, often more than 100 pounds (50 kg) at a time. Only secondarily were ovens used for roasts, pies, cakes, etc. Bread ovens were by no means present in every house in either Europe or colonial America, and the pattern of bread-oven ownership cannot be generalized. In some regions, there were none. In other regions, ovens existed in many private houses, and in still others, they were owned communally by a group of farms or by a village, or the village baker had the sole oven of the community. It is safe to say, however, that only affluent households in either Europe or America could afford to regularly bake nonbread foods in an oven.

Unless there was a village bakery, or the household was very prosperous, baking of nonbread dishes took place only on days when bread was baked, and then only after the bread was taken out of the oven. If a household had access to a bread oven, you should imagine that what was baked where, hearth or oven, was largely a matter of opportunity. Depending on circumstances, a roast might be baked in the bread oven, or in a Dutch oven on the hearth, or roasted in front of the fire from a string or on a spit.

For baking in the bread oven, I identify the kinds of recipes that are often identified as oven dishes in modern cookbooks—stews, roasts, breads, cakes, and casseroles. You can measure the temperature of your bread oven with an oven thermometer. If you operate your bread oven with a fire burning inside the oven alongside the food, you can maintain a temperature that is almost as even as the one maintained by an oven's thermostat. If, more traditionally, you bake in the oven when the fire has been swept out, the heat will always be falling. In that case, start out baking at a higher temperature than you would in a thermostatically controlled oven. Steamed custard should be baked in a water bath; the denser the steamed cake or pudding, the slower the oven should be.

You are not limited to using a bread oven only for foods that we bake in our kitchen ovens. For example, I make the Fava Beans that are in this book in my bread oven by placing a frying pan on a short-legged tripod, and shoveling embers underneath, as I do on the hearth.

Unusual Foods and Special Techniques

Annatto

Brining

Chocolate

Gray Salt

Hand Kneading

Jerusalem Artichoke

Lactarius deliciosus

Pain de Campagne

Porcini, Dried

Truffles

Wild Mushrooms

ANNATTO

Annatto seeds (*Bixa orellana*) are the world's second most common coloring agent for food — following caramel. Annato are small trees or shrubs native to tropical central and south America. The color is in the pulp that surrounds the seeds. It is released in hot water and has no flavor when used in small quantities.

BRINING

The flavor of chicken, quail, and other birds is significantly improved with a short brining. Place the bird(s) in a bowl and cover with cold water to which salt has been added in the amount of 2 tablespoons salt per quart (liter) of water. Set the bowl in the refrigerator for 2 to 3 hours, then remove the bird(s), rinse, and proceed with the recipe. I brine poultry and birds whenever I have the time.

CHOCOLATE

All chocolate is not the same. Modern chocolate is a refined industrial product. Almost all modern chocolate is made with emulsifiers, and has had cocoa butter removed from the natural chocolate. Premium chocolates keep more of the cocoa butter, which is why, if you read labels carefully, you will find that the percentage of fat in a bar of chocolate varies. Premium chocolate is the most flavorful chocolate to use in cooking, and the chocolate that is closest to what was used in the eighteenth century. Premium chocolate usually has a fat content in the range of 22 to 25 percent and, besides the ubiquitous emulsifier lecithin, has no other ingredients beside sugar and vanilla. If vanilla is used, Bourbon vanilla is an indication of quality. Vanillin, which is an artificial flavoring, as well as milk solids, are indications of lesser grades of chocolate. Your ability to whip chocolate drinks into a thick foam is influenced by the quantity and quality of chocolate you use.

GRAY SALT	**When salt is used as an important condiment,** gray salt—salt that is evaporated from seawater and still retains impurities—is, in my opinion, the most visually appealing choice. Where I live, gray salt from France is sold in bulk at the corner grocery store. If it is not available where you live, don't worry about it. Serve table salt.
HAND KNEADING	**All of the dough recipes in this book are mixed and kneaded by hand.** Only small quantities of dough are made, usually for 1 pound (450 g) flour, and all of them are easy to work by hand. I don't own a mixer. If you are more comfortable using an electric stand mixer, adapt my technique as needed. My recipes generally call for a light kneading of the bread dough—just until the dough is smooth and elastic, so be careful you do not overknead in a machine. The most unusual aspect to my bread making is that I sometimes suggest kneading the dough with wet hands. I learned this technique from working with country women in Lithuania. Lithuanian 100-percent rye-flour breads depend on a very sticky dough. Rather than add flour, country bakers keep their hands wet.
JERUSALEM ARTICHOKE	**A few recipes call for a small quantity of Jerusalem artichokes,** also called sunchokes. Jerusalem artichokes are tubers. They are not botanically related to globe artichokes. As a member of the aster family, they are related to the sunflower. They are native to the American midwest and were first documented in the early seventeenth century. Ironically, Jerusalem artichokes are more popular in Europe and China than they are in the United States. They are easy to grow, and are far more productive than potatoes. In the fall, the tall plants are topped by many small sunflowers. Jerusalem artichokes do not store well, so it is best to dig them as you need them. If you live where it snows, they will become sweet like apples after the first heavy freeze and can be dug from under the snow.
LACTARIUS DELICIOSUS	**In Grilled Saffron Milk Caps (page 148),** the European botanical names are used in the introduction because the recipe source is southern Europe. Very similar species occur in North America, Asia, and Australia. As of this writing, the names of some Lactarius mushrooms are in flux. The North American *Lactarius deliciosus* is not identical to the European mushroom of the same name. While the European mushroom is inevitably delicious, the North American one is sometimes bitter. In the United States, *Lactarius rubilactius* is closest in flavor and texture to the European *Lactarius deliciosus.* You can expect the North American mushroom to be given a new name. *Russula cyanoxantha* is another excellent mushroom that is often prepared the same way, and depending on personal preference, may even be considered superior to the *Lactarius* species.
PAIN DE CAMPAGNE	**The technological revolution in Europe** could be said to have started with water-powered flour mills. A survey of England in 1068 recorded almost six thousand such mills. Water mills were still producing stone-ground whole-wheat flour up until the end of World War II. In French, *pain de campagne* means bread of the countryside. When this bread was, in fact, the bread of the countryside, it was

made with stone-ground whole-wheat flour, water, salt, and yeast in the form of a sour starter, or as a piece of dough held back from the previous baking. Also, as bread was mixed and kneaded in dough boxes that were never cleaned out, the yeast from one batch of bread became incorporated into the next simply through the mixing. The dough could take several days to ferment. *Pain de campagne* had a rich, lightly sour flavor and was always baked in huge batches in large stone or brick wood-fired ovens. If a baker near you doesn't produce a bread in the style of *pain de campagne,* use your favorite bakery bread.

PORCINI, DRIED

Italians eat more dried porcini *(Boletus edulis)* than their forests can produce. Italy imports the mushrooms from many parts of the world, including eastern Europe and China, both for domestic consumption and for export. As of this writing, the labeling on dried mushrooms refers to where the mushrooms were packaged, not where they were grown. Dried *Boletus edulis* acquires a more pungent smell and flavor with time. The difference in how dried porcini smell, therefore, may be more a function of how old they are than of where they were picked. My buying advice is to ignore packaging and country of origin information and to purchase the least expensive dried porcini you can find. *Porcino* is the singular of porcini.

TRUFFLES

The truffles of commerce fall into three categories—black, white, and terfez. The three recipes in this book that use truffles—Truffles under Embers (page 142), Potato Tureen (page 132), and Fried Eggs (page 78)—all call for one of the varieties of black truffle.

The most expensive truffle is the white truffle of northern Italy, *Tuber magnatum Pico.* The white truffle is best cooked lightly or not at all. The gourmets of ancient Rome loved truffles, but the truffle they knew was *T. terfez,* which is now more pop ular in North Africa, where it is plentiful, than it is in Europe. Among the many varieties of black truffle, *T. melanosporum,* the truffle most common to France, is the preferred variety for the recipes in this book. However, if you can find fresh, ripe Chinese truffles *(T. sinense),* use them. They are comparatively inexpensive, and, when in good condition, their flavor is excellent. The European summer truffle *(T. aestivum)* is not as pungent as the winter truffle, and does not hold up to baking in ash. In particular, with respect to the white and black truffles of commerce, any truffle you buy should have a strong smell, and it should smell delicious. France is the largest producer of *T. melanosporum,* but small quantities are grown in the United States, and larger quantities in Australia. You can buy truffles over the Internet. If you are in France during truffle season—December through March for winter truffles, and June through October for summer truffles—try to buy truffles from truffle producers. They will still be covered with dirt, which helps preserve their freshness. Terfez are widely sold in North African produce markets in early spring.

Always keep truffles refrigerated in a sealed container (otherwise, the refrigerator will dry them out), and use them as soon as possible after purchase. Truffles infuse anything stored with them with the scent of truffle, so it is traditional to store rice or eggs in the container along with the truffles. As a clerk in a French market explained it to me, when you cook the truffle-infused rice or eggs, you get "a truffle meal for free."

As of this writing, it is legal to carry truffles from France into the United States as long as there is no dirt on them. Buy the winter black truffles, preferably from a producer, and preferably still with dirt, no more than a couple of days before leaving France. Scrub them clean under running water with a brush, such as a medium toothbrush, just before leaving your hotel for the airport. It is essential that there be no dirt on the truffles when you take them through U.S. customs. It is not legal to import eggs into the United States, so pack the truffles in an airtight container with rice.

WILD MUSHROOMS

The cleaner one brings home mushrooms from the forest, the better. As you pick them, trim dirt from the base of the stem, and use a stiff paintbrush to clean leaves, dirt, and sand from the cap. Inevitably, however, the mushrooms will require more washing in the kitchen. If preparing mushrooms to dry, brush them clean under running water and let them dry for a while on a cloth towel. If the mushrooms will be cooked, for example in a stew, they can be washed in a bowl of water. In fact, it is the practice in some parts of Europe to soak mushrooms in a bowl of lightly salted water before frying.

It is also the practice in many parts of northern Europe to parboil, and even boil, mushrooms before sautéing them. Parboiling mushrooms in lightly salted water—1 teaspoon per 1 quart (1 l)—for 3 to 5 minutes, along with 2 garlic cloves and a bay leaf, often improves both texture and flavor. This is a step worth experimenting with, particularly with *Russula, Suillus, Leccinum,* and *Boletus* species. This step may be applied to the recipe for Mushroom Stew (page 150).

A List of Suppliers

An expanded list of suppliers for ingredients and tools mentioned in this book is available at my Web site: *williamrubel.com*.

REPRODUCTION ANTIQUARIAN COOKWARE

Goose Bay Workshops: Bridgeville, Delaware
(goosebayworkshops.com)

Peter Goebel makes a wide range of culinary equipment out of copper, brass, and tin, including a mulling cone. (302) 337-0229

CLOCK-WORK SPITS AND FIREPLACE TOOLS

Le Capucin: La Bussière, France
(lecapucin.com)

This is the largest of the very small number of companies producing reproduction clock-work spits. Le Capucin spits are based on an early nineteenth-century model. Tel: 05 49 48 17 44, from the US: 011 39 5 49 48 17 44

Ball and Ball: Exton, Pennsylvania
(ballandball-us.com)

Specializing in reproduction hardware from the eighteenth century through the Victorian period, Ball and Ball are an excellent source for period American fireplace tools. They also manufacture, on a custom basis, an exquisite, and expensive, eighteenth-century reproduction spit. (800) 257-3711

Historic Housefitters Co.: Brewster, New York
(historichousefitters.com)

This mail order company sells hearth tools, including a crane, a few cooking utensils, eighteenth-century lighting, and a wide range of brass and hard- and machine-forged iron hardware. (800) 247-4111

CHOCOLATE, SPECIALTY GRAINS, GRAY SALT, AND MORE

Scharffen Berger: Berkeley, California
(scharffenberger.com)

Scharffen Berger chocolate, like other premium chocolate, is a good choice for chocolate drinks. If you use a lot of chocolate, then buy the large bars produced for bakers. (800) 930-4528

Kalustyans: New York, New York
(kalustyans.com)

Kalustyans offers an extraordinary selection of grains, salts, spices, and more to satisfy the needs of a large number of the world's cuisines. Prices are usually competitive with your local market. (212) 685-3451

Sweet Marias: Columbus, Ohio
(sweetmarias.com)

This is the preeminent business catering to people who roast their coffee at home. If you need green coffee beans, supplies for home roasting, or just want to learn about coffee, then visit this web site. Sweet Marias has a phone number, but the staff prefers that you contact them online. (614) 294-1816

FIREPLACES

Buckley Rumford Co.: Port Townsend, Washington
(rumford.com)

Buckley Rumford provides detailed information on their Web site about the energy-efficient Rumford fireplace. This is a model for what a company Web site should be. (360) 385-9974

DUTCH OVENS WITH LEGS ("CAMP OVENS") AND CAST-IRON COOKWARE

Lodge: South Pittsburg, Tennessee
(lodgemfg.com)

Lodge is the leading American producer of Dutch ovens and cast-iron cookware. Their cookware is widely distributed in the US and Canada. (423) 837-7181

Lehman's: Kidron, Ohio
(lehmans.com)

This company sells everything you need to set up a farm that is off the power grid. Lehman's offers a wide selection of traditional kitchen equipment, including a crane, and an excellent selection of cast-iron cookware. (888) 438-5346

Sur la Table: Seattle, Washington
(surlatable.com)

Sur la Table is a US chain that offers a fine selection of cast-iron and terra-cotta cookware suitable for hearth cooking. (800) 243-0852

Bibliography

Arora, David. *Mushrooms Demystified: a Comprehensive Guide to the Fleshy Fungi of the Central California Coast.* Berkeley, Calif.: Ten Speed Press, 1979.

Athenaeus. *The Deipnosophists.* Translated by Charles Burton Gulick. Loeb Classical Library, Vol. I–VII. Cambridge, Mass.: Harvard University Press, 1927.

Bachelard, Gaston. *The Psychoanalysis of Fire.* Boston: Beacon Press, 1964.

Beeton, Isabella. *Mrs. Beeton's Every Day Cookery and Housekeeping Book.* London: Ward, Lock and Co., 1865.

Beharn, Helene, and **Philippe Boisseau.** *La Cuisine de Braise.* Paris: Hachette Livre, 1996.

Bertoluzza, Aldo, Pio Dalle Valle, and **Alessandri Mancabelli.** *Saor de la Tera,* Centro Studi per la Val di Sole. Trento: Grafiche Artigianelli, 1997.

Bober, Phyllis Pray. *Art, Culture & Cuisine: Ancient and Medieval Gastronomy.* Chicago: University of Chicago Press, 1999.

Brothwell, Don, and **Patricia Brothwell.** *Food in Antiquity.* Baltimore: Joh's Hopkins University Press, 1998.

Brown, Alice Cooke. *Early American Herb Recipes.* Boston: Charles E. Tuttle, 1966.

Brown, John Hull. *Early American Beverages.* Boston: Charles E. Tuttle, 1966.

Camporesi, Piero. *Exotic Brew, The Art of Living in the Age of Enlightenment.* Cambridge, Mass.: Polity Press, 1994.

Cardoze, Michel. *Ma cuisine dans la cheminée.* Paris: Les Presses du Management, 2000.

Carson, Jane. *Colonial Virginia Cookery,* Williamsburg Research Studies. Charlottesville: The University Press of Virginia, 1968.

Coe, Sophie D. *America's First Cuisines.* Austin: University of Texas Press, 1994.

Coe, Sophie D., and **Michael D. Coe.** *The True History of Chocolate.* London: Thames and Hudson, 1996.

Crump, Nancy Carter. *Hearthside Cooking.* McLean, Virginia: EPM Publications, 1986.

David, Elizabeth. *English Bread and Yeast Cookery.* New York: The Viking Press, 1977.

Davidson, Alan. *The Oxford Companion to Food.* Oxford: Oxford University Press, 1999.

Dembinska, Maria. *Food and Drink in Medieval Poland: Rediscovering a Cuisine of the Past.* Translated by M. Thomas. Philadelphia: University of Pennsylvania Press, 1999.

Flandrin, Jean-Louis, and **Massimo Montanari.** *Food: A Culinary History.* Translated by C. Botsford, Arthur Goldhammer, Charles Lambert, Frances M. Lopez-Morillas, and Sylvia Stevens. New York: Columbia University Press, 1999.

Giacosa, Ilaria Gozzini. *A Taste of Ancient Rome.* Translated by A. Herklotz. Chicago: University of Chicago Press, 1992.

Gimpel, Jean. *The Medieval Machine, The Industrial Revolution of the Middle Ages.* New York: Penguin Books USA Inc.,1976.

Glasse, Hannah. *The Art of Cookery Made Plain and Easy.* Original edition, Alexandria, Virginia: Cottom & Stewart, 1747. Reprint edition, Bedford, Mass.: Applewood Books, 1997.

Grant, Mark. *Roman Cookery: Ancient Recipes for Modern Kitchens.* London: Serif, 1999.

Gray, Patience. *Honey from a Weed.* New York: Harper & Row, 1987.

Grieve, M. *A Modern Herbal.* New York: Dover Publications, 1971.

Guérard, Michel. *Cuisine gourmande.* Translated by Caroline Conran and Caroline Hobhouse. London: Macmillan, 1978.

Hagen, Ann. *A Handbook of Anglo-Saxon Food: Processing and Consumption.* Middlesex, England: Anglo-Saxon Books, 1992.

Hartley, Dorothy. *Food in England.* London: Macdonald General Books, 1954.

Henisch, Bridget Ann. *Fast and Feast: Food in Medieval Society.* University Park: University of Pennsylvania, 1976.

Johnson, Mireille. *Cuisine of the Rose: Classical French Cooking from Burgundy and Lyonnais.* New York: Random House, 1982.

Kasper, Lynn Rossetto. *The Splendid Table: Recipes from Emilia-Romagna, the Heartland of Northern Italian Food.* New York: William Morrow, 1992.

Ladd, Paul R. *Early American Fireplaces.* New York: Hastings House, 1977.

Langsner, Drew and Louise. *Handmade, Vanishing Cultures of Europe and the Near East.* New York:Harmony Books, 1974.

Lecoq, Raymond. *Les objects de la vie domestique.* Paris: Berger-Levrault, 1979.

Luard, Elisabeth. *The Old World Kitchen: The Rich Tradition of European Peasant Cooking.* Toronto: Bantam Books, 1987.

McGee, Harold. *On Food and Cooking: The Science and Lore of the Kitchen.* New York: Charles Scribner's Sons, 1984.

Montagne, Prosper. *The New Larousse Gastronomique.* Translated by M. Hunter. New York: Crown, 1977.

Paston-Williams, Sara. *The Art of Dining: A History of Cooking and Eating.* London: The National Trust Enterprises, 1993.

The Philological Society. *Oxford English Dictionary.* Vol. I–XII. London: Oxford University Press, 1933.

Padulosi, S., Hammer, K., and **Heller, J.,** editors. *Hulled wheats. Promoting the conservation and use of underutilized and neglected crops. 4. Proceedings of the First International Workshop on Hulled Wheats. July 21–22, 1995. Castelgecchio Pascoli, Tuscany, Italy.* International Plant Genetics Resources Institute, Rome, 1996.

Platina. *On Right Pleasure and Good Health.* Translated by M. E. Milham. Asheville: University of North Carolina, 1999.

Pons, Anne. *La maison des jours d'autrefois.* Paris: Éditions Joel Cuenot, 1980.

Reader's Digest Association. *Farmhouse Cookery, Recipes from the Country Kitchen.* London: The Reader's Digest Association, 1980.

Redon, Odile, Francoise Sabban, and Silvano Serventi. *The Medieval Kitchen: Recipes from France and Italy.* Translated by E. Schneider. Chicago: University of Chicago Press, 1998.

Rombauer, Irma, and Marion Rombauer Becker. *Joy of Cooking.* Indianapolis: Bobbs-Merrill, Inc., 1964.

Scully, Terence. *The Art of Cookery in the Middle Ages.* Woodbridge, Suffolk: The Boydell Press, 1995.

———. *The Neapolitan Recipe Collection: Cuoco Napoletano.* Ann Arbor: University of Michigan Press, 2000.

Simmons, Amelia. *American Cookery: or, the Art of Dressing Viands, Fish, Poultry and Vegetables and the best modes of making Puff-Pastes, Pies, Tarts, Puddings, Custards and Preserves, and all kinds of Cakes, from the Imperial Plumb to plain cake, adapted to this country and all grades of life.* Original edition, Albany, NY: Charles R. and George Webster, 1796. Reprint of 2nd edition, Bedford, Mass.: Applewood Books, 1997.

Teubner, Christian. *The Chocolate Bible.* London: Butler & Tanner, 1997.

The American Heritage Publishing Company. *The American Heritage Cookbook and Illustrated History of American Eating and Drinking.* New York: American Heritage Publishing Company, 1964.

Tyree, Marion Cabell. *Housekeeping in Old Virginia.* Louisville, KY: John P. Morton, 1879.

Weaver, William Woys. *Heirloom Vegetable Gardening: A Master Gardener's Guide to Planting, Growing, Seed Saving, and Cultural History.* New York: Henry Holt, 1997.

Weinberg, Bennett Alan, and Bonnie K. Bealer. *The World of Caffeine: The Science and Culture of the World's Most Popular Drug.* New York: Routledge, 2001.

Wilhide, Elizabeth. *The Fireplace, A Guide to Period Style.* Boston: Little, Brown, 1994.

Wolfert, Paula. *The Cooking of South-West France.* New York: Doubleday, 1983.

Wright, Clifford A. *A Mediterranean Feast, The Story of the Birth of the Celebrated Cuisines of the Mediterranean, from the Merchants of Venice to the Barbary Corsairs.* New York: William Morrow, 1999.

Acknowledgments

Irst, to my wife, sonia, who let the runes written in the hearth-fire change her life, and mine, go thanks without measure for having helped in uncountable ways to make this book as good as I was able to make it.

Every project has a beginning. The beginning to this book was a promise I made to write down a few recipes for two friends who had just bought a house with a fireplace. This book began as a letter in a Paris café. Seven years later, I am pleased to acknowledge the inspiration that sparked this project, and to finally be able to make good on my promise to present my friends Ga Lombard and Judith Milton with a guide to open-hearth cooking.

Once it was clear to me that my letter had become a book, I sought the collaboration of Ian Everard, a friend and gifted artist. What was to be a few illustrations for a small book grew to over one hundred illustrations for a big book. I cannot thank Ian enough for the extraordinary effort he put into this project.

How to learn to write a book? From David Arora, fine writer and gifted mycologist with whom I have traveled in pursuit of wild mushrooms, I learned so much, including the vital importance of paying attention to details. I hope that I have managed to record the details that will make these recipes a success for everyone who tries them.

David Craig and Roberta Cairny proved to be the best friends a friend can have. They told me the truth about the manuscript when I thought it was done, sending me back to my computer for another year and a half of work, a favor for which I cannot thank them enough.

While it feels, as I write this, that all I have ever done is write this book, however long it has taken me, it would have taken significantly longer had I not had a country cabin to go to where I could write for uninterrupted stretches of time. Arvydays Sabonis and Ramunė Januševičiūtė, my Lithuanian friends, let me take over their lives, and their country house, on more occasions than is polite for a guest to demand. You will hear the spirit of the Lithuanian countryside in this text, the sound of the cuckoo, and the spartan life of the subsistence farmer.

PERMISSIONS

Page 72: Reprinted with permission of Simon & Schuster from *Popul Vuh* by Dennis Tedlock. Copyright © 1985, 1996.

Page 118: *The Silver Chair* by C.S. Lewis copyright © C.S. Lewis Pte. Ltd. 1953. Extract reprinted by permission.

Page 150: Excerpt from Vladimir Nabokov's *Speak, Memory: An Autobiography Revisited,* courtesy of the Estate of Vladimir Nabokov.

The miracle of the Internet brought me recipe testers whose dedication to this project cannot be overstated. Each tester was so kind and worked so hard that it would be unfair to call one out above the other. With a depth of emotion that I cannot express in words I thank Liam Hughes; Diane Albracht; Brion Sprinsock; Liza and Allan Grissino; The Historical Cooking Guild of the Catawba Valley, Barbara Goodwin, Carolyn Dilda, Pam Dudeck, Janet Dyer, Wanda Hubicki, Audrey Mellichamp, Quinn Moore, Sharon VanKuren; and the Historic Foodways Society of Delaware Valley, Mercy Ingraham, Lisa Price, and Susan McLellan.

I thank my friends who "suffered" through several dozen testing dinners offering their comments between mouthfuls and read all or part of the manuscript: Anthony Chennels, Joel Leivick, Mary Scott, Chris Connery, Sandy Connery, Jozseph Schultz, Kelly Porter Sanchez, and Mark Sanchez.

Several of the recipes are the product of field research. I thank Marco and his sister Sandra for help with the mushrooms of Trento, Italy, and their wonderful parents, Silvano and Lina Florinao, Trentino masters of polenta from seed to table. Noccola Sitta, Giorgio Bonelli, and Niccolino Fabbreschi are to be thanked for a warm introduction to the mushrooms and chestnuts of Mt. Amiata.

It took two trips to Italy, and many days of searching, to finally track down *crescentine,* the tile-baked bread of the mountains above Modena. I thank Alberto Bettini who answered an e-mail from a stranger and set me on the right path. Massimo Turchi was a gracious guide while I was in Fanano. He magnanimously tolerated me for several days of endless questions and introduced me to friends who demonstrated *tigelle* baking. For an expert lesson and a wonderful evening I thank Giovanni Degli Antoni and his family.

When it comes to French truffles, I would have left Provence as ignorant as I came had it not been for the warm hospitality of one of France's great truffle families. Gilles Aymes and Falla took my wife and me under their wing, introducing us to their friends including the indomitable truffle collector of wild truffles, Louis Barbesier. I also wish to acknowledge Louis' friend Jean Claude Girard and his sweet dog Nora, whose pictures are in the book, and the proprietors of Les Buisses in Saint-Restitut, who let me commandeer their fireplace to test my truffle recipe.

I have asked so many people so many questions. I thank Carolyn Burke, who helped me with French translations and provided moral support; Renée Flower for her thoughtful advice on a range of subjects; William

Menchine, my neighbor and an engineer with the Raytek Corporation, for introducing me to the wonders of the infrared thermometer; Roger Taylor, who always responded immediately to transatlantic e-mails to check something in his extensive cookbook collection; Anton Poler, master Slovenian mycologist; Letina Letua, Babu and Rose Zakau, my guides in Wamba, Kenya; Jim Buckley, Rumford fireplace king who helped with the technical description of fireplaces; Raphael Bedos, a dealer of culinary antiques on Pont Neuf, Paris; Philippe Irrman, whose extraordinary meal cooked for strangers is partly memorialized in the recipe Philippe's Veal Roast; Jadvyga Meiduvienė who has so patiently demonstrated Lithuanian dishes; Subhash Chandar Khosle (Sharod) of Deeg, India, for lessons in the fine art of *chai*; Gildas Hamal, Karen Yamshita, Peter Haas, Richard Wolfheiler, Ryuta Imafuku, and so many others who answered specific questions and whose answers, hopefully, I understood and recorded properly.

In the last few months, as *The Magic of Fire* was transformed from a manuscript into a book, I was surrounded by an incredible team of copy editor, keyboardist, and proofreader. Credit for the final polish goes to my wonderful editor Sharon Silva, who wields her red pencil with wisdom and sensitivity, and to the sharp eye of Linda Bouchard, a talented proofreader. Jacinta Monniere, an amazing keyboardist, transferred Sharon's "light" edit into the manuscript at a speed that didn't seem possible. Ken DellaPenta, has done a fabulous job creating an index that lets you find what you are looking for. Although my Ten Speed editor, Holly Taines White, came into the project late in its life, I'd like to thank her for her good spirit and thoughtful advice.

As Web sites, including my own, begin to compete with books as ways of disseminating information, book designers become all the more important. If the book isn't beautiful, why not publish the material on a Web site? Jim MacKenzie worked many fourteen-hour days to create a book that is worthy of being held in your hand and read beside the fire. An author couldn't have a more supportive designer. He worked with me in unfailing good spirits to realize my dream for a cookbook that tells its story of taste, poetry, and technique through a weaving of pictures and words.

Lastly, there is no book without a publisher. And it is not mere formula to say that in Phil Wood, a wonderful man of boundless enthusiasms—including for that of a good meal—a collector with a keen eye, and a man willing to take risks, I found the perfect publisher for this book.

Page 154: *The Master and Margarita,* by Mikhail Bulgakov, excerpt reprinted with permission, Ardis Publishers.

Page 178: Photograph by Drew Langsner, from *Handmade, Vanishing Cultures of Europe and the Near East* by Drew and Louise Langsner, Harmony Books, 1974.

Page 224: *Sir Gawain and the Green Knight* by Marie Boroff, ©1973 by W.W. Norton, excerpt reprinted with permission.

Index

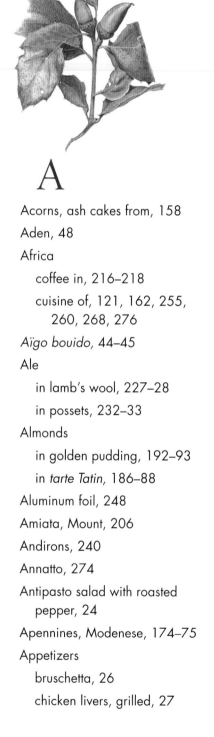

as polenta topping, 93

in potato tureen, 132–33

raclette, 84

waffles, 169

Cherries

in clafouti, 194

dried, in infusions, 215

Chestnuts

ash cakes from, 159

leaves, mushrooms grilled over, 147

leaves, tile-baked breads with, 174, 175, 176

roasted, 206–7

in stuffing, 66

Chicken

baked in wrappings, 58–59

breasts, grilled stuffed, 102–3

brining, 274

in clay, 75–76

in flour crust, 68–69

in frittata, 82–83

grilled strips of, 120

Gypsy, 75

hobo, 75

livers, grilled, 27

in a pot, 60–61

in pot-au-feu, 114–17

roasted, 70–71

Chicory, coffee with, 219–20

Chiles, in chocolate, 234, 236

Chimney

function of, 243

sweeping, 244

China

cuisine of, 58, 158, 260, 267, 275, 276

tea in, 230

Chocolate

cake, 192, 193

French *chocolat ancien*, 237

hot, 232–37

Mayan chile, 236

quality of, 274

Spanish Baroque, 236

supplier of, 278

Chops, grilled stuffed, 102–3

Cinnamon, 215, 235–36

Clafouti, 194

Clay, chicken in, 75–76

Cod

preserved, 55

stew, 54–56

Coffee

and bread, 229

with chicory, 219–20

spiced, 216–18

Coffeepots, 216, 248

Colonial America, 40, 58, 158, 159, 160, 200, 248, 249, 255, 273

Commissioned tools and cookware, 227, 248–49

Cooking times, 11

Cookware

cast-iron, 249, 279

commissioning, 249

kitchen, 249

suppliers of, 278, 279

terra-cotta, 252

Coppersmiths, 248–49

Corn. *See also* Cornmeal; Polenta

bread, 160–61

ember-roasted, 138

grilled, 135

Cornish game hens

baked in wrappings, 58–59

in a pot, 60

Cornmeal

ash cakes from, 158, 159

in brown bread, 180–81

in corn bread, 160–61

grinding your own, 90, 160

Crab apples, in lamb's wool, 227–28

Crane, 249, 258

Crème caramel, 208

Crêpes, 172

Crescentine, 174–75

Crumpets, 165–68

Currants

in baked apples, 204–5

in Irish soda bread, 170–71

Custard, steamed, 208

D

Damper, 245

Dandelion, in sautéed greens, 141

Daube, French, 106–7

Daubière, 106, 258

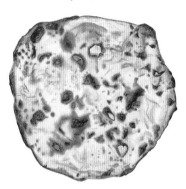

O

P

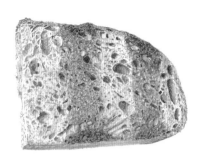

T

Tarte Tatin, 186–88

Tava, 162

Tea
    brewing, 230–31
    chai, 222–23
    in England, 230–31
    herbal, 214–15
    rituals, 230–31

Techniques. *See* Methods

Terra-cotta cookware, 252

Thanksgiving, 65, 145, 189

Thermometer, infrared, 253

Thyme tea, 215

Tiberius, Sea of, 48

Tigelle, 175–76

Tile baking, 174–77, 253, 268

Toast, English, 182–83

Toasting fork, 183, 250

Tomatoes
    in chicken in a pot, 60–61
    grilled, 135
    in salt cod stew, 54–56
    in winter bean soup, 38–39

Tongs, long-handled, 253

Tools. *See* Equipment

Tourtière, 258

Trento, 88, 90

Tripods. *See also* Boiling; Pot beside the fire method
    hearthside/short-legged, 253, 262

long-legged, 253, 262

Trout
    baked in salt, 57
    baked in wrappings, 58–59
    ember-baked, 48–49
    grilled, 50–51

Truffles
    collecting, 142, 143–44
    under embers, 142–44
    fried eggs with, 79
    in potato tureen, 132–33
    storing, 276–77
    through U.S. customs, 277
    using, 142–43
    varieties of, 276

Tureen, potato, 132–33

Turkey (bird)
    string-roasted, 65–67
    stuffing for, 66

Turkey (country)
    coffee in, 216, 248
    cuisine of, 30, 178

Turnips
    in drippings, 140
    in Philippe's veal roast, 128–29
    in pot-au-feu, 114–17

Tuscany, 36

V

Veal roast, Philippe's, 128–29

Vegetables. *See also individual vegetables*
    in drippings, 140
    ember-roasted, 136–39
    in French daube, 106–7
    in frittata, 82–83
    grilled, 134–35
    larding with, 111

as polenta topping, 93
in pot-au-feu, 114–17
in veal roast, Philippe's, 128–29

Venison
    chops, grilled stuffed, 102–3
    pot roast, 122–23
    roast, 110–11

Venues, key to, 270–73

W

Wafers, 196–97

Waffles, cheese, 169

Walnuts
    leaves, tile-baked breads with, 174, 176
    in persimmon pudding, 200–1

Water
    bath, 266
    boiling, 257

Web site, 269

Wheat berries, 95

Williamrubel.com, 269

Wine. *See also* Port
    in the bishop, 212
    mulled, 224–25
    in possets, 232–33
    in stewed dried fruit, 198

Winter bean soup, 38–39

Wood, 245

Wrappings, 58, 248, 251

Z

Zucchini, grilled, 135

COLOPHON

The Magic of Fire was designed by Jim MacKenzie using Centaur and Futura types. Centaur—used in the recipe narratives—was designed in the early 1900s by American typographer and book designer Bruce Rogers, who had been asked by the Metropolitan Museum of Art in New York to develop a new typeface for its exclusive use. Rogers accepted the museum's challenge and modeled his design after Nicolas Jenson's Roman letterforms used to print Eusebius' De Praeparatione Evangelica in Venice in 1740. Rogers' new design—a typeface that a little over a decade later would become widely known as "The Centaur Type"—first appeared in a slim, limited-edition quarto of Maurice de Guérin's The Centaur, designed by Rogers and published by the Montague Press in 1915.

The museum's Centaur quickly became noticed—and much sought after—by the commercial printing trade. When the Lanston Monotype Corporation finally coaxed Rogers into allowing them to release his design for machine composition in the late 1920s, it became apparent that Centaur's Roman was missing an italic complement. Rogers, according to type historian Alexander Lawson, feeling that he "lacked the skill to produce a competent chancery to accompany his Roman," persuaded another American typographer, Frederic Warde, to allow his elegant cursive italic, Arrighi—which Rogers considered "one of the finest and most legible cursive letters ever produced"—to be adopted as Centaur italic. Warde designed a version of Arrighi specifically for use with Centaur, creating the exquisite "inclined" capitals so bountifully evident in the recipe headings throughout this book.

Futura, the family of sans-serif types used extensively throughout The Magic of Fire, was designed by German book designer Paul Renner in the 1920s. Renner's design, inspired by the "form follows function" dictum of the Bauhaus, reduced letterforms to almost pure geometry—the o being perfectly round, and with a number of lowercase letters (a, b, d, e, g, p, and q) also based on the circle, with single strokes added to complete the character forms. The result, issued by the Bauer Typefoundry of Frankfurt in 1928, is a typeface of exceptional readibility—especially when illuminated by the flickering glow of a hearth cook's fire.